Reviews of *God*

"You have a well-resea~~rched and~~ ~~well~~ draws an appealing portrait of the Major. I enjoyed reading it, was impressed at the breadth of resources underlying your statements about him, and learned much about him that I had not known before. In today's world, when there are so few encouraging models for our youth to imitate, it is heartening to read this portrayal of a man whose energy and faith are transparent and whose frailties are even inspirational."

> – Dr. Malcolm C. Doubles, Coker University Provost Emeritus, St. Andrews Visiting Professor. Author of *A Century Plus: A History of Sonoco Products Company*; *In Quest of Excellence: A History of Coker College on Its Centennial*, and *The Seduction of the Church*.

"Will's success in consolidating the many threads of Major J. L. Coker's life and legacy into this biography is a Herculean effort. He not only explains how Coker's ability, leadership and strong faith brought success in his own time, but demonstrates how they continue to show a moral and ethical way to success for future generations."

> – Hartsville native Edgar H. Lawton, Jr., Princeton graduate and Harvard MBA. Lawton's career included the management and governance of ongoing Coker business enterprises and Coker College. He is Major Coker's great-grandson, and the grandson of J. J. Lawton, who was like a son to Major Coker.

"God, Guts and Gallantry" is a very timely book that reminds us of those men who were of strong moral character during the dark period of the history of slavery in the American South. Without trepidation, Major Coker transcended the racial barriers and societal norms of the time and created gainful employment opportunities for African Americans after the Civil War. In spite of hardships along the way, he lived so the light of Christ within him shone brightly in a time when light was so desperately needed. Surely, he was an example of what is good and right in a world divided between good and evil and right and wrong, even today."

Rev. Henry Caldwell of Raleigh, NC. Used by permisison.

–   Rev. Henry Caldwell, Pastor of First Church of God Ministries of Raleigh, NC

"God, Guts, and Gallantry tells the fascinating story of Major James Lide Coker, a Christian gentleman seriously wounded in the Civil War who became one of the most outstanding citizens this country has ever known. It is an inviting book with great 'curb appeal.' It I highly recommend this inspiring book about an individual who accomplished so much while serving God and his fellow man."

–   Susan D. Reynolds, M.D. Dr. Reynolds is a highly respected Hartsville physician, author, and historian. She was voted "Best Family Physician" in Darlington County in 2012 and 2013. Susan is the county's Medical Director for Hospice Care, and she volunteers at the free medical clinic in Hartsville.

"This biography of Major James Lide Coker is well researched and provides the reader with an understanding of his Christian witness as well as his impact on the economic development of the New South."

    –   Dr. Lloyd Johnson, Professor of History and Director of Historical Studies, Campbell University.

"The author has done his homework with "God, Guts and Gallantry!" Beyond the usual biography, this book clearly speaks to us today as an objective analysis of an outstanding man and his life. Descriptions of Major Coker that capture my attention are lion-hearted and adventurous, yet, humble and full of spiritual integrity. As a business owner, I know the courage it takes to step out with limited resources and the need for a foundation built on a strong inner life to keep persisting despite difficulties. My favorite visual of the Major is "a crutch, a hoe … and dirty overalls." I haven't been in that cotton field exactly, but I know the feeling! You will greatly benefit from the inspiration and instruction resourced from the courageous life of Major James Lide Coker!"

    –   Amanda J. Bew, Flux & Flow Coaching, Certified Coach (International Coach Federation), Coach Trainer, Christian Coach Institute, Certified Human Behavior Consultant and Trainer, Master's, Reformed Theological Seminary, B.A., UNC - Chapel Hill. Amanda trains and inspires coaches and leaders to cultivate lasting change in others.

"I have heard and read shorter accounts of how Major James Lide Coker impacted Hartsville and our state. However, *God, Guts, and Gallantry* brought previously unknown facets of the Major to light. The author goes into deep details of the Major's personal and business life, and explains how he faced challenges with strategic business thinking and his faith in God."

- Joshua Tadlock, Hartsville, South Carolina native and Coker University history major.

GOD, GUTS,

and

GALLANTRY

The Faith, Courage, and Accomplishments
of Major James Lide Coker

Dr. William H. Joslin

WESTBOW
PRESS®
A DIVISION OF THOMAS NELSON
& ZONDERVAN

WestBow Press books may be ordered through booksellers or by contacting:

WestBow Press
A Division of Thomas Nelson & Zondervan
1663 Liberty Drive
Bloomington, IN 47403
www.westbowpress.com
844-714-3454

ISBN: 978-1-9736-9765-7 (sc)
ISBN: 978-1-9736-9767-1 (hc)
ISBN: 978-1-9736-9766-4 (e)

Library of Congress Control Number: 2020913315

Print information available on the last page.

WestBow Press rev. date: 02/05/2021

Contents

Opening Remarks

Truth be known, we all have blind spots. Abraham Lincoln was responsible for the cruel and unjust deaths of well over five thousand imprisoned southern soldiers from 1863-1865 at Camp Douglas prison camp near Chicago.[1] The Apostle Paul once persecuted Christians, even unto death.[2] George Washington, Thomas Jefferson, and Patrick Henry owned slaves. Almost all heroes have faults. But in spite of the failures of these leaders, we stand to learn from their good qualities.

All of us today—Northerners, Southerners, and everyone else—are imperfect. Though perhaps not as outwardly obvious as owning slaves, we have faults of our own. We are all guilty of faults such as pride, greed, lust, contempt, neglect, or prejudice. America's founders and some of their Southern successors like James's father Caleb Coker, Jr. were not worse people than we are. However, they needed to recognize and repent of their blind spots. They should have restructured their plantation economies around wages rather around slavery. To some extent, the Civil War happened because they were too slow to do so.

For the record, Confederate Major James Lide Coker was happy when the slaves were freed.[3] And as evidence of his good treatment of African Americans, just after the Civil War, James endorsed a political platform calling for "full recognition of the legal and political rights of the Negro."[4] And James concluded his own book on the war with these words: "There is one great result of the war between the States for which we are truly thankful: *slavery is abolished.*"[5]

ENDNOTES FOR OPENING REMARKS

1   Carl Sandburg, *Abraham Lincoln: The War Years*, Volume III (Harcourt, Brace & Company: New York), 1939), p. 641. Sandburg quotes Confederate prisoner Henry M. Stanley: "Henry M. Stanley, on what he saw at a human 'cattle-yard' at Camp Douglas at Chicago. On the way to the latrines Stanley saw 'crowds of sick men who had fallen prostrate from weakness, and given themselves wholly to despair, [who] crawled or wallowed in their filth....' Every morning came wagons whereon Stanley saw the corpses rolled in the blankets 'piled upon another, as the New Zealand frozen mutton carcasses are carted from the docks!'".

2   Acts 7:1-8:3; 1 Timothy 1:13.

3   George Lee Simpson, *The Cokers of Carolina, A Social Biography of a Family*, (The University of North Carolina Press: Chapel Hill), 1956, p. 184.

4   George Lee Simpson, op. cit., pp. 90-91

5   James Lide Coker, *History of Company G, Ninth SC Regiment, Infantry, SC Army and of Company E, Sixth SC Regiment, Infantry, SC Army*, (Attic Press: Greenwood, SC), 1899, quoting D. H. Hill, p. 210. Hereafter this work will be referred to as *History of Company E and G*.

God, Guts, and Gallantry

The faith, courage, and accomplishments of Major James Lide Coker

By Dr. William H. Joslin

This biographical anthology of Major Coker is roughly chronological, with some exceptions for the natural development of themes.

NOTE TO THE READER: For further exploration and growth, I've posted discussion question sets on Major Coker's life and principles at https://www.willjoslin.com/major/. Both general and Christian readers can profit from them.

The cover picture of Major Coker is in the public domain.

Dedication

To all who thirst for the highest reason to live, and long to fully redeem the balance of their lives. May Major Coker's faith and shining example inspire you to a victorious quest.

WHY I HAD TO WRITE THIS BOOK

I'm a southerner. I grew up in Raleigh, North Carolina, my father William Joslin's hometown. My mother, Mary Coker Joslin, was from Hartsville, South Carolina. When I was a boy—

The Brown House, where the author and his siblings played as children. It is the former home of Major Coker's son D.R. and his wife May Roper Coker. The Major lived across the street and would visit here. Artist M. Tallon Chalmers. Used by permission of Coker College Press.

from the late 1950s to the mid-70s—our family would spend the week after Christmas in Hartsville with my grandmother, Margaret ("Miss May") Roper Coker in the house pictured. My siblings and I spent many happy hours sliding down the sturdy banisters, playing hide-and-seek in the endless rooms, and climbing the Darlington Oaks and magnolias in the yard of her beautiful brick home. Known in the neighborhood as "The Brown House" for its distinctive brick color, it is now the Coker University administration building.

As we got a little older, we discovered that Sonoco Products, the town's big industry, had sprung from two companies started by our great grandfather, Major James Lide Coker. We also learned that Major Coker was an outstanding Christian citizen who was instrumental in the settling and early progress of Hartsville. His portrait, along with that of our grandfather, D. R. Coker, hung prominently in Miss May's home.

Even with a simple boyhood knowledge of the Coker legacy, there was a glorious aura surrounding those visits. In about 1969, I distinctly remember exploring the streets of Hartsville with my brother David. We could not help but notice Coker College, then the Coker Department Store, and a little farther, the Coker Pedigreed Seed Company. A few blocks away was the huge Sonoco Products plant. As we absorbed the cumulative impact, my brother and I looked at each other with a sense of amazement, wondering how our ancestors had accomplished so much. There was also a sense of challenge about it all - that we in turn live useful lives.

I was nineteen when Miss May died in 1976, and my memories of those wonderful times in Hartsville receded as my wife Becky and I raised three children, served in ministry for two decades, and then owned and operated our own technology consulting business for two more decades.

Then it happened. Early one morning in June of 2018, just before waking from a restful night's sleep in Raleigh, I had a stark and compelling dream. I was back in the 1960s, walking the streets of Hartsville with my brother. Suddenly the aura was magnified a thousand times. A burning curiosity to investigate these fascinating roots, and a consuming desire to rise up and become a faithful conduit of Major Coker's legacy, ignited in a flash that burned into my brain.

I woke up with a start and in a sweat. When I greeted my wife Becky a few minutes later, I told her that something transcendent—a "God moment"—had just happened. I believed God was calling me to undertake an important work: to get to the fountainhead of the river of Coker accomplishment. I realized that such an undertaking would mean carefully searching out the history and legacy of my great grandfather, Major James Lide Coker.

Normally, I don't make too much out of dreams, but in this case, the compulsion in the dream was grounded in scripture – specifically, the example of Luke being called to document history. I would never claim inspiration in the same sense that it came to the writers of the Bible. However, I think I felt like Luke did when he opened his gospel with these words: "Many have undertaken to draw up an account of the things that have been fulfilled among us ... I too decided to write an orderly account... so that you may know the certainty of the things you have been taught" (from Luke 1:1-4 NIV).

As I began to dig for more information, I found partial descriptions and anecdotes of Major Coker in various newspaper and magazine articles, and in archives, and genealogical records from the late 19th century to the mid-20th century. I read Major Coker's own writings and books, and I read all the works by others I could find. The late Dr. George Lee Simpson Jr.'s fine work, *The Cokers of Carolina* (University of North Carolina Press, 1956), was perhaps the most substantial, devoting two and a half chapters to him. I included details from the booklet by his mother Hannah Lide Coker, *A Story of the Late War (Walker, Evans and Cogswell,* 1887), and quotations from those who had observed Major Coker's life in *Recollections of the Major: James Lide Coker, 1837-1918* (Hartsville Museum: 1997).

Yet there remained a good-sized void. First, nothing approaching a complete biography had ever been written. Second, many previous writings have downplayed his life's driving force, his faith. In order to fill in gaps and reveal the full dimensions of this man for the benefit of current and future generations, I've drawn upon more than 165 additional sources and interwoven previously under-represented and overlooked characteristics into this biography of 15 chapters and five appendices. I've researched the archives of the University of

South Carolina's Caroliniana Room, the University of North Carolina's Wilson Library, Coker University, The Citadel, and the Darlington County Historical Commission. I've also visited and gathered information from the Major's industrial legacy, Sonoco Products, his birthplace at Society Hill, and his church, First Baptist Church of Hartsville, gaining as much information as possible.

In all, I found more on his dramatic life than I could fit into a reasonably sized book, so I have placed additional important material, along with several sets of discussion questions at https://www.willjoslin.com/major.

James suffered terribly in the Civil War, escaping death only by a miracle, and he remained lame for life. His plight of pain helped him fully identify with others who suffered. When he rose up to incredible business success, he intentionally lifted up needy people, white and black, in his wake. Fueled by his faith, his passion was that his life and service reflect the goodness and grace of God to hurting people in the destitute, war-torn South.

Mahatma Gandhi (1869-1948), former leader for independence in India, said to some Christian clergymen: "I like your Christ. I do not like your Christians. Your Christians are so unlike your Christ."[1] Well, Gandhi never met Major Coker, for he was one of the most constructive, powerful, and loving personalities for social redemption who has ever lived. But if the Major's faith does not necessarily resonate with you, I can relate, since before my own conversion, my perception of Christians who took the Bible seriously and thought Christ was still alive was that they were, at best, naïve, and at worst, a social problem. But I assure you, as revealed in this book, Major Coker was neither naïve nor a social problem.

Since the Major lived in the Civil War era, which is, almost by definition, controversial, I very much doubt I will be able to please everyone. I am also aware that some, male, female, white, black, and otherwise, will come to this book with different religious, social, and historical perspectives. I want them to know that I fully share the grave concerns voiced by the African American author Emory L. Waters, who, in his book on growing up in Hartsville, wrote: "The 2016 presidential election has subtly turned back the educational gains and accomplishments made after the Brown v. Board of Education decision."[2] I too, was taken aback by some of the things that happened during those four years, and I look forward to a more united future.

On the other hand, I not a socialist. I think the kind of socially sensitive, discerning capitalism that Major Coker exemplified, and that he used to help make winners of all ethnic groups whom he influenced in the decades after the Civil War, brings the greatest good to the greatest number. Perhaps this book and his example can provide some constructive economic talking points as our nation hopefully comes back together under succeeding administrations.

A Little About Myself, and my Vision for this Book

I was privileged to speak personally with the aforementioned Emory L. Waters, and we both believe, as Major Coker did, that the ultimate answers to our social problems lie in individual life transformation through Jesus Christ, multiplied and played out collectively and redemptively in society. To that end I've invested twenty years of my life in ministry, including six years in hands-on urban youth work. I've shared life with them through sports, business ventures, and meals. I've helped train African-American youth in Christian discipleship, leadership, and in running their own businesses. These youth are hungry for the word of God, which is not sourced in me, but in heaven (1 Thes. 2:13). The training gives them confidence in both their foundation and their future.

I was once a young man growing up in the uncertain 60's

and early 70's, gasping for my life's purpose. I needed hope, a life vision, and someone to model genuine and resilient faith to me. Needing answers, I went to a guidance counselor at UNC – Chapel Hill. I said to him: "I have no idea who I am, why I exist, or what will happen when I die. So how am I supposed to know what subject to major in?" He answered with these deflating words: "You come by it honestly – nobody really knows who they are or why they exist." But something deep inside told me the counselor was wrong. With a sincere prayer, I continued my search until thankfully, I found a stable leader and friend who pointed me to Christ.

Today, we see the same hunger for reality among millennials and Generation Z-ers as they try to navigate the mists of modern relativism. I listen to their conversations in coffee shops and hear them groping for truth. Their hunger is reflected in U2's song, "I Still Haven't Found What I'm looking For," and Linkin Park's 2017 release, "Looking for an Answer." Younger generations need answers, and I believe that, by upholding the torch of Major Coker's faith, redemptive life, and timeless principles, we can help inspire these future leaders with substantive hope, constructive vision, and some of the motivational and ethical resources needed to live out satisfying and purposeful lives.I believe that, for his times, the Major is an example of someone who moved mountains toward racial reconciliation. Furthermore, his dynamic integrity and vision, along with his spotless business principles, should be heralded, for they can powerfully inspire and benefit all peoples of all times.

ENDNOTES FOR PREFACE – WHY I HAD TO WRITE THIS BOOK

1   Goodreads, "Mahatma Ghandi Quotes," 2019, https://www.goodreads.com/quotes/22155-i-like-your-christ-i-do-not-like-your-christians (last accessed December 29, 2019).
2   Emory L. Waters, *The City We Knew But Everybody Forgot, Hartsville, the African American Experience,* (Lyndon Williams, Saving Ourselves Publications, 2020), back cover.

Acknowledgments

God, Guts, and Gallantry was a collective effort involving family, extended family, friends, librarians, professors, editors, and dozens of helpful South Carolinians, who are now newly made friends.

I am grateful to Hartsville history expert Dr. Malcolm C. Doubles, Coker University Provost Emeritus, who, early on, encouraged me to pursue this project and volunteered valuable historical information. Two of Dr. Doubles' books, *A Century Plus* on the centennial of Sonoco Products and *In Quest of Excellence* on Coker College's centennial, helped immensely. Sincere thanks to Dr. Lloyd Johnson, Director of Historical Studies at Campbell University, who reviewed and validated my work. I owe much gratitude to Matthew Turi, the Manuscripts and Research Instruction Librarian of the University of North Carolina's Louis Round Wilson Library, for helping me to locate UNC's Coker family collection.

The people of the Palmetto State have an almost universal attitude of neighborly friendship unlike any other. I am thankful to Kathy Dunlap, Andrea Steen, Matthew Winburn, and the team from the Hartsville Museum Commission for permitting me to use pictures from Hartsville Museum Press books. Gratitude goes out to Dr. Susan D. Reynolds, respected Hartsville physician, author, and historian, who gave me permission to use material from historical publications on First Baptist, many of which she wrote herself.

Hats off to Brian Gandy, his mother Doris, and Ann Chapman from the Darlington County Historical Commission for giving me access to county information and pictures, and to Hartsville City Councilman and regional historian Johnny Andrews, who encouraged my research, diligently read my entire manuscript, and gladly met me in person to give creative and valuable feedback.

I am indebted to Roger Schrum, Sonoco's Corporate Vice President for International Relations and Corporate Affairs, for his interview and a tour of the plant. In addition, Carolyn D. Johnson in Sonoco's Corporate Communications, provided valuable pictures and helped me get permissions. And hats off to veteran employees Eugene Thompson and Walter Britt, both of whom granted me personal interviews. I also owe thanks to Eileen Johnson at Sonoco for facilitating my communications at the company.

I'm indebted to many from Coker University. Dr. William D. Carswell, Vice President for Advancement, permitted me to use pictures from Coker College Press and the Coker University archives. I am grateful to Coker's Library Acquisitions and Cataloging Coordinator Nancy T. Matthews for guiding my research in the archives and to Director of Retail Operations Emily B. Phillips at the bookstore, who helped me make contacts at the university. Thanks to Dr. Susan Daniels Henderson, Provost and Dean of Faculty/Professor of Education, for granting access to some valuable materials at the Administration Building and to Tracy Laffidy and Shannon Flowers at the office of academic records.

Susan Henderson let me nostalgically re-explore my grandmother's old home, the Brown House. I thought about surprising her by sliding down those sturdy bannisters like I did as a boy, but it occurred to me that, fifty years later, a little more gravitas might be in order. From across the street at the Drengaelen House, now the Office of Advancement, I want to thank Advancement Officer Peggy Smith for graciously giving me three or four pertinent books with local lore that greatly aided me in my research.

From the South Caroliniana Library at the University of South Carolina, I am very appreciative of Library Specialist McKenzie Lemhouse in providing me with boxes of papers and pictures from the Coker Family archives and granting me digital images and permissions. From The Citadel, I want to thank Tessa Updike and Alexandra Adler of The Daniels Library for valuable pointers in navigating their archives and for helping me to discover a most important publication from one of the Major's contemporaries, the *Journal of Cadet Tom Law*.

Thanks to other patient manuscript readers. My dear wife Becky corrected grammatical errors and provided some valuable style suggestions, and my children Joel, Lydia, and Andy, gave needed feedback in the early stages. Lydia again gave feedback in the later stages, helping me keep the spiritual emphasis commensurate with the records of Major's spiritual life. My beloved sister, Furman University Art Professor Dr. Carolyn Coker Joslin Watson, helped me to determine exactly what kind of book this was going to be and pointed me toward some valuable sources. My dear deceased mother, Mary Coker Joslin, bequeathed to me some rare Coker family biographical sources, such as *Chronicles of a Worthwhile Family*, by Kate Chambers, that otherwise would have been difficult to find. My mother also wrote two helpful books on her own on other aspects of the Coker legacy.

This book would not have reached its final form without my main editor, Pat Stainke, whom I found on Thumbtack. Very capable intellectually, she completely understood the vision I had for the book and boosted the quality in many dimensions. I also wish to thank Joel Jupp of PaperBlazer for his proofreading.

Thanks to my brother James Joslin, named for Major James Lide Coker, and my friends Wynn Cleveland, Paul Olson, and Dean Howard, for helping with the book's expenses.

Finally, I want to thank my friend, Rev. Henry Caldwell, African American pastor of First Church of God Ministries in Raleigh, NC. Like myself, he is a strong believer in the power of forgiveness and in racial reconciliation under the cross. He read the whole manuscript, and helped me present some of the sensitive parts of southern history in what we think is a balanced way. Our intent is to open up the riches of Major Coker's life to as many people as possible.

Introduction

WHY MAJOR COKER'S PRINCIPLES APPLY TO EVERY ERA

Early in World War II, American lawyer Robert D. Abrahams was leisurely playing cards with his friends. Conscious that thousands of Chinese civilians were being brutally murdered that very instant as Japanese invaders burned Shanghai, he suddenly became intensely embarrassed at the stark contrast between the victims' sufferings and his ease. Later, he lamented his cowardice, writing:

> Some men die in shrapnel; some go down in flames, But most men perish inch by inch, in play at little games.[1]

Too many men of our day display this languid passivity as well. Perhaps that's why shows like *Seal Team* and WWII movies like *Fury* have been so popular among both men and women. They fill a void in our culture by portraying brave men who sacrifice for others. But because these men are actors, something is still missing, and we know it.

Today's Muddled Masculinity Needs Clarity

Men were designed to use their God-given strength and drive for worthwhile ends such as bettering their communities, defending their nations, and/or marrying and protecting their wives and families. But masculinity is in crisis today. Some men are turning to destructive devices such as pornography, Internet sex, and drugs for so-called satisfaction. These unworthy pursuits degrade men's souls and weaken families, and will never fulfill the God-given longing each man has to be a hero.

Author Bob Schultz writes: "Books, magazines, and movies often make fun of authentic masculinity. The current pursuit of pleasure, leisure, early retirement, and selfishness stunts the growth of many men. An [immature man] … shrinks from the cold, from climbing mountains, from fighting battles—and then wonders why life is dull and meaningless."[2]

Some would-be cultural influencers try to persuade us that faith and morality are old-hat and that life is without transcendent meaning. We witness the tragedy of this influence when we see selfish, purposeless men who wander through life, never accounting for much. Middle-aged white men now suffer the highest rates of suicide in our country[3] and men of all races need inspiring leaders to encourage them to press forward into productive manhood. There is no better model than Major Coker. He was no actor! He filled the void of courageous manhood in reality.

As a male writing about a male, my book naturally has masculine themes. But the book is intended for both sexes, for both women and men need heroes. And just as men can learn from leading women like Joan of Arc or Florence Nightingale, so women can gain inspiration from men like Major Coker.

The Major's story includes wise and influential females who surrounded him, Including his mother Hannah, his wife Sue, and Coker College alumni Josephine Erwin, Evelyn Snider, and Mrs. Charles Kupfer. And Major Coker was a leader in building up women educationally and spiritually.

Self-serving and materialistic values have always been present, but in the last several decades they have become predominant in our culture. Need we wonder why most people feel empty, and have no larger meaning for life? Men and women need to discover they have a larger purpose and grow to their full potential in ways that benefit others and bring themselves true satisfaction. To this end, Major Coker's principles of courageous leadership and a servant's spirit are needed now more than ever.

Goodness and Greatness

Genuinely good people, such as devoted mothers, faithful school teachers, and dedicated pastors of small churches, may attain greatness in God's eyes (which ultimately is sufficient), but do not usually attain greatness in the world's eyes. And many "great" people, such as former United States Presidents John F. Kennedy and Thomas Jefferson, had serious underlying moral and/or ethical problems that tend to neutralize their greatness. But the Major was both good *and* great. By "great," I mean that he had an inspiring, far-reaching cultural influence as a servant-leader, an influence which continues today.

Many South Carolinians consider him the best businessmen in the history of the state.[4] At the same time, he was a valiant, energetic spiritual leader. George Wilds, business partner and grandson-in-law of the Major, who lived until 1951, said "How much this present generation needs a few Majors."[5] Today's world, rife with corruption in politics, academia, sports, and business, is no different – we are screaming for strong leaders who are trustworthy. We need mentors, and Major Coker's life can mentor us today.

Distinctive of this Biography

Many previous writings on Major Coker, including Simpson's *The Cokers of Carolina*, acknowledge James's Christian faith, but essentially minimize it. This may be because James had a period of doubt between c. 1879 and c. 1894. Even during this time of wrestling with God, the Major never ceased teaching Sunday School, and never retracted his beliefs. He clearly emerged, and strongly re-expressed his devotion to God in 1894 and 1908, when he established two Christian schools, gracing their curricula with Bible classes (and classic education), their founding documents with Christian principles, and their purpose with Christian service. Also, James approved of the invitation of the famous orthodox Christian orator, William Jennings Bryan, to speak at Coker College, in 1911.[6] So there is no need to minimize his faith, and I will present the Major as he was: a humble, intelligent, courageous man of God. In addition to where James quoted God's word, I've included some Bible verses that match his life principles, and his Christian world view.

For more on the Major's beliefs, and challenges to them, Appendix 5 (p. 283) gives a well-documented, detailed account.

The Major Became a Passionate Leader of Social Progress

Major Coker grew up in the old South, and when he came of age, he did not buy slaves. His younger contemporary, J. W. Norwood, said that before the Civil War James "did not believe in slavery."[7] However, when his father Caleb gave James a thousand acres in Hartsville in 1857, he included ten slaves, and James received them with the land. How do we reconcile this irony? It is possible that James received them reluctantly, to avoid appearing ungrateful to his father; it's also possible he felt he needed them to run his farm profitably. But when we consider that, after the war, in 1865, 1866, and every year thereafter, the Major turned a profit on his farm while paying freedmen who stayed on to work for him, the first explanation remains plausible.

In any case, James's reception of the slaves is indeed regrettable. However, he repented of that blight, and immediately after the war, showed his sorrow by initiating and leading the fight for voting rights and economic opportunities for African Americans in his county and state, as described in the section on Reconstruction in Chapter 6 (p.77) and in Appendix 4 (p. 269). By his works, James showed his faith was real.

Today, in churches comprised of blacks, whites, and other ethnic groups, we joyously sing "Amazing Grace," heralding the depths of God's forgiveness and His power to change lives. Should we stop singing it because the songwriter, John Newton, was formerly a slave trader? On the contrary, that's what makes amazing grace so powerful! There are repentant slaveowners in heaven because they received God's pardon.

Examining Ourselves

Some remain unwilling to forgive those slaveowners who repented, and whom God has forgiven. Are these critics wiser than God? Are their standards more legitimate than God's? Are we being hypocritical? Perhaps we should first repent of our own sins. I know some will disagree with me, and that's OK, but I personally know people from both parties who agree with my view of the moral issue I address here. Shouldn't we be more concerned over 60 million aborted babies (half of them women) since 1973, including babies aborted alive and trashed?[8] [9] Why do we allow these lynchings? Why haven't we emancipated our babies? This is not just directed at women who have abortions, for some are stressed out and unaware of better options, but at the piggish men who pressure them, at the current culture which allows it, and at the businesses that drive it. Abortion was infrequent in the Major's time. Instead of pointing the finger back at slaveowners, shouldn't we first examine ourselves? The Lord says it is not us, but He, who knows all, and He who judges with equity:

> Therefore do not go on passing judgment before the time, but wait until the Lord comes, who will both bring to light the things hidden in the darkness and disclose the motives of human hearts" (1 Corinthians 4:5).

When we consider our own culture's sins, I thank God that His forgiveness of the repentant extends beyond the Major's time to ours as well. "Christ gave Himself for our sins, that He might deliver us out of this present evil age, according to the will of our God and Father," for "whoever calls on the name of the Lord will be saved" (Galatians 1:4, Romans 10:13).

Fresh Perspectives on Southern History are Needed

Revealing the steadily progressive leadership qualities of this Confederate man should introduce fresh perspectives on southern history, and help moderate some of the negative tenor of our national conversations about Confederates. Yes, slavery was wrong, and many Confederates were cruel, and even diabolical, slave masters. But there has been a tendency to indiscriminately stereotype all who fought for the Confederacy as white supremacists, throw them into the same box, and close the lid. These stereotypes are far from being universal.

Aside from the Major, another progressive Confederate was Virginia's Calvary Commander, John S. Mosby, who never owned slaves. He said, "I think as badly of slavery as [Union abolitionist] Horace Greeley." But Mosby said he fought for the South "because the South was my country."[10]Other former slaveowners who cannot be stereotyped are Moses and Susan Carver, whites who adopted and nurtured black agricultural genius George Washington Carver, taught him to read, and encouraged his interest in plants and higher education.[11]

A Clear Conscience, and Spiritual Unity across Cultures

A clear conscience under God brings joy that cannot be touched by unforgiving people. The repentant are privileged to "draw near to God in faith with a clear conscience, having our hearts sprinkled clean from an evil conscience" (Hebrews 10:22). But being forgiven does not mean instant maturity. It means that, beneath the cross, the redeemed of all cultures progress together as one family, mutual victors over selfishness, sin, and division. They grow thoughtfully together in grace, truth, and in working out justice, even after tragedies like the murder of George Floyd in May of 2020 at the hands of a white Minneapolis police officer.

The Sunday after his death, In George Floyd's home city of Houston, white parishioners apologized on their knees for years of racism to their black brothers and sisters, who accepted the apology, then they all knelt and prayed together.[12] Afterward, they got up off their knees to work together for justice and peace. George Washington Carver said of Christians: "We are brothers, all of us, no matter what race or color or condition; children of the same heavenly Father. We rise together and we fall together."

I am aware that many across our nation still have racist attitudes, and that much more work must occur, including an examination and weeding out of some in our police forces, before anything close to complete reconciliation is finally achieved. But there is good news. In 2018, the city council of Charleston, former hub of slave trade in South Carolina, officially apologized for the city's previous role in slavery.[13] Charleston's repentance was, of course, not without precedent. And over 140 years before Charleston's apology, Major Coker was living out his repentance from the same nefarious tradition.

In Appendix 4 (p. 269), "How Major Coker Grew Beyond the Mindset of the Old South," Major Coker's racially progressive journey is addressed further, along with a look at some of the author's own "hands on" work toward racial reconciliation.

A Daring Ride Awaits

As we discover this lionhearted man, we'll take an adventurous ride—one of mortal danger, bravery through agony, and unsurpassed initiative and genius. We'll learn the character qualities that led him to purposeful and spotless success. These qualities, if embraced, can help us to do the same today. And if we discover the source of his power, we can become part of the grand, ongoing redemptive drama that endlessly blesses others as he did. Like the Major, we may even change the world.

ENDNOTES FOR INTRODUCTION – TO BE READ! WHY MAJOR COKER'S HEROICS APPLY TO EVERY ERA

1   Robert D. Abrahams, "The Night They Burned Shanghai," *Saturday Evening Post* November 13, 1943, p. 91, as cited in Josh Moody's book *Seven Days to Change your Life*, (Abingdon Press: Nashville, TN), 2017. Also found on Jose Silva's The Intuition website, https://www.intuitionmission.com/fight_apathy.htm (accessed December 29, 2019).

2   Bob Shultz, *Boyhood and Beyond: Practical Wisdom for Becoming a Man*, (Great Expectations Books: Eugene, Oregon), 2004, pp. 40-41.

3   April Baumgarten, Grand Forks Herald November 20, 2019 article "With nation's highest suicide rate, middle-aged white men often don't seek mental health care, " https://www.grandforksherald.com/lifestyle/health/4779091-With-nations-highest-suicide-rate-middle-aged-white-men-often-dont-seek-mental-health-care (accessed December 29, 2019).

4   Ned L. Erwin, "Coker, James Lide, Sr.," on the South Carolina Hall of Fame website, wrote: "At the time of his death on June 25, 1918, Coker was considered the wealthiest citizen of the state and, perhaps, its most versatile postbellum entrepreneur."

5   George Wilds, *Recollections of the Major: James Lide Coker, 1837-1918* (Hartsville Museum: Hartsville, SC), 1997, p. 67. In citations hereafter, this work will be abbreviated as *Recollections*.

6   Editor, Bishopville, SC's *Leader and Vindicator* newspaper, "Local Items," Thursday, June 11, 1911, Vol. 10, No. 1 p. 1.

7   J. W. Norwood, as quoted by Harvey Toliver Cook, *Rambles in the Pee Dee Basin, South Carolina*, (The State Company: Columbia, SC, 1926, Volume I, pp. 162-163, p. 425.

8   Schu Montgomery, Jan. 22, 2020, "Opinion: The fight against abortion is a fight for women's rights," https://www.courier-journal.com/story/opinion/2020/01/22/abortion-march-life-theme-shows-pro-life-pro-woman/4523169002/, accessed January 2021.

9   Editors, The Christian Lawyer, volume 8, no. 4, Summer 2013, "Roe v. Wade, Reflections After 40 Years," https://www.christianlegalsociety.org/sites/default/files/2017-07/2013%20Summer%20Christian%20Lawyer%20Magazinetest.pdf

10 Virginia Commander John S. Mosby, letter to Sam Chapman, June 4, 1907, Wayback Machine, Gilder Lehrman Collection, https://www.gilderlehrman.org/history-by-era/reconstruction/resources/former-confederate-officer-slavery-and-civil-war-1907.

11 Barbara Maranzani, Biography.com, 2016, 2020 article "How George Washington Carver Went From Enslaved to Educational Pioneer," https://www.biography.com/news/george-washington-carver-slave-educational-pioneer, accessed January 2021.

12 Web team, WION TV web site, June 3, 2020 article, "White parishioners kneel down, ask for forgiveness in George Floyd's hometown Houston," New Delhi, https://www.dailymail.co.uk/news/article-8376907/White-people-pray-George-Floyds-hometown-Houston-ask-black-communitys-forgiveness.html, accessed 12/29/2020.

13 M. L. Nestel, ABC News site, June 20, 2018 article "Charleston formally apologizes for its role in slavery," https://abcnews.go.com/US/charleston-formally-apologizes-role-slavery/story?id=56026589 (accessed March 2, 2020).

PART I

BEGINNINGS: JAMES'S LIFE AND ADVENTURES FROM BOYHOOD TO AGE 24

CHAPTER 1

ANCESTRY AND BOYHOOD

James Lide (rhymes with "tide") Coker was born in Darlington County in northeastern South Carolina, about fifty years after the American Revolution. His life covers a critical span of American history, stretching from 1837 the frontier days, to 1918, the year World War I ended.

Revolutionary War General Francis Marion, "The Swamp Fox." His band who attacked the British in the Pee Dee included two of James's great-grandfathers, Captain Thomas Coker and Major Robert Lide. Painting by artist Robert Wilson, https://www.robertwilsonsrfineart.com. Permission of Jeff and Toni Hesla.

James's family on his mother's side was Welsh, and on his father's side, English.[1] They lived in an area originally settled by Welsh Baptists who called themselves the Saint David's Society,[2] named after the patron saint of Wales. The oldest community in Darlington County, their town was named Society Hill because it rested on high ground west of the Pee Dee River. The town has been called "the birthplace of the Pee Dee"[3] because most early leaders

2

of Darlington County hailed from there. Later James would establish his own home just a few miles southeast, in Hartsville.

James's Heritage of Valor

Backcountry South Carolinians have never lacked for mettle, and they played a key role in the American Revolution. Two of James's great grandfathers, Lieutenant Thomas Coker[4] on his father's side, and Major Robert Lide,[5] on his mother's, fought the Redcoats in the Pee Dee

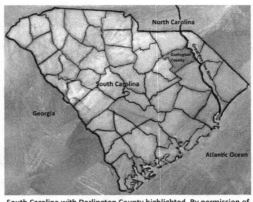

South Carolina with Darlington County highlighted. By permission of professional artist Dan Nelson of Raleigh, NC.

River area under "The Swamp Fox," South Carolina's famous General Francis Marion.[6] In the movie *The Patriot*, released in 2000, Mel Gibson represented a composite character that included the courageous and cunning Marion,[7] and two of the men in Marion's band represented James's great grandfathers. Marion taught his men stealthy battle strategies that he had learned from the Cherokee Indians when he fought them in the French and Indian War.[8] Marion's men would hide behind Cypress trees in the Pee Dee swamps, then suddenly jump out to attack the unsuspecting British. Along with General Nathanael Greene, Marion's troops played a key part in helping to win our war for independence, depleting the British forces, then forcing them northward where they were pinned down by Washington in Virginia. And the valor of these two great grandfathers would show up conspicuously in James as well.

Even before the Revolution, as some of the first settlers in Darlington County, Lieutenant Thomas Coker and Major

Robert Lide, owned a fair amount of land in the county. After the Revolution, they were awarded larger tracts. An official deed states that Lieutenant Thomas Coker was granted an additional "tract of one thousand acres ... surveyed and granted for Thomas Coker the fifth day of February 1787, by His Excellency William Moultrie [the] Governor...."[9] To these lands, Lieutenant Thomas Coker added at least three hundred more acres "adjoining other Coker lands."[10]

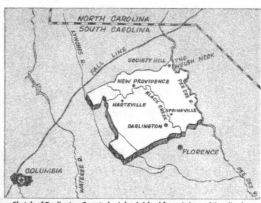

Sketch of Darlington County by John Ashford from *Cokers of Carolina* by George Lee Simpson, Jr. Used with permission from UNC Press.

Thomas Coker was active in the community, helped establish the Cashaway Baptist Church near Society Hill in 1804[11] and served as one of its lay preachers.[12] Major Robert Lide was a member of this church.[13] Thomas Coker also "helped mightily to establish the community, to give it shape and identity out of the raw shapelessness of new lands."[14] He married Mary Prestwood, for whom Hartsville's Prestwood Lake is named.[15] Their son, Caleb Coker Sr., was described as "a substantial farmer and landowner in the community."[16]

These two would go on to acquire more land, and though it is difficult to assess the total acreage that Lieutenant Coker and Major Lide passed on to their descendants, it is safe to say it was a sizeable chunk of the upper half of Darlington County. Consequently, two generations later, their grandchildren, including both of James's parents, Caleb Coker, Jr. (1802-1869) and Hannah Lide (1812-1900), were heirs to substantial plantation tracts. They also were some of the leading citizens of the county.

James's Parents and Home Life

James's father, Caleb Coker, Jr., was a partner in a successful general store in Society Hill, Coker and Gregg, founded in 1828. He was also a cotton trader, the director of the Cheraw and Darlington Railroad, a charter member of the Society Hill Agricultural Society, and the local librarian. He was known as an honest and diligent merchant. He usually attended church and often gave some of his products to the pastor, yet he declared himself an agnostic,[17] once saying he was "not good enough to join the church."[18] This statement seems curious because the church is made up of those who join on those very grounds—that they are not good enough.[19]

James's father Caleb Coker, Jr., c. 1855. From George L. Simpson's *Cokers of Carolina*. Permissions of UNC Press and portrait owner Caleb Fort.

James's mother, Hannah Lide Coker, was a pivotal person in her son's life. She had "lively eyes, where even at the age of eighteen, there were indications of firmness and character."[20] She had "her happy, vivacious side, and a sense of humor that eventually appeared in time to lighten moods in troublous times."[21] She and Caleb were married in 1830, and Hannah bore him ten children. James was the oldest boy and the third child of ten: Jane Lide, Anna

James' mother Hannah Lide Coker, daguerrotype from c. 1840. From Coker College Archives. Retouched by Diane Henry Studio of Raleigh, NC.

Maria, James Lide, William Caleb, Charles Westfield, Francis Elizabeth Pugh, Mary Lide, Edward Thomas, Emma Sarah, and Florence.[22] The family worshipped at the Welsh Neck

Baptist Church, established in 1738, the second oldest church in the state. It was named "Welsh Neck" Baptist because it is situated in the northeastern neck of Darlington County (see maps above). The church and its related school, Saint David's Academy, founded 1777, were virtually extensions of the Coker home.[23]

Unlike many women from her era, Hannah had a good education from two private academies, including the Misses Ramsey's School for Young Ladies on Broad Street in Charleston.[24] She also had a strong faith, owning Christ as her Savior in c. 1825 during America's Second Great Awakening,[25] a national religious revival that lasted from c. 1790 to 1860. South Carolina state historian Walter Edgar writes that this revival had a tremendous impact on the people of upstate South Carolina.[26] In 1841, John L. Hart, son of Hartsville namesake Thomas E. Hart, wrote to his uncle, Colonel T. C. Law of Hartsville: "I was extremely happy to hear of the great revival of religion in that section of the country [the Pee Dee area]. I hope that it may not cease and that there may be as it were a perpetual springtime."[27] For more on America's awakenings, see this endnote[28] and accompanying chart.[29]

James's sister, Jane Lide, spoke of their mother's zeal for the things of God: "My dear mother, Mrs. Hannah Lide Coker, was always the kind, sympathizing and helpful friend of every pastor and she was loved and honored by each one."[30] "I learned more about Christianity from my mother than from all the theologians in England," said John Wesley, founder of Methodism.[31] Similarly, with devoted love, James's godly mother gave him and his siblings a solid biblical foundation and a transcendent purpose for life. Though not personally converted until age 19, as a child, James accepted Christian values, and built his life on that bedrock.

It is interesting that James's childhood houses also had firm foundations. The house in which he was born in Society Hill, built in 1832, is still standing. In 1844, the family moved to another house two miles away in an area known as Camp Marion. That house also still stands today.

The native soil was rich sandy loam,[32] and their ancestors had used the land profitably as planters of cotton, corn, small grain, indigo, and tobacco. Though not as wealthy as South Carolinian aristocrats, such as the John C. Calhouns of Fort Hill Plantation or the Wade Hamptons of Columbia, by the standards of country life, the Cokers were wealthy.

The sturdy house in Society Hill, built in 1832, where James Lide Coker was born. Permission of Jim Lyles, unitedbrokerage.com, and Agnes Lyles, agneswilcox.com

James, Jane, and Anna walked two miles each day to Saint David's school. The first year, James's homemade boots blistered him so badly

A southern cotton field like young James Lide Coker worked in the mid 1800's. Permission of Depositphotos.com.

that he often went barefoot. In later years, he wrote that this gave him "a great deal of glee."[33] In those days, the teacher in the one-room schoolhouse assigned the girls to sit on one side and the boys on the other. When James started first grade, just before turning six, he sat on the girls' side with his sisters. After allowing this arrangement for two days, the teacher told James, "From now on, you must either wear petticoats or sit on the boys' side."[34] James changed his seat and matured rapidly after that.

James excelled in school, and later, with his characteristic modesty, wrote: "I could read a little when I started to school, having been taught at home by my mother."[35] He also wrote, "It seemed to me that going to school was a very serious matter, and I remember that it caused me real grief if I missed a single word in any of my lessons."[36] George Norwood, a lifelong friend who attended Saint David's with James, described the robust Coker boy as follows: "In playing ball and other games, young Coker displayed noticeable energy, activity, and earnestness… and these characteristics were shown in his every undertaking throughout his life."[37]

Hannah had a natural hands-on instinct for farming. She saw to it that James and his brothers each worked their own plots of cotton, with each responsible for his own production.

James thus grew up participating in two worlds: farming and merchandising. On the farm, he experienced the hard, physical work of planting and harvesting, and felt the rhythms of agricultural cycles. He also identified with the toil and hardships of his poorer neighbors, fostering empathy and compassion in his character.

As far as merchandising, he paid attention to his father's market savvy and entrepreneurial skills, and acquired a good nose for business. The combination of these diverse sensibilities equipped James with many capabilities for service.

James also loved the outdoors, and observed the plant and animal kingdoms with a keen mind. While quite young, he caught and

Established in 1828, James's father Caleb Coker Jr.'s store as it still stands in Society Hill, SC. Permission from Jim Lyles of unitedbrokerage.com.

raised a young sparrow hawk. He taught it to hunt for sparrows, finches, and thrushes. He often carried it on his finger and dispatched it to flush birds from the bushes, then dart down, catch its prey, and come back to perch on his finger.[38]

James grew up before slavery was outlawed. From his childhood, he was kind to the slaves whom he knew, and he had a deep desire to improve their lives. For example, he developed a close bond of friendship with a slave his own age named York. They farmed together, hunted and fished together, went to the

James and York grew up to be best friends.
Conception of professional artist Dan Nelson

swimming hole together, and laughed and cried together. Because York was a slave of James's father, it cannot be said it was a friendship of equals. Nevertheless, they were so close that each pledged that he would take care of the other for life.[39]

James's Observations

As James worked hard on the farm, his keen eye noticed many things. He thought there had to be more efficient ways to profit from cotton. Whereas his father kept detailed records of his store inventory, expenses, and income, he observed he kept minimal records for their farm tracts. They did not record methods of soil preparation, grades of seeds, or which fertilizers were being used on which plots, so there was no objective basis for crop performance comparison.[40] Although most young people would not have noticed these subtle deficiencies, James knew instinctively that keeping better records would improve efficiency and maximize farm production. His niece, Kate Chambers, reflecting on James's boyhood, wrote that the "young man was intelligent and progressive beyond his time."[41]

Even in his youth, James thought as an entrepreneur. He asked questions like, "Why do we have to ship our cotton to the companies in Charleston[42] so that they make the big profits

Young James pondering how the Cokers could ship their goods more efficiently. And why couldn't they build their own cotton mill? Conception of Professional Artist Dan Nelson.

reselling it? Why can't we build our own machines and spin the yarn ourselves?" and "Why don't we build a railroad to ship our goods instead of using our slow, low-volume overland wagons?"

Community Needs and Early Impressions

Young James also had a tender and sympathetic heart toward others. His grandparents on Hannah's side moved to Alabama just two years before his birth because of problems with malaria from mosquitoes in the Pee Dee swamps and because they had exhausted their farmland due to repeated cotton planting.[43] It saddened young James to be separated from his kin. These public health and agricultural problems made a deep impression on him, and in his lifetime he remedied them for the good of all. His mother's relatives did not move back to the Pee Dee, but later, while visiting them, James would find a prize in Alabama.

As he rubbed shoulders with poor sharecroppers, he noticed most farm families were extremely uneducated and often penniless due to farming debts. He was deeply moved in spirit when he saw they had almost no hope of improving their lives. It also grieved him that the churches and schools were not reaching out to them. His boyhood friend George Norwood noticed: "In addition to his energy and sound common sense, Major Coker had a remarkable natural intellectual ability, and was blessed with a noble, unselfish character, and a sound physical constitution."[44]

His Life Purpose

James had no identity crisis. Even as a youngster, his life purpose was taking root. His calling from God would be to provide better economic, educational, and spiritual opportunities for his fellow South Carolinians, both white and African-American. These noble intentions would be severely challenged by his sufferings. But in the end, his trials made him more selfless and his faith more genuine, and combined with his gifts, forged him into one of the most remarkable men who has ever lived.

For those who want to reinvest Major Coker's childhood values into the lives of today's children and youth, see the discussion questions built off James's boyhood and designed for them at https://www. willjoslin.com/major/questions/children and https://www.willjoslin. com/major/questions/youth.

ENDNOTES FOR CHAPTER 1: ANCESTRY AND BOYHOOD

1   Editor, Coker Family History site at https://www.ancestry.com/name-origin?surname=Coker (accessed December 29, 2019). and Lide Family History Site at https://www.ancestry.com/name-origin?surname=lide (accessed December 29, 2019).

2   Editor, The Federal Writer's Project, *The WPA Guide to South Carolina: The Palmetto State,* (Trinity University Press: San Antonio), 2013, Tour 2, Section a., Google Books, https://books.google.com/books?id=YbLpCAAAQBAJ&dq=saint+david%27s+society+society+hill+named+for+patron+saint&source=gbs_navlinks_s.

3   Behre, Robert, 2019 "Preservation South Carolina" article at https://preservesc.org/saving-society-hill-the-birthplace-of-the-pee-dee-looks-to-its-past-for-new-life/ (accessed December 29, 2019).

4   George Lee Simpson, op. cit., p. 20.

5   Editor, Singleton Family's website, "Major Robert Lide (1734-1802), http://www.singletonfamily.org/getperson.php?personID=I4021&tree=1 Major Robert Lide was "Captain of the Militia of the Continental Army in 1776, Major in Marion's Brigade. Robert was a major in the South Carolina Militia and was present at the defense of Charleston in 1779. Escaping capture, he was attached to Francis Marion's brigade" (accessed March 5, 2020).

6   George Lee Simpson, op. cit., pp. 6,20.

7   Editor, The Historical Commission, 2018 article "TODAY IN SOUTH CAROLINA HISTORY: THE PATRIOT WITH MEL GIBSON," https://dchcblog.net/2017/06/30/today-in-south-carolina-history-the-patriot-with-mel-gibson/ (accessed December 29, 2019).

8   Carole Bos, Awesome Stories, 2013, updated 2019, "Francis Marion, 'Swamp Fox,'" https://www.awesomestories.com/asset/view/Francis-Marion-Swamp-Fox-//1 (accessed February 29, 2020).

9   George Lee Simpson, op. cit., p. 20.

10 Malcolm C. Doubles, *A Century Plus: A History of Sonoco Products Company* (Coker College Press: Hartsville SC, 2005, p. 4).

11 Harvey Toliver Cook, *Rambles in the Pee Dee Basin, South Carolina,* (The State Company: Columbia, SC, 1926, Volume I, pp. 162-163, and similar information on Lieutenant Thomas Coker is found at George Lee Simpson, op. cit., pp. 161-162, and George Lee Simpson, op. cit., pp. 21-22.

12 George Lee Simpson, op. cit., pp. 20-21.

13 Harvey Toliver Cook, *Rambles in the Pee Dee Basin, South Carolina,* (The State Company, Columbia, SC), 1926, Volume I, pp. 162-164.

14 Ibid, p. 21.

15 Malcolm C. Doubles, *In Quest of Excellence, A History of Coker College on its Centennial*, (Coker College Press: Hartsville), 2008, p. 4, where he quotes Janie Lide, "Founder's Day Address," Coker College, April 1951, Coker College Archives.

16 George Lee Simpson, op. cit., p. 21.

17 William (Will) Chambers Coker, *Recollections* p. 67.

18 George Lee Simpson, op. cit., p. 40, as told by Dr. W. C. Coker to his mother.

19 Romans 5:6: "For while we were still helpless, at the right time Christ died for the ungodly."

20 George Lee Simpson, op. cit., p. 4.

21 Ibid., p. 28.

22 The dates for James's siblings are Jane Lide (1831-1923), Hugh (1833-?), Anna Maria (1834-1899), James Lide (1837-1913), William Caleb (1839-1907), Charles Westfield (1841-1862), and Francis Elizabeth (1844-1910), Mary Lide (1847-1929), Edward Thomas (1850-?), Emma Sarah (1853-1923), and Florence (1854-1934). From George Lee Simpson, op. cit., p. 37.

23 George Lee Simpson, op. cit., p. 38.

24 Editor, United Brokerage Real Estate Services, https://unitedbrokerage. com/wp-content/uploads/2018/02/Coker-House-and-Family-History. pdf (accessed February 17, 2020).

25 Robert W. Fogel, see review of his book, *Phases of the Four Great Awakenings* at https://www.press.uchicago.edu/Misc/Chicago/256626. html (accessed December 29, 2019).

26 Walter Edgar, *South Carolina: A History*, (University of South Carolina Press: Columbia, SC, 1988), p. 292.

27 Dr. Susan D. Reynolds, *First Baptist Church Scrapbook*, (History Committee Books 2005-2008, Hartsville, SC). The letter is recorded on p. 124.

28 Robert W. Fogel, op cit.

29 The chart below gives the author's synopsis of the four great awakenings.

America's Great Awakenings	Approx. Dates	Leading Evangelists
1st	c. 1730-1760	Jonathan Edwards, George Whitfield
2nd	c. 1790-1860	Lorenzo Dow, Charles Finney, Hannah Whitall Smith
3rd	c. 1860-1930	Dwight L. Moody, Billy Sunday
4th	c. 1949-	Bill Bright, Billy Graham, Nicky Cruz, Luis Palau

30 From Jane Lide Coker Wilson, *Memories of Society Hill, S.C.*, Pee Dee Historical Society, 1909-1910, p. 19, (South Caroliniana Library, University of South Carolina: Columbia, SC).

31 Editor, Grace Quotes, 2016 "John Wesley," https://gracequotes.org/author-quote/john-wesley/ (accessed March 5, 2020).

32 George Lee Simpson, op. cit., p. 5. For more on the Pee Dee's sandy loam soil and suitable crops, also see 2019 website "Darlington County, SC" at http://www.carolana.com/SC/Counties/darlington county sc.html (accessed December 29, 2019).

33 Vivien Gay Coker, *Recollections*, p. 1.

34 George Lee Simpson, op. cit., pp. 38-39.

35 James Lide Coker, *Recollections*, p. II.

36 Ibid.

37 J. W. Norwood quoting his father George Norwood in Appendix 1 of Furman Professor Harvey Toliver Cook's book, *Rambles in the Pee Dee Basin, South Carolina,* op. cit., p. 414.

38 Ibid., p. 82.

39 William (Will) Chambers Coker, *Recollections,* pp. 10-11.

40 James A. Rogers and Larry E. Nelson, *Mr. D. R.: A Biography of David R. Coker*, Coker College Press, 1994, pp. 4-5, and also Vivien C. Coker, *Recollections*, p. 3. These sources indicate that James was very eager to learn about accurate and scientific agricultural recordkeeping at Harvard, implying that his family did not practice much of it in James's youth. James A. Rogers and Larry E. Nelson will hereafter be referred to as Rogers and Nelson.

41 Kate Chambers, *Chronicles of a Worth-while Family*, a book on the Chambers and Stout families, published in only twenty copies in 1919. In 2004, one hundred more volumes were published by Edgar H. Lawton Jr. with help from Coker College and Frank Bush. The quote is from p. 77.

42 J. W. Norwood from his recorded speech "Major James Lide Coker as Citizen and Business Man," from *Memorial Exercises*, Coker College, subtitled *Founders Day, April 9, 1919*, op. cit., p. 15.

43 Miss Jane Lide, from her typed speech "An Attempted Character Sketch" [of Major Coker] given on Founder's Day, Coker College, Friday April 27, 1956. p. 2, from Coker College archives.

44 J. W. Norwood, *Rambles in the Pee Dee Basin, South Carolina*, op. cit., p. 414.

CHAPTER 2

THE ARSENAL, THE CITADEL, AND HARVARD

James finished Saint David's in 1853 at age sixteen. It is no coincidence that he went on to the South Carolina Military Academy; there were already pre-Civil War rumblings of a conflict with the North. His military training would consist of a year at The Arsenal in Columbia followed by three years at The Citadel in Charleston.

The Citadel Academy in Charleston in 1860 with cadets performing drills in case of "emergency" as storm clouds gather. By permission of Citadel Archives.

His Mother's Concern

Beyond the worldly conflicts of the day, Hannah also recognized that as a young man now on his own, James was facing spiritual battles. She cared deeply about his spiritual welfare and prayed for him. Other than that he had not yet been converted, we don't know if James did something to prompt this warning, but she wrote him these passionate words of concern in 1853:

Nothing can give us more heartfelt satisfaction and comfort or cause us deeper grief and woe than the conduct of our children. They are our hopes and expectations. For their good, we are willing to make many sacrifices of comfort and pleasure, hoping to be repaid by seeing them grow up to be good, useful, and respectable

James as a Citadel cadet, c. 1856. From *Recollections of the Major*, published by Hartsville Museum and used with permission.

citizens. If, on the contrary, they should become idle, immoral profligates, we would rather follow them to their graves or be carried there ourselves than live to endure such sorrow and disgrace.[1]

In another letter, seven months later, she quoted Proverbs 1:10 to him: "My son, if sinners entice you, do not consent."[2] And on more than one occasion, she said to him: "Always remember that you are a gentleman."[3]

James progressed to The Citadel, where from the beginning, he achieved high marks. Later, his son Will Coker described James's progress in mathematics: "He had a splendid mathematical mind, leading his class at the Citadel where mathematics might be called the main subject of study. The second student in his mathematics classes was Mr. Benjamin Sloan who later became Professor of Mathematics and Physics at the University of South Carolina and was one of my professors there."[4] And as far as his progress in military training, by the end of his second year, James had attained the rank of second lieutenant.

James's Conversion

His mother's warnings about his human sin nature seem to have helped James discern its murky undercurrent in his life.

In his first year at The Citadel, James saw that his high breeding, noble intentions, and religious background would never justify him before God. He remembered the truths in 2 Timothy 3:15: "From childhood you have known the sacred writings which are able to give you the wisdom that leads to salvation through faith which is in Christ Jesus." The flash point came as he repented of his sins, trusted Christ, and received forgiveness.

His fellow cadet Thomas Hart ("Tom") Law was a friend from Hartsville, only one year younger than James, and their friendship strengthened. Tom was a devout young man who became Citadel valedictorian[5] and was later ordained as a minister. He kept a detailed journal of their time at The Citadel. On Sunday, March

Tom Law, James' fellow cadet at The Citadel. From *Journal of Cadet Tom Law*, reprinted by John Law, PC Press, 1941.

30, 1856, he wrote about James desiring to own Christ as his Savior. Tom's journal entry reads:

> It rained almost the whole day, so much that we did not attend church. In the afternoon, I heard the report that JLC intended uniting with the church on the next Sabbath…. That evening, I got a letter from Julia [Tom's oldest sister], who mentioned that she had heard he [James] said he "was indulging a hope." Soon after, getting in private with him, he told me that the reports were true, and we then had a religious conversation for the first time. I was much joyed at hearing such news.[6]

Tom's journal for the following Sunday reads that James followed up his decision by being baptized:

> On account of J. L. Coker's baptism, we were excused from marching to [The Citadel's campus] church. A good many of us went to the Morris Street Church to attend the service.[7]

What did James mean by "indulging a hope?" *Merriam-Webster's Dictionary* defines "indulge" as "to give free rein to, to take unrestrained pleasure in," and "to yield to the desire of."[8] "Indulge" implies that there is something lavish to be gained, which is the same vocabulary God's Word uses to describe the hope of salvation as "the riches of His grace, which he lavished upon us" (Ephesians 1:7-8). The apostle Peter also wrote that believers are indulging a hope when they are "born again to a living hope through the resurrection of Jesus Christ from the dead" (1 Peter 1:3). The Second Great Awakening had claimed James along with his mother.

James shed more light on his conversion in 1859 when he wrote in his farm journal:

> The character of the Supreme Being is a subject of such sanctity that we must, like the [Old Testament] High Priest, when he would go within the veil of the temple, purify ourselves, putting away all import and remember that our license thus to deal with these sacred terms and penetrate into the most Holy place is derived from our communion with Christ our Lord and granted us through His most comprehensive merits.[9]

Note: For more detail on James's lifelong faith, see Appendix 5 (p. 283) which addresses his own confessions of faith and his response to the teachings of Darwin, which were published near the time of his conversion.

Debates and Academics at The Citadel

James's classmates elected him president of The Citadel's Polytechnic Literary Society, which by design had oratory duels with their campus rival, the Calliopean Society. In the debates, James actively exercised his vigorous mind, increasing his skills in rhetoric and sharpening his intellectual powers. James was ranked sixth in a class that included some of the best young minds in the state of South Carolina. But just six weeks before graduating in the top third of his class, his life at The Citadel took an adverse turn.

Courses and Textbooks at The Citadel for 1856, James' 4th Year
From *Journal of Cadet Tom Law*

Studies	Text Books
Civil and Military Engineering	Mahan, Halleck, and Lectures
Intellectual Philiosphy	Thomas C. Upham, Mental Philosophy
Moral Philosophy	William Paley, Principles of Moral & Political Philosophy
Political Economy	Droz. (in French)
National and Constitutional Law	Constitutions of U.S. and S.C., and Calhoun's Disquisition
Astronomy	Gummere
Chemistry	Fowne
Mineralogy	Dana
Geology	Lyell
Topographic and Architectural Drawing	Eastman
Artillery and Infantry Tactics	U.S. Tactics, Kingsbury and Scott

Misfortune, Conflict, and Honor

On September 15, 1856, when James flawlessly worked out a theorem on the board, his math professor, Major F. W. Capers, accused him of plagiarizing—a charge Capers could not prove. James knew himself to be innocent and his classmates believed he had not done this. He felt that Capers had not only called his honor into question but had attacked his family name. As a result, he took issue with the professor. In his journal entry of September 15, 1856, Tom Law gave a fuller picture of the incident and James's response:

> A circumstance took place today, which from its consequences has become a matter of some moment. While reciting to Major Capers, Jim Coker was called up to the board. When he went to demonstrate, Major Capers insinuated that he suspected him of taking his figure from the book. This being quite offensive to sensitive gentlemanly feeling, J. L. C. was somewhat touched by it and told Major Capers that he did not think he had any reason to think him guilty of such a thing, which led on to some pretty sharp words.

21

> That afternoon, J.L.C. resigned to Major Capers his office of 2nd Lieutenant—said he did not wish to hold it since it was the gift of the latter. He also wrote to [General] Ben. Jones in regard to the affair, appealing to him for justice, which he saw plainly could not be obtained from the very unworthy Superior of our officers [Major Capers].[10]

There is a YouTube video suggesting that James actually challenged Professor Capers to a duel.[11] Dueling was still legal at the time, but Tom Law did not hint at this in his detailed journal, and finding no other evidence for it, the duel challenge may have been an exaggeration.

Law's entries from September 15 to 26, 1856 included the following:

> Many of the Cadets seemed quite indignant at this. As for myself, I could scarcely contain myself. J. L. C. seemed quite mortified at it, though he did not appear to care very much on his own account, principally that of his parents.

> He tells us today [Sept. 25] that he and Jones have split on a still smaller matter. Gen. Jones tells him that Major Capers disclaims all intention of insulting him in the section room. He (J. C.) therefore agreed to retract what he said provided that it [what Major Capers had said about not intending any insult] be mentioned in the order (as above). This, however, Gen'l Jones would not consent to do, and as J. L. C. was unwilling to retract without it, he was determined to bid them adieu.

James summarized the unhappy incident this way:

> I did not graduate at The Citadel, although I finished the course and was ready for graduation standing high up in the class. A difficulty with the Superintendent was the cause of my leaving the Academy a few weeks before graduation. I resented an unjust charge involving my character and was expelled from the institution, the Board of Visitors offering to restore me if I would make apology to the Superintendent which I declined to do, as by so doing, I would have been admitting a fault that I had not committed. My literary society gave a diploma, the same as they gave to those who receive the graduating diplomas, and nearly all of the class approved of the position I took. [12]

In Chapter 15 on his character qualities, under "Did Youthful Pride Get the Best of James at The Citadel?" we discuss whether or not James could have handled this delicate situation better.

James came home. Because of his earlier diligence with his cotton field, Caleb Jr. and Hannah gave him ownership of a plantation "of a little more than one thousand acres"[13] in the Hartsville area. This was half of the land that Caleb Jr. had purchased in 1854[14] from John Lide Hart, son of Captain Thomas Edward Hart (1796-1842), for whom Hartsville is named.[15] [16] James was grateful, but felt he could help his family and community more if he first studied scientific farming methods. He asked if he could attend Harvard's Lawrence Scientific School [17] for a year before beginning his agricultural work in earnest. His parents agreed, and he left for Harvard in March of 1857.

Harvard

When he arrived, the professors told him they could not help him unless he had soils from his native land. James calmly replied, "I have samples of the soils with me."[18] Journalist Mabel Montgomery commented: "With meticulous thoroughness... he had brought with him in his small trunk, samples of the soils of Darlington County."[19] That trunk is now in the Hartsville museum.

At Harvard James received many answers to questions he had since childhood about farm production as he learned about the chemical needs of plants, soil chemistry, the testing of fertilizers, how to rebuild soil that had been depleted by cotton planting,[20] and about selectively breeding crops. He "learned to lay off measured fields and label what was planted in each, to observe continuously, to record the growth of each plant accurately, and to measure and compare results."[21]

J. W. Norwood, son of the Major's boyhood friend George Norwood, commented on James's diligence and his fascination with chemistry: "While at Harvard, he frequently took his lunch with him to the chemical laboratory in order that he might spend the day with his experiments and thereby get more thorough knowledge."[22] James returned to Hartsville early in 1859 with a chemistry set that he would use to refine his fertilizers and augment agricultural production throughout his life. He kept accurate records of fertilizers, plots, and weather conditions in his farm journal and implemented what he learned at Harvard.[23] In this way, he was able to continue making a profit for three straight years before the Civil War—even during the long, unfortunate spans of weather that threatened other farms in the area. And setting a pattern that would characterize his life, he unselfishly gave back to the community the blessings of his wider knowledge[24] by organizing an agricultural club, later called the Hartsville Agricultural Society.[25]

ENDNOTES FOR CHAPTER 2: THE ARSENAL, THE CITADEL, AND HARVARD

1   George Lee Simpson, op. cit., p. 296, quoting from the letter from Hannah Coker to James Lide Coker, February 24, 1853 (R. E. Coker).

2   Ibid., p. 296-297, quoting from the letter from Hannah Coker to James Lide Coker, September 9, 1853.

3   Ibid., p. 297, quoting from D. R. Coker, "Major James Lide Coker: A Son's Tribute," typewritten copy of talk made by D. R. Coker at Coker College, January 5, 1937.

4   *Recollections*, p. 2

5   Editor, "Law, Thomas Hart (1838-1933)", Citadel.edu, http://www3. citadel.edu/archivesguide/index.php/LAW, THOMAS HART, 1838- 1923 (accessed March 5, 2020).

6   John Adger Law, *The Journal of Cadet Tom Law*, chronicling Tom's Citadel years from 1855-1858, (PC Press: Clinton, SC), published in typewritten form in 1941, p. 15.

7   Ibid., p. 18.

8   Editor, Merriam Webster website, 2019, definition of word "Indulge," https://www.merriam-webster.com/dictionary/indulge   (accessed December 29, 2019).

9   James Lide Coker's personal farming journal, essay on the transcendence of his personal God over natural law, p. 28, according to the journal page enumeration of The Caroliniana archives storage system, courtesy of South Caroliniana Library, University of South Carolina, Columbia, SC Box 2, File "Plantation Records 1858-1860."

10 Thomas Hart Law, op. cit., p. 50.

11 James Lide Coker, IV, March 12, 2013 video "James Lide Coker," https:// www.youtube.com/watch?v=7GmNV9zy00E(accessed June 16,2020).

12 James Lide Coker's own written account of his leaving The Citadel, as published, *Recollections*, Foreword, p. VI.

13 Malcolm C. Doubles, *A Century Plus: A History of Sonoco Products Company*, op. cit., p. 2.

14 Editor, "South Carolina Plantations" 2019 website by SCIWAY.net, LLC, https://south-carolina-plantations.com/darlington/hartsville. html (accessed December 29, 2019).

15 Editor, WikiTree website 2019 article "John Lide Hart," https://www. wikitree.com/wiki/Hart-10757 (accessed December 29, 2019).

16 George Lee Simpson, op. cit., p. 49.

17   Editor, article "James Lide Coker, *"Who's Who in America?* from Volume VIII, 1914-1915 (Marquis Press: Berkeley Heights, NJ), 1915, mentions the Major's work at Harvard as being in its Lawrence School of Science.

18   Mabel Montgomery, South Carolina's *The State* magazine (not to be confused with the present newspaper by the same name), December 18, 1949. Pp. 1-8

19   Ibid.

20   Vivien G. Coker, *Recollections*, p. 3.

21   Rogers and Nelson, op. cit., pp. 4-5.

22   J. W. Norwood from his recorded speech at *Memorial Day, Founder's Day,* at Coker College in Hartsville, SC, on *April 9, 1919*, p. 15.

23   Simpson, op.cit., p. 53.

24   J. M. Napier, *Recollections*, p. 14.

25   Will Coker, *Recollections*, p. 4.

CHAPTER 3

MARRIAGE AND CHILDREN

After Harvard, James spent more than two years over a plow looking at the south end of a northbound mule. Needless to say, he was ready for a prettier companion. A man blessed with a wonderful mother tends to look for a bride like his mother; accordingly, James wanted someone like Hannah: a woman of God who was devout, strong, purposeful, attractive, and funny.

In January of 1860, he was the best man at the wedding of his first cousin on his mother's side, Rebecca Lide, of Carlowville, Alabama. He strode in a bit late to the rehearsal dinner and sat near a woman of striking beauty and a stately bearing, Miss Susan (Sue) Armstrong Stout of Wetumpka, Alabama. Sue's cousin, Frank R. Chambers, called her "the

Susan Armstrong Stout Coker, James' wife.
Picture taken c. 1858, is considered public domain.

fairest flower of the family."[1] As it turned out, Sue was the bride's maid, and, foretelling things to come, James walked her down the aisle.

As soon as James discovered that Sue was a devoted Christian with a great sense of humor, and that she loved church work and music, there were no more questions to ask.[2] Later, Sue said of James: "The very minute my eyes lit upon James, I knew I was going to marry him." And James said: "Well, I guess you might call it love at first sight on both sides."[3]

Sue's parents were Rev. Platt Stout (1796-1867) and Margaret Armstrong Stout (1801-1888). Witnessing the courtship was Kate Chambers, Sue's niece on her mother's side. Kate's eventual husband, Frank R. Chambers (who, along with Kate, appears later in the book), was James's nephew. Kate wrote about Sue and the short courtship:

> Aunt Sue, like her sisters, had grown into lovely young womanhood. She was possessed of an exquisite complexion, a delicate blush mantled her modest face, her profile was classic, her hair was soft, brown, and abundant. She had the voice of a bird, and her music possessed a rare soul quality. She was an earnest Christian, distinguished by an utter absence of self-consciousness, merry, social, and always kind…. She secured a position to teach music in a Female Seminary in Tuskegee, Alabama. She made a success of her teaching and was much beloved in the school. In the early autumn of 1859, she was invited to be a bridesmaid for her special friend and schoolmate, Rebecca Lide, who resided in her old home, Carlowville.
>
> A cousin of her hostess, James Lide Coker, had journeyed from Society Hill, Darlington County,

South Carolina, to be an attendant at this
marriage…. James Coker was fascinated by Sue
Stout's charm and sweetness. She soon lost her
heart for this young man, who proved singularly
congenial and who joined in her songs with his
rich voice.[4]

Rebecca Lide's wedding festivities lasted two weeks,
and all the while, another wedding was brewing up in the
midst. Vivien Gay Coker, James's future daughter-in-law, later
described James and Sue's rapid courtship:

At the end of that time [two weeks], there was no
question about it having been love at first sight.
Father and Mother went down the Alabama River
on one of the delightful boats that happily made
part of the journey by moonlight. When they
arrived in Mobile, Father accompanied Mother
to her house—still by moonlight, I think. Aunt
Mamie came to the door, and Mother greeted
her with the explosive remark, "Sister Mary Ann,
this is James Coker, and I am going to marry
him!"[5]

They were married just two months afterward on March 28,
1860. In addition to romance, their love had substance. James's
lifelong friend George Norwood described the marriage
this way:

He was happily married early in life, and his wife
was entirely in sympathy with him, intellectually,
financially, and morally, or spiritually, if you
please…. She was gentle, kind, refined, cultured.
She was the daughter of Rev. Platt Stout, a highly
respected Baptist minister, and accepted all of

the doctrinal part of the religion. Major Coker
was reared in a similar atmosphere.[6]

To their delight, James's parents gave her a piano as their
wedding present. [7] After Sue moved to Hartsville, Kate
Chambers observed: "Her husband's father, Caleb Coker Jr.,
commanded her deep respect and confidence, and in his
[James's] mother, she found a source of inspiration, comfort,
and wisdom."[8]

Newlywed Church Leaders

From the outset, Sue and James were devoted to church work at
First Baptist Hartsville and beyond. They taught Sunday School
together, and she played piano. Frank R. Chambers wrote:
"They set up at the beginning a home altar for family worship
as became people of such Christian ancestry—how the local
church and Sunday School engaged their warmest interests,
how their Christian influence reached out to neighboring
congregations in helpful co-operation—busy, happy people
they were."[9]

Sue's Humor and James's Devotion to Her

W. C. Wilson recalled Sue's sense of humor: "I was at Uncle
James's house when I was just a little fellow, and I heard him
call Aunt Sue and ask her where his pen was. She said: 'No,
I haven't seen your pen, but what's that you've got in your
mouth?'"[10] James was good to Sue throughout their marriage.
His nephew Arthur Rogers boarded with them while attending
Welsh Neck High School about 1898-1991.[11] An eyewitness to
their domestic life, he commented: "He was devoted to Aunt
Sue, of course, just as gently and considerate as he could be of
her; her health wasn't so good at the last."[12]

Discussion Questions on Dating and Marriage for Christians, touching on James and Sue's principles, are found at https://willjoslin.com/major/questions/datingandmarriage.

The Children

The Major and Sue would go on to have ten children, seven of whom survived childhood: Margaret, James Lide Jr., David Robert (D. R.), William Chambers (Will), Jennie, Charles Westfield, and Susan. All of them married; all but Will had children, and all were active in one or more of the following: commerce, agriculture, the church, and academics.

Margaret	*James Lide. Jr.*	*David Robert*	*William Chambers*	*Jennie*	*Charles Westfield*	*Susan*
(1861–1912)	(1863–1931)	(1870–1938)	(1872–1953)	(1874–1914)	(1879–1931)	(1882–1960)
m. Joseph James Lawton (1861–1941)	m. Vivien Gay (1868–1952)	m. Jessie Richardson (1874–1913)	m. Mararet May Roper 1915 (1890–1976)	m. Louise Venable (1885–1983)	m. Duncan Gay (1865–1948)	m. Carrie H. Lide (1877–1948)	m. Richard F. Watson (1879–1957)

James and Sue's seven children. From *Growing Up in the Brown House* by Mary Coker Joslin. Used by permission of Coker College Press.

Margaret and James Jr. were born during the Civil War. An eyewitness of Sherman's destruction, these two hid under the bed as Yankee soldiers stormed into their house. Like her parents, Margaret became active in the First Baptist Church. While a student and the Greenville Baptist Female College in 1878, she met Joseph James (J. J.) Lawton, from Allendale, South Carolina, then a student at Furman University in the same town. She never forgot him, and a few years later asked her father to hire J. J. to help on the farms, which he did They were married in 1883, and J. J. became like a son to James, helping him in his enterprises before the Major's sons came of age. Extremely capable, soon the Major asked him to manage of all his farms, and more. Lawton's story is picked up throughout the book, especially in Chapter 10 on the Sunday School.

James Jr., the Major and Sue's first son, later partnered with his father in industry and was instrumental in the founding of The Carolina Fiber Company. He married Vivien Gay, sister of Jennie's future husband, Duncan Gay. Vivien had a gift for hospitality. Once, just for fun, she slyly spiked the dessert at a Coker party with an alcoholic drink, a story described in Chapter 13. We will pick up the story of James Jr. and his business ventures with his father in Chapter 8 on The Carolina Fiber Company.

D. R., their second son, after attending South Carolina College (precursor of the University of South Carolina), took over his father's general store. However, his passion was plant breeding, and the Major helped him start The Coker Pedigreed Seed Company, chronicled in Chapter 6 on the Major's businesses. D. R. was also on the boards of several large schools and companies. A full story of D. R.'s life is told in James A. Rogers and Larry E. Nelson's book, *Mr. D. R.: A Biography of David R. Coker.*[13]

Their third son, Will Coker relished the nature walks that he took with his father as a boy, and this love of all things green foretold his destiny. He attended South Carolina College, and after trying his hand at banking in Wilmington with reasonable success, he decided his true calling was botany. In 1897, he left banking and began a doctorate in biology at Johns Hopkins University. In 1902, he became a botany professor at UNC-Chapel Hill,[14] and the UNC campus arboretum now bears his name. He specialized in and wrote on a wide variety of plants, including the Venus flytrap, many species of trees, and various fungi. His life and writings are featured in *Essays on William Chambers Coker, Passionate Botanist*, by Mary Coker Joslin.

Jennie, the second daughter, had a sense of adventure and a keen intellect. She became a poet and short-story writer of some renown. Her husband, Duncan Gay from Mount Vernon, New York, was a famous artist in his own right and illustrated many of her works, among others. After her mother developed a severe heart condition, Jennie helped to nurse Sue during the last four years of her life until Sue died in 1904.

Charles Westfield Coker, the fourth and youngest son, was named for his uncle who died at Malvern Hill in the Civil War. He married Carrie H. Lide, and his accomplishments are mentioned in <u>Chapter 9</u> in connection with his financial and executive leadership in his father's Southern Novelty Company.

Susan, the third daughter and youngest child, lived until 1960. She told a wondrous story from her childhood that gives us insight into how Major Coker's children viewed him:

> My first memory of Father was on a snowy day when I was still a very little child. We had a heavy snowstorm with great fluffy white flakes, and the whole world was white and beautiful. The evergreens were so piled with their loads of snow that Father was determined to go to their rescue. He invited me, and I was buttoned up in a red wool cap and many other red warm things and went out hanging on to Father's hand. He moved the snow from the bending evergreens, and I had a feeling only of delight and the security and strength of Father. [15]

Susan married Richard F. Watson from Greenville, South Carolina. As a true southern lady of genteel breeding, she was kind, generous, and hospitable. When her mother health declined in her later years, along with her sister Jenny and sister-in-law Vivien, Susan was a tremendous help to her parents. She stepped into Sue's shoes, continuing the art of Southern hospitality in the Major's home. She was an ardent fan of her father, as evidenced by her many admirations published in the Hartsville Museum's book, *Recollections of the Major.*

We now resume the Major's adventures following their wedding.

ENDNOTES FOR CHAPTER 3: MARRIAGE AND CHILDREN

1   Frank R. Chambers, nephew of the Major, in his talk "Major J. L. Coker, Christian and Philanthropist," *Memorial Exercises*, subtitled *[Coker College] Founders Day, April 9, 1919*, op. cit., p. 55.

2   Vivien G. Coker, *Recollections*, p. 60.

3   Ibid., p. 9.

4   Kate Chambers, op. cit., pp. 75-76.

5   Ibid, p. 9.

6   Cook, op. cit., p. 435.

7   Ibid, p. 9.

8   Kate Chambers, op. cit., p. 78.

9   Frank R. Chambers, op. cit., p. 56.

10 W. C. Wilson, *Recollections*, p. 64.

11 The 1900 Census for Susan Stout Coker, who was from Alabama, lists Arthur Rogers as a resident at the Major and Sue's household in Hartsville, courtesy of Stephen Posey of the Selma, Alabama library census records.

12 Arthur Rogers, *Recollections*, p.86. Note: both Arthur Rogers and Paul Rogers were nephews of the Major.

13 Rogers and Nelson, op. cit.

14 Mary Coker Joslin, *Essays on William Chambers Coker, Passionate Botanist*, University of North Carolina at Chapel Hill Library, Botanical Garden Foundation, Inc., Chapel Hill, NC, 2003, p.23.

15 Susan Coker Watson, *Recollections*, p. 119.

PART II

BATTERED BY WAR: GUTS THROUGH VIOLENCE, TRAGEDY, AND LOSS

CHAPTER 4

THE EARLY CIVIL WAR

In April of 1860, James and his bride returned to Hartsville, where he continued farming until 1861. But the simmering national conflict was about to boil over. As J. W. Norwood said, "His conspicuous agricultural success was interrupted by the Civil War."[1]

Causes of the War

As a Southerner, James was familiar with the background of the conflict. From the late 1700's, the manufacturing economy in the North was suffering from competition with low-priced imported goods from Europe. The Southern states, which at this point manufactured few of their own goods, benefitted from the low-priced European imports. To protect themselves, in 1828, Northerners wanted to impose a strong tariff on imports. They had little need for these imports, since they manufactured their own goods. Northerners were largely joined by their political and economic allies in the midwestern and western states.

The Tariff of 1828

In the House of Representatives on May 19, 1828, South Carolina, Mississippi, Louisiana, Georgia, Virginia, North Carolina, Tennessee, Alabama, and Maryland, voted against the tariff, 64 to 4. But when the northern and western states outvoted them, Southerners were forced to pay tariffs, and from the beginning, they called it the "The Tariff of Abominations."[2]

> Southerners, including South Carolinians, justifiably felt abused by the import tariffs, and planters like the Cokers were hit hard. It was a trap. For decades, Europeans had been buying Southern cotton, in part because Southerners bought European manufactured goods. But when the South became reticent to buy their goods at tariff-inflated prices, the Europeans, in turn, became wary of buying Southern cotton, so the South had to keep buying the foreign goods at higher prices.

The implications were huge. The higher prices were not on just a few peripheral goods. Records of the 20th Congress, Session I, Ch. 55, state that import duties were required on the following essential items, all produced in the North and in Europe, and all needed in the South: iron, steel, axes, knives, sickles, scythes, hooks, shovels, bridle bits, chisels, vices, wood screws, lead, minerals, wool, any clothes containing wool, window glass, and other absolutely essential items.[3]

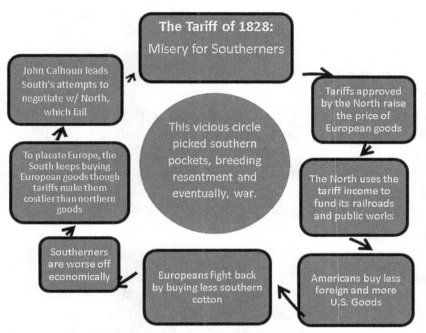

The Tariff of 1828:
Misery for Southerners

John Calhoun leads South's attempts to negotiate w/ North, which fail

Tariffs approved by the North raise the price of European goods

This vicious circle picked southern pockets, breeding resentment and eventually, war.

To placate Europe, the South keeps buying European goods though tariffs make them costlier than northern goods

The North uses the tariff income to fund its railroads and public works

Southerners are worse off economically

Europeans fight back by buying less southern cotton

Americans buy less foreign and more U.S. Goods

Chart showing the escalation of tensions caused by the Tariff of 1828, which The South called "The Tariff of Abominations." Chart by author. Content paraphrased from sources linked to endnotes cited in proximity.

The South's prices for these foreign goods soared up by 30 to 50 percent, and the whole Southern economy was affected. All Southerners, not just slaveowners, were hurt. Only about 30%[4] of Southerners were slaveowners, but since the conflict affected the South's broader slaved-based agricultural economy, this effectively tied slavery in with the tariffs as a cause of the Civil War.

Northern industries prospered from the tariffs, and expanded their trade with the mid-western and western states. It amounted to three regions of the country exploiting the South.[5] Matters became even more insufferable for Southerners when they saw that the tariffs collected were in large part used to build railroads and infrastructure in the North, with nothing allocated for the South. According to the *Daily Progress* website: "Between 1830 and 1850, thirty thousand miles of track were laid [in the North]," and "at the time, 90 percent of the federal government's annual revenue came from these taxes on imports."[6]

The northern economist and magazine editor Thomas P. Kettell (1811-1878), author of *Southern Wealth and Northern Profits*, produced statistics showing that the North "took from this section [the South], between 1789 and 1861, $2,770,000,000 of her wealth." In 2020 dollars that would be over 81 trillion confiscated from the South's economy.[7] It was pretty much extortion.

South Carolina's eloquent and fiery U.S. Senator, John C. Calhoun (1782-1850) made passionate attempts to negotiate a better deal for the South. On the U. S. Senate floor, referring to the fact that a majority of Congressmen voted for "The Tariff of Abominations," and the North's subsequent abuse of the South, Calhoun said:

John C. Calhoun (1782-1850), U.S. Vice President, 1825-1832, U.S. Senator from South Carolina, 1845-1950. Prior to the Civil War, he was a fiery orator for states' rights. Permission of shutterstock.com.

> The Government of the absolute majority instead of the Government of the people is but the Government of the strongest interests; and when not efficiently checked, it is the most tyrannical and oppressive that can be devised.[8]

Calhoun also warned the North that Southerners would rather die than be treated as inferiors:

> I would rather meet any extremity upon earth than give up one inch of our equality, one inch of

> what belongs to us [Southerners] as members of
> this republic! What! Acknowledged inferiority!
> The surrender of life is nothing to sinking down
> into acknowledged inferiority![9]

His passionate speeches failing, Calhoun attempted to have the tariffs nullified in South Carolina, arguing that the state had rights to be exempt.[10] But nothing improved, and Southern resentment only became more intense.[11]

Slavery came to the fore with the question of whether slavery would exist in new states. But I think it would be a mistake to say that when the war started in April of 1861, it started just over slavery, for in Lincoln's First Inaugural Address on March 4, 1861, he promised: "I have no purpose, directly or indirectly, to interfere with the institution of slavery in the States where it exists. I believe I have no lawful right to do so, and I have no inclination to do so."[12]

But at the same time, he promised he would invade any state that failed to collect tariffs. Lincoln's harsh words of "pay the tariffs or be invaded" were received from Baltimore to Charleston as a declaration of war on the South,"[13] and the Civil War started just five weeks later.

But Lincoln's later Emancipation Proclamation declaring freedom of slaves did not occur until 21 months and 24 battles after the start of the war,[14] on January 1, 1863.[15] Only after that proclamation did the Northern cause and the end of slavery overlap.

Secession and formation of the Confederacy

J. W. Norwood, son of James's boyhood friend George Norwood, commented on James's thoughts on the start of the war: "[He] did not believe in slavery, but he did believe that the tariff laws operated against the best interest of the South, and he accepted for the time being the popular idea in South Carolina that it was wise to secede, and that we had the constitutional right of secession."[16]

Jefferson Davis from Kentucky, who had previously served as a U. S. Senator and as U.S. Secretary of War, was elected as the President of the Confederacy. Prior to that, he successfully influenced South Carolina to be the first state to leave the Union on December 20, 1860. Within six weeks, six Southern States joined in the Confederacy, and shortly afterward they had eleven states across the south and southwest from Virginia to Texas. Border states Maryland and Kentucky were split between the two.

The Start of the War

When Confederate soldiers fired on Union-held Fort Sumter in Charleston, South Carolina, on April 12, 1861, the war was on. Across the South, it was seen as a young man's duty to fight in order to protect his family, property, and community. Southerners felt this was their second war for independence, so fighting was their patriotic duty. James wrote, "If there were a few able-bodied men exempt from service for one reason or another, if they had not good cause, they got but poor encouragement from their neighbors, especially from the true Southern women, who looked upon all shirkers with contempt."[17]

James immediately volunteered. With his natural leadership qualities and Citadel training, he quickly organized a regiment from the Pee Dee and was elected Captain of Company G, Ninth S.C. Infantry, which later became Company E, Sixth S.C. Infantry. York went with him to the war, as an assistant. Also volunteering were his brothers William and Charles. Charles was the youngest and was known for his faith, gentleness, and sense of duty. In college at the time, he was not expected to enlist. Nevertheless, he chose to enlist and found himself in William's company. Not long afterward, James was promoted to infantry commander, then field captain. Later, he would be elevated to the rank of major.

James's Plight in the War

In August of 1861, James's regiment fought with Robert E. Lee and Stonewall Jackson during the overwhelming Confederate victory at the Battle of First Manassas, also called the First Battle of Bull Run. This battle is where Jackson was seen "standing as a stone wall," and his fortitude resulted in "the Yankee skedaddle" to Washington.[18] Lee and Jackson could have pressed this advantage against cautious Union General George B. McClellan by immediately attacking Washington. Some historians say that if they had, the South would have threatened the North enough to bring them to the negotiating table then and there.[19] However, for whatever reason, Lee and Jackson missed this critical opportunity.

In 1861, his first child, Margaret, was born while James was at Frayser's Farm near Richmond with his brothers William and Charles. After suffering sweltering heat before, during and after the Battle of Seven Pines that summer of 1862, James was afflicted with camp fever and mumps. Sue came up to Richmond to nurse him back to health during the battle of Malvern Hill. He soon regained strength, and before summer's end, fought again at Second Manassas, Harpers Ferry, Boonsboro, and Antietam.

Later James also fought in the western campaigns at Chickamauga and Lookout Mountain.

Battles in which Major Coker Fought	State	Date(s)
First Mannassas	Virginia	8/21/1861
Seven Pines (Fair Oaks)	Virginia	5/31/1862 – 6/1/1862
Malvern Hill (present but sick)	Virginia	7/1/1862
Second Manassas	Virginia	8/28/1862 - 8/30/1862
Harper's Ferry	Virginia	9/12/- 9/15/1862
Boonsboro	Virginia	9/14/1862
Antietam (Sharpsburg)	Maryland	9/17/1862
Chickamauga	TN/GA border	9/19/1863 - 9/20/1863
Lookout Mt. (severely wounded)	Tennessee	10/28/1863

His Brother Charles is Killed

Tragedy struck the Cokers in that summer of 1862. Charles, who by duty was not supposed to be on the front lines, felt compelled to enter the fray and was shot to death at the Battle of Malvern Hill on July 1st, 1862. His brother William found his body. Reflecting the crushing heartbreak at the death of a beloved Civil War son, J. O. B. Dargan of *The Charleston Mercury*,

James' brother Charles Westfield Coker, who died at The Battle of Malvern Hill in 1862. Used by persmisson of the South Caroliniana Library, University of South Carolina, Columbia, S.C.

wrote Charles' obituary, lamenting this tragic loss of a Civil War son as well as any words ever could:

Being Ordnance Master [with the duty of staying behind the lines to watch the weapons], he occupied a position of comparative security. But impelled by patriotism and a conscientious sense of duty, he determined to participate with his brave comrades in all the dangers of the terrific and unequal strife of that memorable afternoon of July 1st.

With touching and unfaltering intrepidity, he advanced through the crimson and heaving surges of that gory contest and laid his own costly garland – amid the votive offerings of multitudes of the true, the noble, the lofty in soul and deeds – upon the bloodstained altar of his country. Struck by a ball, which severed an artery, he fell, and soon expiring, entered the portals of that invisible Temple, where, from the hand of the Most High, a bright coronal awaits the pure in heart, the good, the Christlike of earth….

Farewell to thee, dear son of memory! To us on earth thou comest no more, but ever green as the pine which stands as sentinel beside thy lonely grave, whose leafy hand by unseen fingers touched wails forth in sweet but saddest strains thy requiem to every breeze, will live in many fond hearts thy name, thy virtues, thy image.

Comforted by Faith

Upon Charles' death, James grieved for himself but immediately thought of his dear mother Hannah, and wrote this Christ-centered letter to comfort her:

My first impulse after learning that God had stricken us by taking from us noble Charlie was to write to you. I thought of the terrible blow which the sudden tidings would inflict, and then of your bursting heart after the realization of the awful truth. But the sweet promises of the One who is good even while He afflicts, presented themselves to me and I felt sure you would have grace sufficient and could give unto our Father praise and thanksgiving—for have we not, Mother, many causes for thanksgiving... We know that Charles was a Christian, he professed to be one, and he lived as a follower of the Lamb.[20]

James's faith sustained him, and as the war ground on, with terrors on every side, many of his fellow soldiers also fled to Jesus for peace and hope. James wrote in his book, *History of Company G and E:*

It is true that the camp life of the Army was a severe test of religious character. I am glad to say those who influenced our war men most were strongly religious. President Davis was a devoted Christian; General Robert E. Lee possessed in extraordinary fulness the sweet characteristics of a true religion; Stonewall Jackson stands forth as a "burning and shining light," praying as he fought and fighting as he prayed.... Religious meetings were always encouraged throughout the armies, and thousands of men professed a true conversion before the assembled congregations of their comrades.[21]

The Major also wrote:

> "Around the campfire hymns of praise were
> heard, and as they plodded wearily on the march
> they cheered themselves with… "Am I a Soldier
> of the Cross,"… Cross and Crown,"…, [and] "I'm
> going Home to Die no more." Even Cromwell's
> [Oliver Cromwell, Puritan English General and
> statesman of the 1600's] army did not acknowledge
> their dependence on God more fully than did
> General Lee's Army of Northern Virginia."[22]

However, under the same threat of imminent death, other
Confederate soldiers did not turn to the living God for hope,
and some turned to drugs. His cousin, Miss Jane Lide, reported
that "Not a few men sought solace in alcoholic beverages, and
some became compulsive drinkers. Unable to free themselves,
they switched to narcotic drugs…. This resulted in pathetic
lives and pitiful deaths."[23]

James's Bravery Fired up His Company

Captain James Lide Coker's own faith and courage also inspired
many. One of his men said of James that even "Stonewall
Jackson was not more beloved or respected by his men than
Captain Coker was by the members of his company."[24] James's
courage was proven on the field of battle. Later his son Will
Coker said that his father

> quickly made a reputation for extreme courage in
> battle. At Seven Pines, for instance, I have heard
> privates in his company tell about how he rushed
> through the woods considerably ahead of the
> company, calling to them to follow on quickly,

and while under heavy fire. One of his own men
told me Father was very brave in battle.[25]

On April 29, 1863, Colonel John Bratton, under whom James
served, wrote of his bravery under rifle and cannon fire in the
days just before the Siege of Suffolk, Virginia. In his words,
"The conduct of Captains Coker and Crawford, engaging
and repulsing the gunboats on the Nansemond River, has
deservedly won the admiration of everyone."[26]

Misfortune continued to strike the Cokers in 1863. James's
brother, Captain William Coker, was wounded at Gettysburg
and carried on a stretcher to a prison at Johnson's Island on
Lake Erie in Ohio.[27] All communication between William and
the family was cut off, and only months later did they learn of
his narrow survival.

At Death's Door in the Western Campaign

In mid-1863, James's company was transferred from Virginia
to the western campaign in Tennessee. It was now called the
Sixth Regiment under General James Longstreet, the foremost
Confederate General
under Robert E. Lee,
whom Lee called his
"Old War Horse."

Captain Coker
fought again
at The Battle of
Chickamauga on the
Georgia-Tennessee
border. Thus far, he
had escaped serious

Battle of Lookout Mountain, TN on Oct. 28, 1863 where a Yankee bullet shattered James'
left thigh. Painting by Louis Kurz, published by Allison and Kurz. Now in the public domain.

injury. Then on October 28, 1863, during the Battle of Lookout
Mountain, James's company was still fighting at the end of

the day. Generals Bragg and Longstreet gave the order for a brigade, including James's company, to make a surprise attack and capture a Yankee wagon train and the troops guarding it. James had just scouted the area and had reported to them that one brigade would be insufficient because there was a massive body of infantry behind the wagon train. However, the generals insisted they go right then. James himself described the battle and his part in it:

> The mountain was crossed after dark. Company E, 6th Regiment... was designated as one of the pickets to form a long skirmish line in advance of the line of battle. As it was night, and the country very rough and wooded, it was very difficult to prevent mistakes and keep the direction for this skirmish line....
>
> The orders were to capture the pickets of the enemy, and press rapidly towards them, and engage them, our battle line following the skirmishers as closely as possible. When the brigade came up... the enemy was surprised when attacked by the skirmishers but

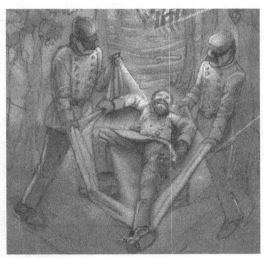

Seriously wounded James L. Coker is carried by Sergeant Nettles and Corporal Wilkins at Lookout Mountain, TN.

soon began to get into ranks and to return our fire. When [Commander John] Bratton got up with the Brigade, he attacked them vigorously, aiming at the light of the discharging musketry in front. The enemy soon brought up their artillery and made good use of it until our fire grew too near and too hot for them. The Confederates made progress, taking possession of the wagons and teams, and were pressing their advantage when the order came from General Jenkins for us to retire. This order was caused by a movement up the valley from Brown's Ferry, which seemed to be successful, and would soon cut us off from our crossing at Lookout Creek.

I was sent in to bear this order to a part of the line, and while delivering it to Colonel Mart Gary on the right, I was shot down.

James's femur was shattered as he was shot just below the left hip joint. A Minié ball, shot from one of the powerful advanced grooved-bore Yankee rifles, did the horrific damage. James describes the scene just after he fell:

Gary directed those near me to take me up and bring me off the field, but no one being designated by name, I was not taken up until Sergeant Samuel J. Nettles and others of our company, hearing my name, came up, and with the willing help of some of Gary's men, got me on a blanket and bore me to the rear, after all our troops had retired.[28]

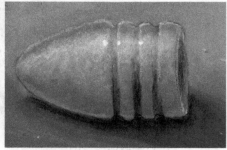

Advanced Yankee Minié Ball with grooves for spin, distance, and maximum damage. Drawn by Raleigh, NC artist Dan Nelson and used by permission.

Kate Chambers, from James's own tortuous description to her of the plight, wrote "After he received his wound he was carried across the mountain, through this rough country, in a blanket, by his comrades. He afterward told me of his intense suffering, when he had begged to be allowed to die, and found that the spur of his boot on the foot of his injured leg was catching in the bushes."[29]

Kate was describing when Sergeant Samuel J. Nettles, and Corporal Wilkins accompanied by York, carried him in a blanket to a house near Lookout Mountain, owned by a sympathetic family named Hicks. At that point, James was still on the Confederate side of the lines. But with the Yankee camp in full view, it was not a peaceful rest.

Colonel Bratton wrote of his terrible injury: "I have to regret the loss of the services of Captain J. L. Coker, 6th regiment, South Carolina volunteers, acting Assistant Adjutant General on my staff. He was seriously wounded while nobly performing his duty."[30]

The Damage

The ball had passed through his body but left bone and lead fragments lodged in his leg. The Confederate manual of military surgery, in reference to the Minié ball's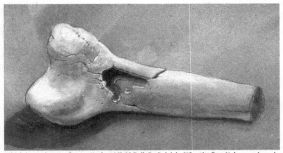

Thigh bone damage from a Yankee Minié Ball. By Raleigh, NC artist Dan Nelson and used by permisson.

"fearful velocity," stated: "Should they impinge upon a bone, the splitting and crushing is so extensive as to necessitate more frequently amputations and resections." [31] Worse yet, James's bed was unsanitary; the infections only became abscessed, and fever, sores, and lack of food pushed him to the very brink of death. At this hour of Captain Coker's greatest need, York, his friend since boyhood, chose freedom and went north. [32] This was understandable, but given the timing of his best friend's departure at the very lowest point of his life, it was very discouraging to James.

Conditions were practically beyond hope, but James managed to send a message. Kate Chambers wrote: "On the morning of the 30th of October of 1863, his family (Aunt Sue was at that time [with them] at Society Hill) received a telegram from James saying, 'I am severely wounded, thigh fractured near hip. Sue and mother, please come and ask Dr. Griffin to come with you.'" [33]

Hannah's Valiant Mission

Hannah had lost Charles already and would do everything in her power not to lose another son. As the brave young officer lingered precariously at death's door, Hannah rushed up from Society Hill with almost superhuman speed and determination. Miraculously avoiding enemy bullets and cannonballs, she got through the lines with food and with the family physician, Dr. Griffin. They found James delirious with a high fever. [34]

When a sane moment came, James was delighted to see his mother, but asked, "Where is Sue? Didn't she come?" [35] As for Sue's inability to make it, Miss Jane Lide wrote: "She was completely broken-hearted because, awaiting the birth of her second child, she felt sure her husband would not have asked her to come if he had any hope of living." [36] Later, she tried to make the journey, and came within thirty miles of him, but could not get through war lines, and returned home. [37] Sometimes James would cry out, "Oh! Mother, I will never see Sue again!" [38] and she reminded him of Isaiah 26:4: "Trust ye in the LORD forever: for in the Lord Jehovah is everlasting strength" (KJV). [39]

Later his mother wrote of his harrowing condition: "The surgeons had delayed for several days performing any operation, for they were sure the wound was mortal and wished to spare him unnecessary suffering; but when they found his strength kept up so well, they decided there was *some* hope of his recovery, and so they proceeded to operate."[40] The Confederate surgeons removed many pieces of shattered bone and bound him in splints. Afterward, Dr. Griffin helped a great deal, but could only stay a week. James's condition was still tenuous as nourishing food, so necessary for his recovery, was scarce. James and his mother were still not sure if he would live. But at this time, his father Caleb Jr. managed to sneak through the lines with a large box of provisions,[41] which helped a great deal.

November 24th and 25th brought the battle of Missionary Ridge, which raged dangerously close to the Hicks house. It

ended in a decisive Yankee victory, allowing the Union to gain complete control of Chattanooga and its environs, including the Hicks house. This left the Cokers behind enemy lines. They were allowed to stay in

Battle of Missionary Ridge Nov. 25th of 1863, where James, his mother, and Sergeant Nettles fell behind enemy lines. Painting by Louis Kurz, published by Kurz and Allison. Part of public domain.

the house but were now prisoners. The Union allowed only one soldier to stay with James. It was decided that Corporal Wilkins would quickly return to the Confederate camp and Sergeant Nettles would remain with Hannah and James.

Hannah wrote of their dependence on God: "How dependent we felt on 'the friend that sticks closer than a brother.'"[42] They refreshed themselves in the Lord, reading a chapter from the Bible every night, and remained remarkably cheerful and strong in spirit.[43] Throughout his life, James loved to sing, especially hymns. Those in other rooms at the Hicks house and enemy soldiers passing by must have marveled as they heard mother and son, from their place of prison and pain, joyfully singing out:

> From every stormy wind that blows,
> From every swelling tide of woes,
> There is a calm, a sure retreat,
> 'Tis found before the mercy seat.[44]

With their display of overcoming faith, the scene was reminiscent of the New Testament account of Paul and Silas in Philippi in 52 A. D., when the Romans beat and jailed them, and they responded with songs of joy. (Acts 16:22-27). On his bed of suffering, Captain Coker also committed Psalm 27, KJV to memory[45] and comforted himself and Hannah with these words:

> The LORD *is* my light and my salvation; whom shall I fear? the LORD *is* the strength of my life; of whom shall I be afraid? When the wicked, *even* mine enemies and my foes, came upon me to eat up my flesh, they stumbled and fell. Though an host should encamp against me, my heart shall not fear: though war should rise against me, in this *will* I *be* confident....
> I would have fainted unless I had believed to see the goodness of the LORD in the land of the living."

At Christmas of 1863, James received the cheering news from Sue that their first son, James Lide Jr., had been born. However, war dangers and James's dire condition prevented his return to South Carolina for another eight months. He and Hannah eventually received needed parole papers from a considerate Yankee officer, General Thomas. Upon leaving the Hicks house, they spent a week at a field hospital in Chattanooga, where a

Dr. Perrin came to see James and remarked to him, "The rule in such a wound as this is to die; the exception, to get well."[46]

The Arduous Journey Home

To begin the trip home, they had to take a detoured route from Tennessee to Kentucky, either dodging or enduring unsympathetic Yankees all the way. From Kentucky, they took a steamboat across the Big Sandy River to West Virginia. Of this trip, James wrote:

> There were northern men who came to my stretcher with other feeling than sympathy. One hard-looking man, after abusing the South in brutal fashion, said to me: "Yes, you went to war to get your rights; you got part of them there" (pointing to my fractured thigh). "You should have them all, there" (pointing to my head).[47]

James said another abusive Yankee, presumably a civilian of fighting age, "was greatly offended because I suggested that his ardent hatred could better be exhibited at the front with Grant."[48]

After this difficult leg of the journey, mother, son, and the sergeant made it from West Virginia to the Yankee prison hospital at Fort McHenry in Baltimore. However, they were crushed upon learning that their parole papers were no longer honored. In the ensuing delay, James's condition degenerated due to poor food and the stress of the difficult task of getting new release papers.

From either ignorance or spite, the Yankee hospital authorities receiving them in Baltimore insisted on separating Hannah and Sergeant Nettles from James, causing him to regress for lack of attention. It was then that the upstanding

Union General Lew Wallace – who would go on to write the famous historical novel (later a movie) *Ben Hur– A Tale of the Christ*, graciously intervened. Later James wrote: "[The] Provost Marshall had charge of the prisoners. This humane officer procured a special order from General Lew Wallace, then in command in Baltimore, who overruled the hospital authorities, and sent my good friend and nurse back to my bedside."[49] Without General Wallace's order to restore his helpers, once again, James probably would have died.

Finally, after Hannah telegraphed the Commissary of General Prisoners in Washington, they were given permission to cross battle lines. They went on to Ft. Monroe, Virginia, then to Richmond. There James was promoted to his final rank of major at his honorable discharge. They went on to Florence, South Carolina, where Sue and James's father greeted them heartily. They finally returned to Society Hill at 11:00 p.m. on July 21, 1864, ten months after James had been shot. Greatly relieved, the rest of the family greeted him enthusiastically, and with great joy, the Major saw his son James Jr. for the first time.

Another Doctor Comments on James' Miraculous Survival

Back home, he regained a measure of health, but the shattered thigh was beyond recovery, and James used a crutch or cane for the rest of his days. Another medical doctor, Dr. W. L. Byerly of Hartsville, commented on his uncanny escape from an early grave: "Aseptic surgery was not then known, and most wounds of this character meant death from gas gangrene, tetanus, or bloodstream infections. The survival of Major Coker can only be attributed to a rugged physique, tender common sense nursing of his mother, a devoted soldier companion, and the will of God."[50] James wrote these words of gratitude: "To their [his mother and Sergeant Nettles'] attention, with the blessing of God, I owe my life."[51] The Major later included Sergeant Samuel J. Nettles' son James in his will.[52]

Two decades later, James had another near death experience when he was in Charleston during the great Charleston earthquake of 1886, which registered seven on the Richter scale. He was on the porch of a brick building, and when the rumbling started, most people flew off the porch into the street and were killed or injured by falling bricks. The Major stayed on the porch and was unharmed.[53] Once again, amid life-threatening danger, he was miraculously spared. Were these repeated escapes from death merely coincidental?

ENDNOTES FOR CHAPTER 4: THE EARLY CIVIL WAR

1   J. W. Norwood, as quoted by Harvey Toliver Cook, op. cit., p. 415.
2   Walter Edgar, op. cit., p. 331.
3   Editor, American Memory, "A Century of Lawmaking for a New Nation: U.S. Congressional Documents and Debates, 1774 – 1875," pp. 270-274, https://memory.loc.gov/cgi-bin/ampage?collId=llsl&fileName=004/llsl004.db&recNum=317(accessed June 15,2020).
4   Editor, The Conversation web site, "American slavery: Separating fact from myth," http://theconversation.com/american-slavery-separating-fact-from-myth-79620 (accessed February 18,2020), and Sarah Pruitt, History web site, May 3, 2016 article "5 Myths About Slavery, https://www.history.com/news/5-myths-about-slavery (accessed February 28, 2020). The first site said southern slaveowners comprises 25% of southern whites; the second said southern slaveowners comprised 32% of southern whites, so I split the difference at 30%.
5   See 2010, 2020 article entitled "Tariffs and the American Civil War" by Phillip W. Magness at http://www.marottaonmoney.com/protective-tariffs-the-primary-cause-of-the-civil-war/ (accessed December 29, 2019).
6   David John Marotta, and Megan Russell, June 23,2013 article "Protective tariffs: Primary cause of the Civil War," https://www.dailyprogress.com/opinion/guest_columnists/protective-tariffs-primary-cause-of-the-civil-war/article_63b77f5c-dc0c-11e2-8e99-001a4bcf6878.html (accessed December 29, 2019).
7   James Lide Coker, *History of Company G, and E,* op cit., p. 210.
8   Richard K. Cralle, Editor, *Speeches of John C. Calhoun,* (D. Appleton and Co., New York, NY), 1888 accessed at Google Books, https://books.googleusercontent.com/books/content?req=AKW5QadyT n8FkXrjQjBgXWwyA lleBqHl 4JFh-FpGsQPKMeLtMyeQGr7ATHFjf gL0XuQF--Er T UY6BgkHFQm--v6yQuhzWZ7Q4 DRPXGlZHxBs ZXj2EHs-RMalu7f9RDLFU9sBZOIAw pOI6WPkEl0ON2Mf aUMQt515ghTZ0FsJwJkov5szoxSkBBQdBek2SCNAD1oUc0 liduW0mKT3UZYLFioV9LETvNQ5sMyl6ORw1bfPbzKuOL wJ4Dd8yZ8dVl5mjGAdi7YAkYp6NZ24Q8ES3NZ5AYw (accessed March 5, 2020).
9   John C. Calhoun, speech at the U.S. Senate on February 19,1847 as recorded by editor, last updated March 2, 2020 "John C. Calhoun," Wikiquote, https://en.wikiquote.org/wiki/John_C._Calhoun (accessed May 22, 2020).

10 Editor, History, Art and Archives, web article "The Tariff of Abominations: The Effects" at https://history.house.gov/Historical-Highlights/1800-1850/The-Tariff-of-Abominations/ (accessed December 29, 2019).

11 Editor, Library of Congress Web Guides "Nullification Proclamation" article at https://www.loc.gov/rr/program/bib/ourdocs/nullification.html (accessed December 29, 2019).

12 President Abraham Lincoln, First Inaugural Address, March 4, 1861, U.S. Embassy & Consulate in The Republic of Korea, https://kr.usembassy.gov/education-culture/infopedia-usa/living-documents-american-history-democracy/abraham-lincoln-first-inaugural-address-1861/#:~:text=I%20do%20but%20quote%20from,no%20inclination%20to%20do%20so, last accessed 11/4/2020.

13 David John Marotta, and Megan Russell, op. cit.

14 Editor, American Experience website, "Significant Civil War Battles," https://www.pbs.org/wgbh/americanexperience/features/timeline-death/ (accessed March 5, 2020).

15 See National Archives "The Emancipation Proclamation" article at https://www.archives.gov/exhibits/featured-documents/emancipation-proclamation (accessed December 29, 2019).

16 J. W. Norwood, op. cit., p. 425.

17 James Lide Coker, *History of Company G and E,* (Attic Press: Greenwood, SC), 1899, p. 193.

18 Betty Carlson Kay, *The Civil War from a to Z: Two Points of View* (Author House: Bloomington, IN(, 2010 as found at https://books.google.com/books?id=0MsrwRga3hQC&pg=PT18&lpg=PT18&dq=stonewall+Jackson+standing+as+a+stone+wall+Yankee+skedaddle+to+Washington&source=bl&ots=Pq-m8_Vsm-&sig=ACfU3U1SjrEvdJEHDovYzqmOoqPcFeGjUQ&hl=en&sa=X&ved=2ahUKEwin3IaUiv3hAhUOh-AKHaF_AY8Q6AEwAnoECAgQAQ#v=onepage&q=stonewall%20Jackson%20standing%20as%20a%20stone%20wall%20Yankee%20skedaddle%20to%20Washington&f=false (accessed December 29, 2019).

19 Andrew Knighton, War History Online website, July 21, 2017 article "How the Confederacy Almost Won the American Civil War," https://www.warhistoryonline.com/american-civil-war/confederacy-almost-won-american-civil-war.html (accessed December 29, 2019).

20 George Lee Simpson, op. cit., p. 65.

21 James Lide Coker, op. cit., *p. 204.*

22 Ibid., p. 206.

23 Miss Jane Lide, op. cit., p. 4.

24 J. W. Norwood, op. cit., p. 416.

25 Will Coker, *Recollections*, p. 10.

26 Ibid., p. 417.

27 Ibid., p. 68.

28 James Lide Coker, op. cit., pp. 131-132.

29 Kate Coker, op. cit., pp. 96-97.

30 J. W. Norwood, op. cit., p. 417.

31 Julian Chisolm, *A manual of military surgery, for the use of surgeons in the Confederate States army; with explanatory plates of all useful operations.* Evans and Cogswell: Columbia), 1864 p. 119, https://archive.org/details/manualofmilita00chis(accessed June 15, 2020).

32 William Chambers Coker in *Recollections*, p. 10.

33 Kate Coker, op. cit., p. 96.

34 Hannah Lide Coker, *A Story of the Late War, Written at the Request of Her Children, Grand-Children and Many Friends* (Walker, Evans & Cogswell Company Printers: Charleston), 1887), p. 9.

35 Ibid.

36 Miss Jane Lide, op. cit., p. 3.

37 Ibid.

38 Miss Jane Lide, op. cit., p. 4.

39 Ibid.

40 Hannah Lide Coker, op. cit., p. 8.

41 Ibid., p. 11.

42 Ibid., p. 12, quoting Proverbs 18:24.

43 George Lee Simpson, op. cit., p. 74.

44 Hannah Lide Coker, op. cit., p. 20.

45 Ibid., p. 22.

46 Ibid., p. 26.

47 J. W. Norwood., op. cit., pp. 419-420.

48 Ibid., p. 420.

49 Ibid., p. 421.

50 W. L. Byerly, MD, whose speech was recorded in the *Coker College Quarterly Bulletin*, February 1937, *Centennial Celebration of Major James Lide Coker*, edited by Sylvester Green, p. 8. Hereafter, this work will be referred to simply as "1937 Centennial Celebration of the Major."

51 James Lide Coker, op. cit., p. 135.

52 James Lide Coker's Last Will and Testament, on record at the Darlington County Historical Commission, Darlington, SC. The Major's last revision was May 16, 1916, p. 2.

53 The Major's grandson Richard Coker, *Recollections*, p. 95.

CHAPTER 5

THE LATER CIVIL WAR AND SHERMAN'S WRECKAGE

The Confederacy's war misfortunes paralleled those of the Major. Shortly after his injury, key Union victories turned the tide, and from late 1863 to 1865, the North progressively wore down the South. Lincoln and General Ulysses S. Grant successfully executed their "Anaconda Plan," in which they choked the Confederacy by blockading the South's ports on the Atlantic Ocean and the Mississippi River. After this maneuver cut off Southern supplies from both sides, the infamous General William T. Sherman would make civilians his fodder on his devastating march to the sea.

James was technically no longer a soldier. However, he continued to do all he could to support increasingly pitiful, starving Confederate troops. In March of 1865, he set out with a large box of cornmeal, sausage, and molasses for the Confederate forces in Richmond. On the trip back to Society Hill, he heard the ominous news that Sherman's army was wreaking destruction across his native Pee Dee.

God, Guts, and Gallantry

It was true. While the Major was gone, Sherman's soldiers stormed through his homeland, harassing his family, and severely damaging their plantation. Sue's niece Kate Chambers, who was close to Sue's age, described the threat that endangered her Aunt's life and livelihood:

> Hartsville was directly in the line of Sherman's march, and for three days and nights, she was exposed to the trying experiences caused by the many stragglers who invaded the sanctity of her home…. These ruffians were constantly intruding. She [James's wife Sue] found it difficult to conceal sufficient food to keep herself, her little children, and her friend from starving. Her cotton was burned, all her livestock was taken, the silver was looted, also things valuable and invaluable, like family pictures, etc.

A Yankee soldier one day pointed a pistol at her head and demanded her watch and chain (a gift from her Uncle Will Chambers), which she promptly gave

In the Spring of 1865, Sherman's soldiers ransacked Darlington County, barging into homes, terrorizing civilians, pillaging, and burning whatever they wished. One put a pistol to James' wife Sue's head, demanding her watch. James was taking supplies to Confederate soldiers in Richmond at the time. Courtesy of Raleigh, NC artist Bill Gallagher.

up. The neighbors' houses, two of them, were burned; old people and little children were turned out into the night. The army passed on, leaving devastation and desolation in its wake, but her

faith in her Heavenly Father never wavered, and
she bore her trials with Christian grace.[1]

Kate Chambers was, of course, talking about my great-grandmother, Sue Coker. I forgive Sherman's men, but please don't expect me to forget the pistol at her head, because my family and I would never have lived had that soldier pulled the trigger.

Sherman's men were guilty of nothing short of heathen barbarism. They dismantled or burned many homes, burned cotton fields (worth fortunes), ruined plantations, and looted everything of value from peoples' homes. The Cokers were in no way spared. They stole or drove away the Cokers' pigs, chickens, cattle, oxen, mules, and horses, and took their carts and wagons to carry off the loot. Adding insult to injury, Sherman's men even stole wedding and engagement rings off women's fingers and shot people's dogs.[2] The Major's granddaughter Pauline Lawton Wiggins recalled:

> I remember Mother [the Major's daughter, Margaret Coker] telling how she and Uncle James [the Major's son, James Jr.] were so frightened when Sherman came through that they got some fried chicken and biscuits and went and hid under the bed. These two little children were afraid they would take everything they had to eat, for they stole everything.[3]

W. C. Wilson of Darlington County, an eyewitness to Sherman's march, wrote:

> I can remember the Yankees coming into our house as thick as bees from Monday through Friday. They were camping about five miles away all that week, but Saturday, they had to report back to their camp. They took everything in our

house that wasn't nailed—that is, moveable things—not furniture. They filled pillowcases with groceries. They killed the chickens and cleaned the smokehouse out, and they shot one of our dogs—I remember he went under the house and howled for three or four days.[4]

Before reaching the Pee Dee, Sherman had also burned much of Atlanta and Columbia, South Carolina, to the ground. Major Coker himself decried Sherman's character and deeds. Like many others, the Major never

Sherman's troops celebrate as they burn and loot Columbia, SC on Feb. 3, 1865. Soon afterwards, they marched northeast to devastate the Pee Dee area, including Major Coker's farm. Used by permission from alamy.com.

understood why Sherman allowed his marauders to descend to such cruelty. The Major wrote:

[Sherman's men] left the plantation a picture of desolation. These instances are not singular. Our experience was the common experience of the people all along Sherman's inglorious march. Someday his barbarous practices and spirit will be execrated by the good people of every section. The war left our people poor, indeed, but they were proud of the splendid record of their armies. They continue so until this day. May God bless our Southland and its people forevermore! Amen and Amen.[5]

J. W. Norwood also condemned Sherman, contrasting him with General Lee:

Contrast Sherman's methods with those of Lee. When Lee invaded enemy territory, he gave strict orders to his men not to damage private property... When some soldiers in the regiment conducted by Col. D.G. McIntosh, a native of Society Hill and a boyhood friend of Major Coker, used fences on private property in building a fire with which to cook their provisions, General Lee reprimanded the Colonel for not being on the alert to prevent such a breach of orders.[6]

Civil War Resources Comparison drawn by Raleigh, NC artist Dan Nelson. Used by permission. Data from WorldBook, 1967.

Comparison of War Resources

From the outset, the South had been the underdog. Union armies outnumbered the Confederate troops two to one. And thanks in large part to their pre-war tariff income at the expense of the South, they had four times more money, more than twice the railroad mileage, and four times the industrial base. They also had

Lee's surrender at Appotmattox Courthouse, VA on April 19, 1865. Painting by artist Robbert Wilson, https://www.robertwilsonsrfineart.com. Permission of Jeff and Toni Hesla.

better rifles, bullets, and artillery. Even General Robert E. Lee's considerable skill and bravery could not outlast the superior resources of the North.

From mid-to-late 1864 until surrendering, the South was in desperate straits with starving troops, low munitions, and rampant disease. The war ended on April 19, 1865, when General Lee surrendered the last sizable Confederate force to General Ulysses S. Grant at Appomattox Courthouse in Appomattox, Virginia.

Afterward, Lee showed his noble character, saying to Southern leaders: "Don't bring up your sons to detest the United States.... Recollect that we form one country now. Abandon all these local animosities, and make your sons Americans."[7]

Major Coker always admired Lee greatly, and after the war, he wrote his own historical account of him called "Rawles' Vision,"[8] which he presented to the Pee Dee Historical Commission.

In his *History of Company G and E,* James wrote that from his original Darlington County company of 110 men, a third died, and only six returned unwounded.[9] Lest we forget the bravery of the soldiers and the shattering impact this war had on our nation, we must remember that the Civil War was the bloodiest war in the history of the Western hemisphere.[10] Many do not know this, but the 620,000 Americans who lost their lives in the Civil War are more than those who died in WWI, WWII, Korea, and Vietnam *combined.*[11]

Commentary: "God's Side," Winning, and Losing

In discussing theology relative to the Civil War, I confess there are no easy answers. Human folly, evil, and tragic excess characterize times of war. Beyond this, God alone is in the position to ultimately evaluate men's choices and actions.

Both sides felt God was on their side, and both sides believed they were acting out of a patriotic sense of duty, as each understood patriotism.

For the Union, the "Battle Hymn of the Republic" was written during the war by abolitionist Julia Ward Howe and used by Union soldiers as a battle song.[12] The Puritans had come from the North. Yale Divinity School professor Harry S. Stout wrote that "New England political and religious leaders had long proclaimed themselves God's 'chosen people.'"[13]

On the Southern side, Yale Divinity professor Harry Stout said: "The new Confederate Constitution, ratified on March 11, 1861, officially declared its Christian identity, 'invoking the favor and guidance of Almighty God....'"[14]

Aware that only God has the answers, let us contemplate possible theological scenarios. Did God discipline the South for practicing slavery by allowing it to lose the war? Most Confederate soldiers did not own slaves, but most Confederate leaders did. In the Gettysburg Address, President Lincoln took the view of divine judgment against slavery when he said, "every drop of blood drawn with the lash shall be paid by another drawn with the sword... 'for the judgments of the Lord are true and righteous altogether'" [Psalm 19:9].[15]

Another spiritual dimension, not exclusive of other viewpoints, is the massive conversion of soldiers on both sides. Christianity Today magazine reported that about 10 percent of Civil War soldiers experienced conversion during the war. The article "Religious Revivals During the Civil War" states: "A 'Great Revival' occurred among Robert E. Lee's forces in the fall of 1863 and winter of 1864. Some 7,000 soldiers were converted." Major Coker's own book from 1899, History of Company G and E, [16] gives similar reports of massive conversions.

James described the plight of himself and his South Carolina comrades, bravely marching into the teeth of Yankee bullets and cannon balls, singing:

> Let others seek a home below,
> Which flames devour or waves oe'r flow;
> Be mine a happier lot to own
> A heavenly mansion near the throne.

> *I'm going home, I'm going home.*
> *I'm going home to die no more.*
> *To die no more, to die no more—*
> *I'm going home to die no more.*[17]

Revivals also swept the Union Army. Sometimes preaching and praying continued 24 hours a day, and [Union] chapels couldn't hold the soldiers who wanted to get inside."[18]

In summary, the North had about 2,100,000 soldiers, and the South approximately 1,100,000, making the combined total around 3,200,000.[19] *If 10 percent were converted to the Christian faith, then c. 320,000 soldiers were converted during the war.*

Apparently, staring death in the face caused many to flee to the hope and pardon offered at the cross, leading cumulatively to a revival. From this perspective, we realize that while God hates all the barbarous excesses of war, in the end, souls were saved and lives changed, regardless of which side won.

As to who was to blame for the war politically, while glad for the slaves' freedom, Major Coker strongly believed the North had provoked the war. At the turn of the century, he wrote:

> Who are to be held responsible for the hundreds of thousands of lives lost and for the other terrible consequences of that war? If the states of the South acted according to their constitutional rights when they seceded from the Union and formed the Confederate States of America, they are not to be held accountable, but those who inaugurated the war to prevent this action are the ones to bear the blame for the sacrifices of life and property involved and for the misery and demoralization that followed an unjust war.

In my opinion, peaceable separation would have led to friendly adjustments and a solution to all our problems, and I think all the changes for the better brought about since 1860, even the abolition of slavery, could have and would have been secured without war, but passion governed, unreason prevailed, and no settlement that did not involve blood-letting or abject submission on the part of the South would serve those in charge of the United States Government.[20]

Kate Chambers' own family suffered terribly in the conflict, and she summarized the end of the war as follows:

So ended one of the bitterest and most sincere struggles that have ever occurred in history. The great question of States' Rights had been settled in blood and tears. The Southern people had sacrificed everything but honor... These war-weary men came back to their homes. What did they find? The country swept from one end to the other, the march of the invaders marked by the ruins of burned buildings. Their cattle commandeered by both armies. Many families became refugees; many never to be reunited, their homes fallen into disrepair. Their wardrobes reduced to the lowest possible ebb. Their bonds and currency, wastepaper.[21]

ENDNOTES FOR CHAPTER 5: THE LATER CIVIL WAR AND
SHERMAN'S WRECKAGE

1   Kate Chambers, op. cit., p. 99.
2   W. C, Wilson, *Recollections*, p.12.
3   The Major's granddaughter Pauline Wiggins, *Recollections*, p.11.
4   W. C. Wilson, *Recollections*, p.12.
5   James Lide Coker, *History of Company G and E.*, p. 195.
6   J. W. Norwood, op. cit., p. 424.
7   Editor, Wikiquote, "Robert E. Lee," https://en.wikiquote.org/wiki/Robert_E._Lee (accessed December 29, 2019).
8   I have a copy of Major Coker's typed copy of "Rawle's Vision," an admiring account of Robert E. Lee in my files, obtained from either the Darlington County Historical Society or the Coker College archives.
9   Ibid., p. 209.
10 H. V. Traywick Jr., Reckonin' website, "The Apostate," p. 1, https://www.reckonin.com/hv-traywick-jr/the-apostate (accessed December 29, 2019).
11 Editor, American Battlefield Trust's "Civil War Facts" article at https://www.battlefields.org/learn/articles/civil-war-facts (accessed December 29, 2019).
12 Ruane, Michael E., The Washington Post, November 18, 2011, "How Julia Ward Howe wrote 'Battle Hymn of the Republic' — despite her husband," https://www.washingtonpost.com/local/how-julia-ward-howe-wrote-battle-hymn-of-the-republic--despite-her-husband/2011/11/15/gIQAnQRaYN_story.html(accessed June 15,2020).
13 Harry C. Stout, Yale Divinity School Professor, 2008 web article "Religion in the Civil War: The Southern Perspective," TeacherServe® Home Page, National Humanities Center, http://nationalhumanitiescenter.org/tserve/nineteen/nkeyinfo/cwsouth.htm (accessed December 29, 2019).
14 Ibid.
15 See article "LINCOLN'S GETTYSBURG AND SECOND INAUGURAL ADDRESSES" at http://biblescripture.net/Address.html (accessed December 29, 2019).
16 Major James Lide Coker, *History of Company G, op. cit., p. 209.*
17 James Lide Coker, ibid, p. 193.
18 Editor, *Christianity Today* web article "Christianity and the Civil War: Did You Know?" at https://www.christianitytoday.com/history/issues/issue-33/christianity-and-civil-war-did-you-know.html (accessed December 29, 2019).

19   Editor, American Battlefield Trust's article "Answers to your Civil War Questions" at https://www.battlefields.org/learn/articles/civil-war-facts (accessed December 29, 2019).

20   James Lide Coker, *Hartsville: Its Early Settlers*, originally printed in 1899, reprinted, 1990, (Winmark Inc. / Jiffy Print: 1990), pp. 31-32.

21   Kate Chambers, op. cit., p. 106.

PART III

BOUNCING BACK: THE MAJOR COURAGEOUSLY LEADS THE REBOUND OF DARLINGTON COUNTY

CHAPTER 6

A CRUTCH, A HOE, AND
TWENTY-ONE BUSINESSES

The war had sucked the life out of the South, and few places were worse off than Sherman-devastated Darlington County. The Cokers were as destitute as their neighboring sharecroppers, with no money to speak of, no carts or wagons, and ashes for crops. James had done what he thought was right by going to war, yet the result was utter disaster. Moreover, he now had only one useable leg.

Adding insult to injury, the county was now overrun with "carpetbaggers," the southern term for northern businessmen who took advantage of the defeated South by gobbling up their business markets, often unethically. Dr. Richard Nelson Current, American historian widely regarded as "the Dean of Lincoln scholars," made the point that honorable, informed northerners knew that most carperbagers were up to no good. He quotes from New Hampshire-born Horace Greeley, who founded and edited the well-respected *New York Tribune*. In 1871, after taking a tour of the post-war South, Greeley reported:

> The thieving carpet-baggers are a mournful fact; they do exist there and I have seen them. They are fellows who crawled down South in the track of our armies, generally at a safe distance in the rear…. Some of them got elected Senators, others Representatives, some sheriffs, some Judges, and so on. And there they stand, right in the public eye, stealing and plundering, many of them with both arms around the Negroes, and their hands in their rear pockets, seeing if they cannot pick a paltry dollar out of them…What the Southern people see of us are these thieves who represent the North to their jaundiced vision, and, representing it, they disgrace it. They are the greatest obstacle to the triumph and permanent ascendancy of Republican principles at the South, and as such I denounce them.[1]

Between the ruin of his farm and the plundering of the carpet-baggers, the post-crisis was almost as bad as the war itself. The wolves were snarling at his door; and it was the Major's moment of truth. Both the depth of his character and the authenticity of his faith were on trial – how would James respond?

He refused to blame God. Neither his shattered leg, nearness to bankruptcy, Sherman's barbarism, nor unprincipled men could blur his vision or diminish his faith. He wrote that he and other Confederate Christians were "believing that they would not be altogether forsaken of God, but would receive His guidance in the dark night which enveloped their beloved Southland." [2] Lesser men would have been embittered, but James transcended the circumstances, kept a good attitude, and focused on what he could control. He embraced the principle of Proverbs 24:16: "A righteous man falls seven times and rises again."

They still had one milk cow which Sue had had hidden from Sherman deep in the swampy woods of the Pee Dee basin, and an old mule which Yankee soldiers deemed unfit to steal. James found some cottonseed and seed corn that Sherman's destroyers had overlooked. With his song of faith still in his heart, he gallantly rose up with a crutch in his left hand and a hoe in his right to meet the challenge head on. Aided by five freed African Americans, the old mule, and a pair of oxen borrowed from an uncle, he resolutely planted sixty acres of cotton and forty of corn. [3]

Simpson added that James knew "desolation would not respond to complaint, but it would respond to work, foresight, and care."[4] Modern leadership author and motivator John C. Maxwell put it more bluntly: "Leaders stretch with challenges. Followers struggle with challenges. Losers shrink from challenges."[5] In any case, the lion-hearted Major Coker stepped up to the plate.

His diligence in redeeming what he had yielded twenty-five bales of cotton in the fall of 1865. With his market savvy, he exchanged the bales for $1,700,[6] which in 2020 would be worth

Without complaint over the war's devastations, Major Coker focused on re-establishing his farm and his county's fortunes. By artist Dan Nelson, used with permission.

$27,000. After paying workers and expenses, he netted the 2020 equivalent of $12,500. Other than a few coins, this was the first money he had seen in years, and he invested as much as he could back into the farm. He also resumed his farm journal, with records of crops and fertilizers, and kept improving output according to principles he learned at Harvard.[7]

From this new beginning, wrought from hard farm labor, brains, and dirty overalls, James set in motion an astonishing comeback. Against all odds, over the next few decades he would become the leading businessman in the state and would lift up the prosperity, education, and spiritual life of Darlington County with him. Thomas M. McClellan, a relative who worked with the Major after the war, stated:

> I remember that he [James] told me that he invariably made a dividend on his farm. That he did not remember once in 25 years that he had failed to make a dividend on his farm. This was so unusual that it has stuck in my memory since."[8]

One reason James was able to lead this comeback was that, unbelievably, even with his shattered leg, he stayed physically fit. His nephew Arthur Rogers said of him:

> I remember seeing the Major walking back and forth across the porch in bad weather or a rainy day when he was confined to the house more than usual. He would be walking up and down the porch taking his exercises. He was a vigorous man, you know, even though he was wounded in the war.[9]

It would be a mistake to take Major Coker's faith and tremendous attitude for granted, or to diminish his gallantry as just a product of his times. His younger cousin Miss Jane Lide contrasted his courage with that of another highborn man from the same area. She wrote:

> There was in Darlington County another young captain, home from the war, not related by blood to the Major but of a fine family and blessed with a devoted and magnificent wife. He, too, looked at the wreckage, and he, too, faced serious losses; and he, too, grieved over those who would not return

and over the defeat of their cause. Alas! He did nothing but brood over the tragedies. His health failed, he became mentally ill, and he sank down into the shadows of frustration and futility—a wrecked life. Often I think of the contrast between those two young officers: one yielding to despair, the other singing, "Jesus, I my cross have taken," and looking around to see how to retrieve the losses for himself and *for others* [emphasis in original].[10]

Kingdom Priorities Not Shaken

The Major and Sue did not allow the challenges of protecting their family and re-establishing their farm to distract them from building the kingdom of God. Before the war, James taught Sunday School to children at Hartsville First Baptist Church. Afterward, in 1865, he resumed teaching on his crutch, and became Sunday School Superintendent. He and Sue not only led their Hartsville ministry, but expanded the Sunday School into a rural mission, making two trips a month[11] out in the country to teach literacy and Bible to barefoot children, African American and white.

They led Sunday School together inside and outside the church walls for the next thirty - eight years.[12] The two were quite a force for God. Sue would play hymns on the piano while Major Coker led the singing. Afterward, the Major would teach the older children, and Sue the younger ones.

The Coker couple's sturdy spiritual leadership was sorely needed during the tumultuous time from 1865 to 1877, which is called Reconstruction or Southern Reconstruction. It started as an expression of northern ideals for change in the post-war South, but ended up as a very disordered time when opportunistic northern politicos, carpet-baggers, Southern whites, and freedmen were all vying for power in the defeated

South. Each group had dangerous, even violent, extremists. In contrast, James provided steady leadership with a voice that was both sensible and firm, and a charted path of peace in the midst of the confusion, as told in the section below.

Historical Background: Southern Reconstruction

Southern Reconstruction was the post-war strategy devised on northern terms, to readmit Southern states into the Union. Ideally, its intention was to correct the social, racial, and economic inequalities that remained in the South—as northerners perceived them. However, many Reconstructionists used unnecessarily abrasive tactics and had less than honorable motives, "fixing" injustices with further injustices. Prize winning author and historian Allen C. Guelzo, in his book Reconstruction, a Concise History, wrote: Reconstruction can "reasonably be characterized as the ugly duckling of American history."

Many Southerners felt that the main Northern intent was to continue the economic domination of the South that had, in part, led to the war in the first place. The truth is that some of the northern corrections were desperately needed, while others were a pretext for graft. We'll first describe some very positive changes that came about, then give the other side.

A major positive was that Reconstruction banned the Black Codes, which the South Carolina Legislature had passed in 1865. These were supposed to be South Carolina's post-war improvements to the slave codes, but they changed almost nothing, and they are now considered predecessors of the Jim Crow laws. [13] They were designed to restrict the freedom of African-Americans, forcing them to work by contract labor based on low wages or debt. Even though slaves were guaranteed freedom after the Union victory in 1865, many whites used the codes to reassert total control over freedmen. The codes continued to use the terms "master" and "servant."[14] Something had to be done, and fortunately, in 1865, President Andrew Johnson declared South Carolina's Black Codes "null and void" Then he "appointed military governors to assume complete power in the former Confederate states until new civilian governments could be organized."[15]

78

Another very positive development of Reconstruction was establishment of The Freedmen's Bureau, which provided humanitarian, legal, and economic aid to freedmen. They arranged for African American voters to be registered, and for the first time in American history, some African Americans were elected to Southern state legislatures and the U.S. Congress. And backed by President Ulysses S. Grant, In 1868, the U. S. Congress passed the 14ᵗʰ Amendment guaranteeing all people "equal protection under the law." Major Coker, being racially progressive, helped to implement the positive changes.

Then there's the other side of it. Kate Chambers described the corrupt northern politicians when she said it was a time "when unscrupulous men passed laws to fit certain cases, and the Negro politicians were their tools. She added: "When many people of the South began to recoup their fortunes, they were again swept away by these iniquitous laws enacted by carpetbaggers or renegade Southerners. The taxes were almost confiscatory."[16] Describing the martial law, she said:

> The country was put under military rule and the [Southern] men required to take the Oath of Amnesty, after which they were kept waiting, sometimes for months, before pardon was granted by the United States Government. In many cases, bribery shortened this period, but those too honorable to use bribes felt the consequences.[17]

The aforementioned contemporary historian Professor Allen Guelzo, referring to "New York Tribune" journalist James Shepard Pike, provides evidence that Kate Chambers was not exaggerating:

> Standing in the state house in Columbia [in 1873], Pike watched 'old aristocratic society' replaced by a 'Black Parliament' in which arriviste [newly arrived and ruthlessly greedy] carpetbaggers and treacherous scalawags, in league with their black dupes, created a carnival of corruption: legislative appropriations

intended to purchase land for the freedpeople ended up in the pockets of the politicos; a special appropriation was made to reimburse the [Yankee] speaker of the state house, Franklin Moses, for his losses on a horse race; taxes had risen by 500 per cent since 1860,... and the [Union appointed] governor Robert Scott, "spent $374,000 of the public money to get himself rechosen"[18]

Guelzo also points out that that the South's prewar governments had their own problems with corruption.

A Tension-Packed time for All

What's in the next accounts may seem a bit raw, like an unvarnished war movie. Raw or not, I do not believe we should suppress the truths of history. These are authentic accounts of threats to the Coker home and property. The first was told by James's wife Sue Coker, participant in the event, to her niece Kate Chambers, who wrote it down:

A time of real danger for those white people who live in the country came after the conclusion of the war. The negroes were incited to evil deeds by bad advisors, and a few of them became a menace to life and property. At one time, my uncle [Major Coker] who had been away from home on business, returned unexpectedly, quite ill, in so high a fever that in his depleted condition from his wound he became delirious through the night.

Dear Aunt Sue sat beside the window, watching her sick husband and her three children who were asleep nearby. When the time had gone long past midnight and the beautiful Southern moon was flooding the yard with light, she saw the front gate open very stealthily, and a black man slip through. In the brilliant moonlight, she recognized one of the most dangerous [men] in the community and called out, 'Why, Jim, what do you want?' The man replied in a very plausible tone, 'Miss Sue, is that you? I just want to see Mas' James.' 'He is here,' she said, 'but you cannot see him, and you know you come here for no good reason at this late hour of the night. If you don't leave immediately, I am going to shoot you. I have a pistol here in my hand.' She cocked her pistol noisily. The man hesitated, and she called peremptorily, 'Leave immediately, or I'll shoot you!' He beat a hasty retreat. Then she watched as a sentinel, guarding her family until the morning light brought her protection. I had this story from her own lips.[19]

Simpson also wrote that there were groups of freed slaves and carpetbaggers who tried to intimidate white people, going as far as looting and stealing. He described an armed looting attempt in Society Hill at James's father Caleb Coker Jr.'s store, and of how James's brother, William Coker, minding the store at the time, had to run the looter off with a hatchet.[20]

Federal troops and their allies, carpetbaggers and politically opportunistic Republican radicals, also unnecessarily trampled Southern sensibilities by dividing Darlington County into twenty-one townships, all with Northern names, including "Sherman," "Grant," and "Whittemore." Naming the mid-eastern township "Whittemore" was vainly accomplished by Benjamin Franklin Whittemore, a former chaplain in the Union army. He started a Methodist Episcopal church in Darlington County, but his legacy went downhill from there.

After being elected to the U.S. Congress as a South Carolina Republican from 1868 to 1870, Whittemore was soon found guilty of corruption for taking a bribe in return for an appointment to the Naval Academy.[21] He resigned after the scandal and was censured by the U.S. House of Representatives. Though a minister, Whittemore showed no repentance, because he immediately sought re-election. At that point, The House of Representatives blocked him from continuing in politics. He returned to

his home state of Massachusetts in 1870. When Reconstruction ended,
Pee Dee residents quickly renamed all the townships to Southern names.

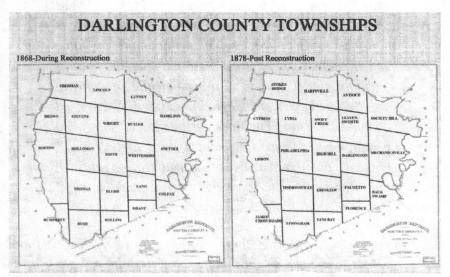

DARLINGTON COUNTY TOWNSHIPS

During Reconstruction, Federal troops and "carpet baggers" trampled on southern sensibilites by dividing Darlington County into 21 townships with Yankee names, including, "Sherman," " Grant," and "Whttemore." After reconstruction, South Carolinians quickly renamed all 21 to reflect southern heritage. Courtesy of Darlington Co. Historical Commission.

Ongoing Prejudice and Legalized Murder

We now return to the South's post-war sins, which were worse. Many
whites, excluding the Cokers and many others, continued barbaric
oppression of the freedmen, carried out in part by the Ku Klux Klan.
The Klan was conceived in 1866 by Southern attorneys who wanted to
alleviate white suffering. Its stated purpose was to be "an instrument
of Chivalry, Humanity, Mercy, and Patriotism," originally founded to
"relieve and assist the injured, oppressed, suffering, and unfortunate,
especially widows and orphans of Confederate soldiers." [22]

But spiteful Kan members quickly pirated the Klan's leadership
and reduced it to a more or less a white terrorist network. They publicly
whipped or lynched African Americans at the slightest appearance of
their being "uppity." Hundreds of people witnessed dreadful Klan
lynchings, yet white juries rarely convicted a white person for killing

an African American person. This amounted to legalized murder, and the atrocities committed can never be minimized. Tragically, many more atrocities were perpetrated by white supremacists against African Americans for decades after Reconstruction. [23]

Then, as today, the unredeemed hearts of unredeemed people produce sin-stained agendas. Mark Twain, a contemporary of the Major, described these times this way: "They [men] squabble and scold and fight; they scramble for little mean advantages over each other." [24] *Then, as today, people on all political sides were in desperate need of the redemptive grace of God in order to treat each other with proper consideration.* [25] *John Wesley said: "Passion and prejudice govern the world; only under the name of reason. It is our part, by religion and reason joined, to counteract them all we can."* [26] *In the name of Christ and reason, Major Coker transcended the hate and did what he could to keep sanity in the equation.*

Major Coker's Response to Prejudiced Whites

Fortunately, Major Coker had the redemptive grace of God, adding extra dimensions of patience and wisdom to his natural leadership abilities. He was able to see outside of the Southern "box."

Even though occupying northerners tried to shame him as a Confederate, with a clear conscience and an inspired mission, he, like Nehemiah, who rebuilt Jerusalem in 444 BC, wasted no time answering his detractors. He remain laser-focused and procured more substantial and enduring political, financial, agricultural, and spiritual opportunities for freedmen than his accusers ever did.

As a peacemaker, the Major perceived evils on both sides and worked for compromise. Simpson wrote: "A great many white people [the Cokers included] came to feel that the only course open was to seek to find a middle ground somewhere between the extreme [northern] radicals who were then controlling and impoverishing the state and the great number of white people who would not give an inch to the new conditions that defeat in war had brought. To this end, the Union

Reform Party was organized in 1870... It aimed to go along with moderated changes, while at the same time attracting enough negro voters to win."

*Simpson continued: "James, along with four other white men and five negroes, formed one delegation from Darlington [County] to the state convention of this party, where a platform was adopted calling for, among other things, **full recognition of the legal and political rights of the Negro." 27 The Major's party also placed at least one black man on the ticket in every state district** (emphasis added). In the end, the Major's Union Reform came up short, primarily because they made more concessions to African Americans than most white South Carolinians of that time were prepared to accept.*

The End of Reconstruction

Reconstruction ended shortly afterward when Republican Rutherford B. Hayes won the presidential election by the narrowest of margins. He was only awarded the presidency after making a deal with Southern Democrats to end Reconstruction. In what was called The Compromise of 1877, he agreed to remove all federal troops from the three states where they remained: South Carolina, Florida, and Louisiana.[28]

The subsequent exodus of federal troops, along with some of the carpetbaggers and Northern Republicans, allowed white Southern Democrats to regain control of their states. Additionally, former Confederate General Wade Hampton was elected governor of South Carolina in 1876. The combination of the exodus, the new governor, and his choice to fill his cabinet with other Confederate generals restored a favorable business climate for whites but meant a significant setback for African Americans. [29]

We have seen the pioneering and progressive attempts of fair-minded whites like Major Coker and his relatives during this period. Unfortunately, despite the efforts of fair-minded whites like the Cokers, in the years after Reconstruction, African Americans in South Carolina lost almost all the political representation they had gained during Reconstruction. Insecure whites with illusions of supremacy continued to harass and marginalize them to keep them away from the polls, and the upward steps of African Americans were stymied. They would not regain full stride until the Civil Rights Movement peaked in the 1960s, due in no small part to the intelligent and resourceful Christian leader, Dr. Martin Luther King, Jr.

There is, of course, much more to American civil rights history than this brief treatment of Reconstruction. Today there are still inequities to be righted in our police force and many other institutions. But for Major Coker's part, he did his best to be an agent of peace and reason during Reconstruction and beyond.

We now resume the Major's entrepreneurial story in late 1865, after he began turning his farm around.

The Major's Strategic Business Responses

When aggressive Yankees tried to steal the customers for his farm and store products, the Major did not retaliate. He simply outclassed them by finding better ways to meet the needs of the customers in his state. After all, they knew he cared more about them than newly arrived northerners did. In the midst of these brutal economic and political conditions, and against all odds, he commenced an almost unbelievable fifty year run of marketplace genius, combined with high-minded cultural leadership, eventually becoming the wealthiest man in his state. As he did, he lifted up the prosperity, educational level, and spiritual life of all of Darlington County along with himself.

J. W. Norwood described the Major's business and personal resourcefulness as follows: "He accumulated one of the largest fortunes ever accumulated in this state, though he was practically insolvent when the Civil War came to an end. He was one of the most versatile businessmen the state has ever produced."[30] We will now follow this legendary, but true account of his business explosion. Then, in Chapter 7, we will learn all we can from his outstanding business principles.

J. L. Coker and Company General Store, 1865

First, the Major opened a general and farming store in Hartsville called J. L. Coker and Company in 1865. He sold neither alcohol nor cigarettes, but the store became the focal point of Hartsville.[31] As folks traded news and stories there, it became the hub for community relationships. The store relocated from its original small wooden building to a larger brick structure on Carolina Ave. Along the way, James delegated management to Arthur Rogers, Tom E. Goodson, his son D. R., and J. J. Lawton. D. R., then Lawton later became store president. By 1881, the Hartsville General Store had become a combination of farm, general, and grocery stores, and it multiplied to several locations across the state.

In 1911, the editor of Bishopville's *Leader and Vindicator* newspaper visited Hartsville and wrote:

> The J. L. Coker fine department store was a marvel to us all. We know of no other town, Columbia not excepted, that has such a splendidly arranged store. Everything on the modern and most approved style. Five stores all in one with every convenience for the comfort of its employees and satisfaction of its customers.[32]

The interior of the J. L. Coker and Co. store in Hartsville, c. 1910. Used by permisison of the Southern Historical Collection, Wilson Library, The University of North Carolina at Chapel Hill.

The Major's son Will Coker commented: "Father's store made a good profit every year, and when any of his sons or sons-in-law would suggest some new business, he would say they always called on the profit of the store [for venture capital] to sustain them. He called it "the old milk cow of the family."[33] Will Coker further observed in 1947: Coker's store [is] an institution that is still running and is now one of the two largest stores in South Carolina after 82 years.[34]

The Staff of J. L. Coker & Company Store, 1913.
Courtesy of the Hartsville Museum.

My siblings and I remember going to a thriving Coker's Department Store in Myrtle Beach, where we vacationed in the 60's and 70's. However, with the advent of behemoths like Walmart, the Coker stores were all closed by about 1990.

J. L. Coker Real Estate, c. 1874

The Major made good use the thousand acres he received from his parents in 1857. He gave generous portions to churches and schools, but businessman that he was, he also traded it profitably. Murray Smith McKinnon, vice president of the Peoples Bank and twice mayor of Hartsville (1902-04 and 1910-12) recounted:

> When those lots were being sold along East Carolina Avenue… often a prospective purchaser would say, "Well, Major, that sounds awful high

for a lot; can't you do any better than that?" The Major would say, "Well, it might sound high, but I have never had anyone to resell one for less than I sold it for, and judging from that, they must be worth what I'm asking for them." And time proved him right.[35]

Even though he sold hundreds of lots as Hartsville grew, over his lifetime, in his trading, the Major actually increased the number of acres he owned by 150 percent. He started with 1000 acres, and in his last will and testament in 1918, he distributed 2,447 acres to his heirs.

As a way of illustrating James's integrity, McKinnon described this event from the real estate business:

This is to show how sacred Major Coker's word was; years ago this land they called the upper farm, I believe, ran across and fronted along Home Avenue there. W. C. Barefoot went to the Major and said, "I would like to buy 100 acres of your land there fronting on Home Avenue." The Major said, "Well, the price might not suit you." "Well, name a price."

One hundred dollars an acre in those times was almost unheard of – Major said: "Well, I will sell you 100 acres at $100 an acre in cash, but I'll have to have the money in hand by sundown tomorrow." And just on the side, I have no idea Major thought Mr. Barefoot could raise that much money. I don't know how he got up the money, but next day he went to the Major and said, "Well Major, I am ready to pay you for that land out there."

Major called David (D. R.), told him about the trade, and asked David to have a deed prepared to Mr. Barefoot for 100 acres. David said, "No, father, you can't sell off this part of the farm. That will just ruin the front of the farm." "Well, David, I gave my word to Mr. Barefoot and he brought the money and so I want the deed prepared. My word is my bond." And Mr. Barefoot got his land.[36] My mother (D. R.'s daughter) taught me and my siblings that a gentleman's word is his bond, and I have also taught my children to do what they say, passing the Major's honor in that sale down four generations.

The Norwood and Coker Naval and Trading Post in Charleston, 1874

The Hartsville general store was just the launching pad. In 1874, he teamed up with George Norwood, his boyhood friend from Saint David's School, to establish Norwood and Coker, a cotton

Picture c\o gograph.com, customized by author.

and naval trading post in the port city of Charleston. This store gave Coker an outlet for his own cotton, along with that of his community. Commenting on the opportune combination of a general store, a cotton distributions center, and a naval supply center in this port city, George Norwood's son, J. W. Norwood, gives us insight into the genius of this enterprise:

Cotton grown in this section [Darlington County] at that time was sold entirely through Charleston. Here was an opportunity for further natural development. He formed a partnership in Charleston to conduct a cotton and naval stores business, which from a small beginning developed in a few years into one of the largest and most profitable businesses in that line in the state.[37]

The Major's Call Back to Hartsville

The Major and his family spent the winters in Charleston from 1876 to 1881, and his interests were divided between Charleston and Hartsville. In spite of the clear success of the naval trading post, something was stirring in James. Deep down he knew his true calling was not to Charleston. He briefly considered a banking opportunity in Richmond, but decided that was not where he belonged either.

His relatives, friends, and the people of his home county were still distressed and downcast from the devastations of the war, and his life's calling since childhood, to redeem them, came back to him clearly. For those familiar with *Lord of the Rings*, the Major's critical decision paralleled the defining moment in *The Return of the King* when Elrond, the King of the Elves, exhorted Aragorn to fulfill his destiny, to rise up and rescue Middle-earth from devastation:

"Put aside the ranger. Become who you were born to be."[38]

Like Aragorn, James decided he must fulfill his destiny. He expressed an acute sense of urgency in a letter to his friend and relative James Lide Wilson:

There is work here [in Hartsville] for which I am responsible that demands from me everything that I can properly perform. Its demands are not

small, nor are they to be set aside... So far as I can
see, no other person is charged with the work to
which I am alluding. I must do what is laid upon
me, or it will not be accomplished.[39]

Shortly thereafter, he sold his interest in Norwood and
Coker and came home with roughly $75,000 in cash, bonds,
and notes,[40] equivalent to almost 2 million dollars in 2020. He
bought a larger home in Hartsville on Home Avenue and from
that point on, Major Coker focused all of his energy on helping
the people of Hartsville and its environs to rebuild their lives,
economically, spiritually, and educationally. His continued
business growth was part of that process, multiplying job
opportunities in the area.

The Darlington Manufacturing Company, 1881

Before Major Coker, Pee Dee farmers grew cotton but did not
make their own yarn. The following is from the Hartsville
Agriculture Society's minutes of August 10, 1869: "The
Chairman, J. L. Coker, discussed the matter at length, arguing
the necessity and propriety of manufacturing our own cotton."[41]

When he returned from Charleston in 1881, the Major
followed through on this project and began a cotton mill
called the Darlington Manufacturing Company in the town
of Darlington, fourteen miles east of Hartsville. His initiative
made it possible for local cotton farmers to control the
manufacturing and marketing of their yarn, multiplying their
profits. The Major then turned the lucrative operations over to
his brother Captain William Coker but retained a majority of
the company's stock.

The Darlington National Bank, 1881

J. L. COKER,
BANKER,
Dealer in Real Estate, Cotton
and Fertilizers.

Hartsville, S. C., _____ 189_0

The Darlington Bank, opened in c. 1881, combined with the letterhead of the store.

As the Pee Dee began to recover from the war, the Major saw a need for a bank. In 1881, he organized and was elected president of Darlington National Bank, the only bank in the county. He rode a buggy fifteen miles through the countryside from Hartsville to Darlington to supervise its affairs twice a week, and made the institution both useful and profitable.

He would leave on Tuesday and come back on Thursday. The Major knew and trained his horses well. One particularly intelligent horse, Joe, was quick to learn the way by heart. On Wednesdays, while he was in Darlington, the Major occasionally lent Joe to a business friend who wanted to go to Hartsville for a day. Joe knew the way so well that no directions were needed. Without fail, Joe and his rider would arrive at the house and stop right in front of the Major's Hartsville porch![42]

Major Coker took classes in drawing at The Citadel and later built his own drawing studio in his home.[43] He was known for creative drawing and for self-sufficiency[44], and he drew his own designs for his business and school letterheads, some of which are pictured in this chapter.

In 1886, the Major turned the presidency of the Darlington National Bank over to Darlington's Bright Williamson,[45] keeping his own stock. Mr. Williamson expressed "his appreciation for the wonderful way that he [Major Coker] had run the bank and the fine condition the bank was in when he left it. He said all the bank papers and records were in such fine shape that all he had to do was sit there and follow up things as they had been running."[46]

The Hartsville Railroad, 1884

As Major Coker's trading success continued, he realized that more than ever, he needed a railroad spur to expedite commercial opportunities for himself and the larger Pee Dee. When he asked his farming and community friends to help him underwrite it, most refused, saying it was too risky. Next, he asked the Atlantic Coast Line Railroad Company if they would pay for it, and they also turned him down, deeming the potential profits unworthy.

So, in a bold move, in 1884 Major Coker partnered with some of his closest associates, J. J. Lawton, Thomas C. Law, the father of his Citadel friend Tom Law, war comrades H. Lide Law and Captain E. W. Cannon, and C. J. Woodruff, who later also partnered in the Carolina Fiber Company later, to manually build a seven-mile extension from Floyds Junction, South Carolina, into Hartsville at their own expense.[47]

The Hartsville Railroad. The Major's son James Lide Coker, Junior, is in the foreground with his new bride, Vivien Gay, in the passenger car, c. 1890. Used by permission of the Hartsville Historical Commission.

J. L. COKER, President.

Letterhead of The Hartsville Railroad, which Major Coker, his son James Jr., and their partners opened in 1884. Courtesy of the South Caroliniana Library, University of South Carolina, Columbia, SC, and used by permission.

The Major found ingenious ways to minimize expenses. The Atlantic Coast Line was in the process of replacing its rails at the same time that the Major wanted to build his track. Simpson informs us: "The Coast Line was replacing its iron rails with steel rails. The Major secured the use of some of these older iron rails, still in good condition, and began to build."[48]

As with his farm, Major Coker did not shy away from the work. At age forty-seven, he was out there with his crutch supervising and helping the men build the track. Mrs. J. F. Ousley, who attended high school in Hartsville, said: "I first saw Major Coker seated on a pile of cross ties for the railroad that connects Hartsville with the Society Hill-Darlington line at a little station [near Darlington] known as Floyds.... He supervised and financed the construction of this railroad..."[49]

When they finished in 1884, the Major asked his son James Jr. to drive the engine for their first ride over the twelve-mile track from Floyds Junction to Hartsville. Overjoyed at having their businesses connected with the rest of the world, Pee Dee merchants, farmers, and suppliers got off the fence and suddenly applauded the Major for his "great idea." They suddenly became enthusiastic in praising him for taking the initiative to make the spur a reality.

As a concrete illustration of the Major's vision to uplift his entire community, his son Will Coker wrote about the Major's decision to locate his railroad terminus to everyone's benefit:

> To me, Father's generosity of spirit was probably more visibly illustrated in his actions in regard to placing the terminus of the railroad. He told those associated with him that he was going to place the railroad station practically on the western boundary of his land. In spite of argument to the contrary, he refused to place it where it would be undoubtedly more advantageous to him; that is, over towards the middle of his own property.

> He said he did not want to be selfish about the
> matter; he wanted other people to get some
> advantage of the increase in real estate values,
> as well as himself.
>
> This resulted in the rapidly growing village
> of Hartsville, now a prosperous town, being
> centered where a large part of the growth would
> be on the property belonging to other people. His
> own store was placed near the railroad station,
> and all the other stores are now in immediate
> vicinity.[50]

Both Major Coker and the Hartsville community profited
greatly from his railroad, and in 1892, he and his partners sold
the railroad operations to the Atlantic Coast Line for a profit.[51]

The Hartsville Electric Light and Water Company, 1899

The light company was made possible in 1899, when the Major
installed an Edison Dynamo generator after he had damned
up Black Creek. Major Coker organized and founded this
utility company in 1899, along with his mentee, J. J. Lawton.[52]
Lawton became the general manager, and it served the needs
of electricity in Hartsville for many years.

The Hartsville Oil Mill, 1900

The J. L. Coker General Store and The Hartsville Oil Mill under one letterhead. Courtesy of the South Caroliniana Library, University of South Carolina, Columbia, SC, and used by permission.

The Hartsville Oil Mill was founded by the Major and J. J. Lawton in 1900, with Lawton as president, treasurer, and general manager. Next Exit History describes this enterprise: "The mill became extremely successful, expanded into soybean oil. As "A cotton oil mill, it crushed cottonseed to produce cooking oil; meal and cake for feed and fertilizer; and lint for stuffing and explosives."[53]

In an interview I had with the Major's great grandson and J. J Lawton's grandson, Edgar H. Lawton, Jr., who was Chairman of the Board, he said the oil mill lasted for 119 years. Company assets were liquidated in 2019.

The Coker Pedigreed Seed Company, 1902

As time allowed, since leaving Harvard in 1858, the Major was working to scientifically optimize his cotton and corn seeds through hybrid breeding using his chemistry set and fertilizers. When he his son D. R. came of age, he too was intensely interested in this work. They became partners, and soon converted some of their land to an experimental farm. But before making it a business, they worked for four or five years purifying the strains of cotton and corn until they reached pedigree perfection.[54]

In 1902, James originally founded the seed company under J. L. Coker and Company stores.[55] In 1918, he separated it, having delegated the presidency and operations to D. R., saying: "David is doing this work much better than I ever could have done,"[56] so he credited David with founding the company. D. R. proved worthy, and over the years expanded experimentation, variety, and production. The Company would go on to share with the world how to breed the highest quality cotton, corn, soybean, and watermelon seeds, as well as how to replenish soils by using the right fertilizers at the right times.

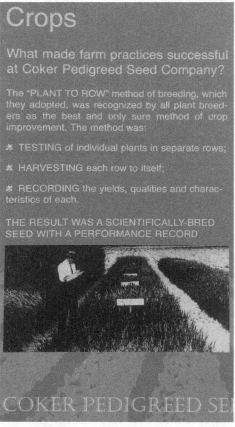

Crops

What made farm practices successful at Coker Pedigreed Seed Company?

The "PLANT TO ROW" method of breeding, which they adopted, was recognized by all plant breeders as the best and only sure method of crop improvement. The method was:

* TESTING of individual plants in separate rows;

* HARVESTING each row to itself;

* RECORDING the yields, qualities and characteristics of each.

THE RESULT WAS A SCIENTIFICALLY-BRED SEED WITH A PERFORMANCE RECORD

COKER PEDIGREED SE

From a sign on the self-guided tour at Coker Experimental Farms National Historic Landmark in Hartsville, S.C. The Major's son D.R. is pictured.

One of the signs at Hartsville's historical landmark for The Coker Pedigreed Seed Company asks and answers the question: "What made farm practices successful at Coker Pedigreed Seed Company? The 'PLANT TO ROW' method of selective breeding."[57] The company's catchphrase, "Blood Will Tell," referred to their improved genetic breeding methods – though, of course, no blood was involved.

They were assisted by Herbert John Webber of the USDA, and by dedicated plant breeder Dr. George Wilds, a key seed team member for life. Later, A. L. M. Wiggins became business manager.

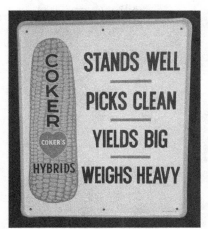

By In 1908, the *New York Times said* that the Coker team "has developed a superior variety [of cotton] with a staple one third larger and from 70 % to 140% more valuable in the market."[58] Major Coker lived to joyfully see the wonderful outcome of these experiments when regional farmers and sharecroppers raised their standard of living by boosting their production with the Coker pedigreed seeds.

Coker Pedigreed Seed Farms Advertising Sign, c. 1918. Permission of Hartsville Museum.

One of their employees, Mr. America Mark, was one of Hartsville's "oldest and most reliable colored citizens." His obituary from the *Hartsville Messenger*, 9/13/1945, states:

> Mr. Mark was one of the best Negro farmers in this community until his health failed him some two years ago. It is said that he was with the beginning of the J. L. Coker's seed breeders and remained with this firm many years, later developing his own farm where he put into practice methods which he had learned.[59]

In cooperation with Clemson College, D. R. and his seed company staff, using a combination of savvy planting methods and beetle poisons, became national leaders in effectively fighting cotton's greatest enemy, the boll weevil, a long-snouted beetle that ruined cotton flowers, which came up from Mexico in the early 1920's. This battle continued under the next two

CEO's, George Wilds (1889-1951), then the Major's grandson through D. R., Robert R. Coker (1905-1987). Robert once said: "I look forward to being a pall-bearer in the funeral procession that carries the casket of the last boll weevil to its grave."[60] In time, the pedigreed seed team revolutionized production for rural farmers and enabled many to weather the Great Depression. The full story of the Pedigreed Seed Company is told in detail in *Mr. D. R.: A Biography of David R. Coker,* by James A. Rogers and Larry E. Nelson. A few articles with a bit more reserved assessment

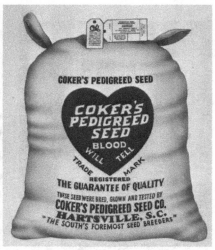

Coker Pedigreed Seed Co. bag, c. 1918, courtesy of the South Caroliniana Library, University of South Carolina, Columbia, S.C.

of D. R.'s impact have been written by UNC History Professor Peter A. Coclanis.[61]

The success[62] of The Coker Pedigreed Seed Company points to the persistent efforts of D. R. and his staff, but its roots go back to the Major and his early experimentation. At the Centennial Celebration of Major Coker's birth, the Major's friend Fred L. Wilcox said, "[Hartsville's] position as the center of agricultural interests not only in South Carolina but in the entire South, is due almost solely to him and to those who have carried on under his influence."[63]

Miss Jane Lide described the Major's "keen sense of community" this way: "His life principle was, 'Everything in my power to help everybody within my reach....' For him, it was never enough that one family should prosper. Experiments in farming must be tried, discoveries made, plans perfected for better crops, that would bring prosperity within reach of every person who was willing to make an effort."[64] The Coker

Pedigreed Seed Company stayed in business until 1988, when the Northrup King Company bought it.[65]

The Hartsville Cotton Mill, 1903

In addition to his Darlington Manufacturing Company cotton mill, Major Coker organized the Hartsville Cotton Mill, which author Malcolm C. Doubles reported "opened in 1903 and operated for more than sixty years. In the late 1960s, it was absorbed into the Milliken organization."[66]

The Bank of Hartsville, 1903

In addition to the Darlington National Bank, Major Coker organized the Bank of Hartsville in 1903 and served as its CEO.[67] Over the next few years, it became one of the most successful banks in the state. The Major became known as the pioneer banker of the Pee Dee area.[68]

The Eastern Carolina Silver Company, 1907

The silver company opened in Hartsville in 1907. Major Coker was president; his son Charles W. Coker, treasurer; and Walter F. Smith, a Massachusetts-born consultant for some of the Major's industries (see Chapters 8 and 9), was manager of manufacturing. In addition to employing Southerners, Smith had recruited some northern workers. The Hartsville Museum informs us that:

Each piece of the silver [which they had manufactured] was stamped on the bottom by a steel marker with the image of a small palmetto tree and the name of the company: E. Carolina Silver Company, Hartsville, SC.

Though profitable, after two years, the Major dissolved

the silver company because the wives of the skilled northern workers could not stand Hartsville's heat and humidity. James just instinctively knew it was time to get out, and he moved the assets to his other businesses.

The Hartsville Fertilizer Company, 1910

With his experimental chemical laboratory in the back of his Hartsville store,[69] as he had time, the Major continued to perfect fertilizers as well as seeds. After D. R. came on to help him with experiments, he patented some exceptionally reliable fertilizers. In 1910, he founded the Hartsville Fertilizer Company,[70] greatly benefitting South Carolina farmers once again.

The Carolina Fiber Company (1899), The Southern Novelty Company (1899), and Sonoco Products Company (1923)

The genius for these last three amazing and interrelated industries started with the Major and his son James, Jr. in the 1880s.

Letterhead of The Carolina Fiber Company, which began production in 1892, but due to early struggles, the Major did not offically found it until quality was assured in 1899. Permission of The South Caroliniana Library, University of South Carolina, Columbia, SC.

All three of these companies grew up making paper, packaging, and spooling products that complemented each other. I have devoted Chapter 8 and Chapter 9 to the exciting history of these three companies.

Summary of The Major's Businesses

In all, from 1858 to 1915, Major Coker founded seventeen for-profit businesses, all of which became exceedingly successful, save one (the Eastern Carolina Silver Company).

1. Coker Farms, begun in 1858, resumed in 1865 after the war.
2. The J. L. Coker and Company General Store, 1865, which expanded to five branches.
3. J. L. Coker Real Estate, c. 1874.
4. Norwood and Coker Naval and Trading Post, 1874.
5. The Darlington Manufacturing Company (cotton mill), 1881.
6. The Darlington National Bank, 1881.
7. The Hartsville Railroad, 1884.
8. The Hartsville Electric Light and Water Company, 1899.
9. The Hartsville Oil Mill, 1900.
10. The Coker Pedigreed Seed Company, 1902.
11. The Hartsville Cotton Mill, 1903.
12. The Bank of Hartsville, 1903.
13. The Eastern Carolina Silver Company, 1907.
14. The Hartsville Fertilizer Company, 1910.
15. The Carolina Fiber Company (started experimentally 1891, founded 1899).
16. The Southern Novelty Company, 1899. Later joined with the fiber company, the two became
17. Sonoco Products Company, 1923.

When we include the four nonprofit businesses institutions he founded, the Hartsville Agricultural Society (1865), the Welsh Neck High School (1884), the Pee Dee Historical Association (1903)[71], and Coker College (1908), then the Major is to be credited with founding 21 businesses.

The Major was primarily responsible for the growth and development of Darlington county and the town of Hartsville, and is universally considered the finest community leader in Hartsville's history. And many residents of the Palmetto State wouldn't argue if we widened that to say he was the finest in the state's history.

In the next chapter, we take a deeper look at the inspiring business qualities in James's character that guided him to his unusual success. Delving into his principles can only help each of us grow in our own success at serving others.

ENDNOTES FOR CHAPTER 6: A CRUTCH, A HOE, AND TWENTY-ONE BUSINESSESS

1 Horace Greeley, as quoted by Dr. Richard Nelson Current in *Those Terrible Carpetbaggers*, (Oxford University Press), 1988, pp. 261-262, as posted by the editor at 1898 Wilmington: Debunking the Myths, http://www.1898wilmington.org/TheCarpetbaggers.shtml
2 James Lide Coker, *History of Company G and E*, op. cit., p. 206.
3 George Lee Simpson, op. cit., p. 86.
4 Ibid., p. 185.
5 Peter Economy, Inc.com article "44 Inspiring John C. Maxwell Quotes for Leadership Success" https://www.inc.com/peter-economy/44-inspiring-john-c-maxwell-quotes-that-will-take-you-to-leadership-success.html (accessed December 29, 2019).
6 Ibid.
7 Vivien G. Coker, *Recollections*, p. 5.
8 Thomas M. McClellan, *Recollections*, p.5
9 Arthur Rogers, *Recollections*, p. 86.
10 Miss Jane Lide, op. cit., p. 4.
11 Kate Chambers, op. cit., p. 78.
12 Mrs. J. F. Ousley, 1900 Welsh Neck High School graduate, in *Recollections*, p. 41, tells of the Major's continuance in teaching Sunday School during her time at the school, which would have been 1896-1900.
13 Editors, History.com, 2010, 2019 article "Black Codes," https://www.history.com/topics/black-history/black-codes(accessed June 15,2020).
14 Editor, Constitutional Rights Foundation, 2020 article "Southern Black Codes," https://www.crf-usa.org/brown-v-board-50th-anniversary/southern-black-codes.html(accessed June 15,2020).
15 Editor, The Constitutional Rights Foundation's web article "The Southern 'Black Codes' of 1865-66," http://www.crf-usa.org/brown-v-board-50th-anniversary/southern-black-codes.html (accessed December 29, 2019).
16 Kate Chambers, op. cit., p. 109.
17 Kate Chambers, op. cit., p. 109.
18 Guelzo, op. cit., p. 100.
19 Kate Chambers, op. cit., pp. 135-136.
20 Ibid., p. 89.
21 Editor, Grand Old Partisan web site, May 18, 2019 article "Benjamin Franklin Whittemore, the SCGOP's first Chairman, https://grandoldpartisan.typepad.com/blog/2019/05/benjamin-franklin-whittemore.html (accessed February 19, 2020).

22 Samuel W. Mitcham, *The Abbeville Blog*," July 15, 2019 article "A History Lesson for Ted Cruz," https://www.abbevilleinstitute.org/blog/a-history-lesson-for-ted-cruz/ (accessed December 29, 2019).

23 Lartey, Jamiles, and Morris, Sam, The Guardian, April 26, 2018 article "How white Americans used lynchings to terrorize and control black people," https://www.theguardian.com/us-news/2018/apr/26/lynchings-memorial-us-south-montgomery-alabama(accessed July 15, 2020)

24 Chad Ashby's posting of quotes from Mark Twain's autobiography at his article "A Depressingly 'Ecclesiastical' Perspective by Mark Twain" at https://chadashby.com/2013/04/19/a-depressingly-ecclesiastical-perspective-by-mark-twain/ (accessed December 29, 2019).

25 Philippians 2:3: "Do nothing from selfishness or empty conceit, but with humility of mind let each of you regard one another as more important than himself."

26 Robert Campbell, editor, April 29, 2011 article, Logos Talk, "Ten Thought-Provoking John Wesley Quotes," https://blog.logos.com/2011/04/ten_thought-provoking_john_wesley_quotes/ (accessed March 5, 2020)

27 George Lee Simpson, op. cit., pp. 90-91

28 Michael Les Benedict. "Southern Democrats in the Crisis of 1876-1877: A Reconsideration of Reunion and Reaction." *The Journal of Southern History*, vol. 46, no. 4, 1980, pp. 489–524. *JSTOR*, www.jstor.org/stable/2207200 (accessed 14 June 2020).

29 Rogers and Nelson, op. cit., p.7.

30 J. W. Norwood, op. cit., p. 429.

31 Rogers and Nelson, op. cit., p.11.

32 Bishopville, SC's *Leader and Vindicator* newspaper, "Bryan at Hartsville," June 22, 1911, p. 1. I have a copy of the article.

33 Will Coker, *Recollections*, p. 19.

34 Ibid.

35 Recollections, p. 71

36 Ibid., p. 72

37 J. W. Norwood from his recorded speech in Hartsville, SC, on *Memorial Day, Founder's Day, April 9, 1919*, p. 15.

38 Tolkien, J. R. R., author. Peter Jackson, Director, *The Return of the King*, New Line Cinema, New Zealand, United States, 2003.

39 George Lee Simpson, op. cit., p. 184, as he quoted from Major Coker's letter to James Lide Wilson of September 12, 1914.

40 George Lee Simpson, op. cit., p. 98.

41 J. M. Napier, *Recollections*, p. 14.

42 W. C. Coker, *Recollections*, p. 16.

43 Susanne Gay Linville, *Jennie: A Biography of Jennie Coker Gay* (the book, written by Jennie Coker Gay's daughter, names no commercial publisher), 1983, p. 2.

44 Ethel L. Miller, *Recollections*, p. 29.

45 Editor, Google Books, 1922 *International Banking Directory* by Banker's Publishing Company of New York, https://books.googleusercontent. com/books/content?req=AKW5QafT6jFiXq7zPSCI7yv338U3qIt-kMA ExUCgNeJAJpppXm9FizNfx4zcp67PmMBrHMPRdGpQyNJxCJgT6 ghM6-EnpkgaJMDeJfYYZiBlinrcn_sjd_pJfWpG47q91AxqQVuOMDh bqnGnOASmEs5iqn5dppdD8Lo1EkpAI-ZihvSPAd_KO7uSlWbGArZ HdnzzqxJCOyrnK920hIpVyp2cAk-A2eoc8cFSiLe7kkuSPAmg-d1iSV CTPFGwj57MFcItxxfLGoctHBsNWjKM93nidsp3zNTZpw (accessed December 29, 2019).

46 W. C. Coker, *Recollections*, p. 18.

47 Edith Cook, *Recollections*, p. VIII.

48 George Lee Simpson, op. cit., p.107.

49 Mrs. J. F. Ousley, *Recollections*, p. 40

50 Will Coker, *Recollections*, pp. 18-19.

51 J. W. Norwood from his recorded speech at *Memorial Day, Founder's Day, April 9, 1919*, p. 16.

52 Malcolm Doubles, *A Century Plus: A History of Sonoco Oil Company*, op. cit., p. 4.

53 Information on the oil mill was given to me in an interview with Edgar H. Lawton, Jr., March 27, 2020.

54 Kate Chambers, op. cit., editorial from the *New York Times* in her Appendix, pp. 174-175. Kate did not include the editorial's date, but it has a reference to 1906 as being two years prior, so I have dated in 1908.

55 Nelson, Larry, 2016 South Carolina Encyclopedia article "Coker's Pedigreed Seed Company," http://www.scencyclopedia.org/sce/ entries/cokers-pedigreed-seed-company/#:~:text=Coker's%20 Pedigreed%20Seed%20Company%20had,of%20superior%20 quality%20and%20length.&text=The%20company%20name%20 officially%20became%20Coker's%20Pedigreed%20Seed%20 Company%20in%201923 (accessed June 15,2020).

56 Kate Coker, *Recollections*, p. 8.

57 These signs are part of the self-guided tour at the Coker Experimental Farms National Historic Landmark, 1257 S. 4th St, Hartsville, SC 29550.

58 Ibid.

59 Editor, *The Hartsville Messenger*, "Aged Citizen Passes," September 13, 1945. Thanks to Coker University professor, Dr. Jennifer Heusel for obtaining me this obituary, and the one below.

60 Robert R. Coker, on sign at the Self-guided tour at Coker Experimental Farms National Historic Landmark, 1257 S. 4th St., Hartsville, SC 29550.

61 Peter A. Coclanis, *David R. Coker, Pedigreed Seeds, and the Limits of Agribusiness in Early-Twentieth-Century South Carolina*, as published in *Business and Economic History*, Vol. 28, no. 2, Fall 1999. Coclanis also wrote similar articles in *The South Carolina Historical Magazine*, Vol. 10 2001, pp. 202-21.

62 Rogers and Nelson, op. cit., p. 255, in referring to context of the 1930's, wrote: "The worst financial times were past, and Coker's Pedigreed Seed Company, Coker Cotton Company, and J.L. Coker Company did reasonably well."

63 Fred L. Wilcox, *Centennial Celebration*, op. cit., p. 41.

64 Miss Jane Lide., op. cit., p. 5.

65 Larry Nelson, 2016 article for the South Carolina Encyclopedia "Coker's Pedigreed Seed Company" at http://www.scencyclopedia.org/sce/entries/Cokers-pedigreed-seed-company/ (accessed December 29, 2019).

66 Malcolm Doubles, *A Century Plus: A History of Sonoco Oil Company*, op. cit., p. 4.

67 Ned L. Irwin, South Carolina Encyclopedia's article "Coker, James Lide, Sr.," op. cit.

68 J. W. Norwood, op. cit., p. 15.

69 Clemson University President E. W. Sikes, in *Centennial Celebration*, op. cit., p. 20

70 Edith Cook, Recollections, p. VIII. For other documentation on the Hartsville Fertilizer Company, see the South Carolina Department of Archives and History, 2014 City of Hartsville site at http://rediscov.sc.gov/scar/default.asp?IDCFile=DETAILSG.IDC,SPECIFIC=5624,DATABASE=GROUP, (accessed December 29, 2019).

71 Samantha Lyles, Staff writer, Darlington's *News and Press*, October 24, 2017 article "Historical Society Celebrates 80th Anniversary," http://www.newsandpress.net/historical-society-celebrates-80th-anniversary/: "Darlington County Historical Commission director Brian Gandy talked about the formation of the first Pee Dee Historical Association, which dates back to 1903.... The evening's program featured a re-printing of the minutes for that October 14 meeting, where a small group of citizens drafted plans to form the Society and dedicate it to the memory of Major James L. Coker and Mr. Bright Williamson as "the primary movers of the now extinct Pee Dee Historical Association."

CHAPTER 7

THE MAJOR'S INHERENT BUSINESS QUALITIES THAT LED TO HIS SUCCESS

Major Coker viewed trading and commerce as opportunities to meet needs of the human race, and business as public service. He believed in capitalism, but the Spirit of Christ within him impelled him to extend his own opportunities into expanded opportunities for

Major Coker as a successful business leader, c. 1877. In all he founded 21 businesses, including four non-profits.

all. In contrast to many of America's post- Civil War "bosses," who built empires of corruption., James never put profits above the public good.

He conducted business with sterling principles that not only allowed him to succeed, but to uplift the business culture of his state. His achievements are still amazing by any standard. Ned L. Erwin, in his article on James Lide Coker for the South Carolina Encyclopedia of Fame wrote: "At the time of his death on June 25, 1918, Coker was considered the wealthiest citizen of the state and, perhaps, its most versatile postbellum entrepreneur."[1] J. W. Norwood added: "He was probably the most highly cultured intellectually of any man who has made a conspicuous business success in the state."[2]

We are now going to examine twelve of the Major's business qualities that led to his success. All of them are still applicable in business today, and anyone aspiring to succeed in business, or for that matter, in life, would do well to learn from them. They read like a manual on "How to Succeed in Business," "How to Live a Productive Life," "How to Serve the Lord in Business," or "How to Earn the Friendship and Respect of Others."

1. Business Intent of Shared Prosperity
2. Uncorrupted Integrity
3. He Gave Money to the Church and His Community
4. Delegation to Trustworthy People Whom He Mentored
5. Openness to the Ideas of Others
6. Excellent Business Judgment
7. Thorough Planning and Quality Control
8. Thrift
9. Manners and Courtesy
10. Well-Dressed
11. Self-Reliant
12. Wise as a Serpent but Innocent as a Dove

Note: Chapter 15 adds a complementary list of the Major's personal qualities.

1. Business Intent of Shared Prosperity

Many successful people act like a dog who grabs the biggest bone and runs off to hoard it for himself. By contrast, the Major had no scarcity mindset; there was plenty for all, and he found happiness in sharing prosperity. E. W. Sikes, Coker College President and later Clemson University President, added: "Major Coker had charity, gave to individuals, and was considerate of the needy, but his vision was much larger. In launching new business enterprises, he talked not about what he would get out of it, but how much it would help the community. He was no exploiter but a builder."[3]

Modern American business leader Patrick Morley calls us back to large-hearted, joyous, self-sacrificing saints like the Major. He contrasted the increasing selfishness of our day with the values that built America: "Our society is trying to tip the scales away from Judeo-Christian values to individual rights. Focus on personal peace and affluence has largely replaced deeply held, self-sacrificing convictions and the resulting community-building causes which benefit the human condition."[4]

Major Coker shared profits with his workers and looked out for them. His enterprises modeled ways to empower and prosper all faithful employees, not just the ones in the boardroom. And in an age when no laws governed unsafe working conditions or abusive child labor, the Major made sure that his businesses steered clear of worker abuses.

The Major created his own model of modified capitalism with built-in social justice. As such, the Major's economic model should appeal to those from a wide range of socioeconomic and political perspectives. Some might say, "That's too idealistic—most leaders just aren't that good at heart." I'd be inclined to agree if we consider leaders who act out of their selfish human nature. However, is it possible that we underestimate the deep changes that Christ made in the Major's heart and in his motivations? Is it possible that under wise and godly business leadership, we can catch real glimpses of God's will being "done on earth as it is in heaven"?[5] Other sincere Christian business philanthropists such as John Wanamaker (1838-1922) of John Wanamaker's Department Store, James Cash (J. C.) Penney (1875-1921) of JC Penny department stores, and Cecil B. Day (1934-1978) of Days Inn Motels have also had a broad and lasting impact for good on their employees, customers, and communities.

Communist founder Karl Marx, blinded by his atheistic assumptions, said that, under capitalism, greed and worker abuse must necessarily accumulate with wealth, as if it were some universal law:

> In proportion as capital accumulates, the lot of the laborer must grow worse. Accumulation of wealth at one pole is at the same time accumulation of misery at the opposite pole.[6]

Major Coker's life disproved Marx's "maxim," because Marx did not anticipate power of Jesus Christ to redirect an entrepreneur's soul from greed to graciousness.

E. W. Sikes commented: "Most men have a great master passion that guides, directs, and explains their activities. For Major Coker, this passion was community service. He was pre-eminently a community builder. He studied the needs of his community and directed his energies toward meeting them."[7]

Around 1905, the Major's daughter Susan commented on his motives in business: "Father's influence in the town, in the county, and in the state was

Southern sharecroppers in the cotton fields, c. 1880. Major Coker and his son D.R. offered folks like these a better way of life. Permission from alamy.com.

112

now very great indeed... I wish to say, too, that his interest in establishing all his business enterprises was much more largely in developing the town and giving occupation to the people of the town and county than in making money."[8]

To appreciate how much the Major lifted up the region with his businesses, we must remember that while the northern and western regions of the United States by and large fared well after the war, the South, especially South Carolina, remained destitute. And most Southerners, white and African American, were rural people who practiced sharecropping and tenant farming, which meant perpetual poverty. Sharecroppers and tenant farmers "shared" up to half of their crop with their landowners in exchange for farm tools and a few basic living staples. There was precious little cash to be found, because they used credit accounts with local stores to buy seed and fertilizer, and store owners charged more for credit than cash. Theoretically, these rural people paid off their debts during the cotton harvest in the fall, but they often did not even break even, and were often lean and gaunt-faced.

In their biography of James's son D. R. Coker, Rogers and Nelson wrote: "the tenant lived from lien [loan] to lien with no hope for the future beyond bare subsistence living."[9] Many were uneducated, did not use scientific planting principles, and ended up with soil exhaustion, further reducing production.

Farmers who worked under Major Coker and D. R. fared better than others. James and son saw to it that they used their pedigreed seeds, crop rotation and scientific farming methods, thereby boosting their crops' market values.

As his business and

African-Americans in Spartanburg, SC doing business with Coker Pedigreed Seed Co. and its Clemson affiliate, the SC Crop Improvement Association. These superior seeds helped SC's rural farmers see real profits and a better life. It all started in 1859 with Major Coker's fertilizer and crop experiments. Photo date is 1953. Permission of Linda Harris of Spartanburg.

industrial expansion took off, so did local job opportunities. Mr. Edward Fleming, an African American, was one of Hartsville's first citizens. He helped clear the land for the Coker Pedigreed Seed Farm, and helped build the first Methodist church in Hartsville. As described in his obituary in *The Hartsville Messenger* in the 1940's, he was employed for much of his life with the Coker Pedigreed Seed Company, and in his later years, by the Hartsville Oil Mill.[10]

Additionally, many tenant farmers left their fields to take advantage of jobs at the Major's mills and plants, and gained more financial stability.

Tom E. Goodson, store partner, described the Major's ambitions to share prosperity this way: "Major Coker was a man of vision. His ambition was to build here a town and community that would be outstanding for its high standards of citizenship. A town of good churches and schools, a town with thriving industries and with a happy, prosperous and contented people, and in realizing this ambition, he spent his time, his talents, and his money."[11]

2. Uncorrupted Integrity

The Major's nephew Paul Rogers, who helped lead The Carolina Fiber Company, wrote:

> I have always thought for many years that Major Coker did a great deal to uplift the standard of doing business. He had such high standards of right and wrong in business, and he demanded them of himself and those he dealt with. And his many connections near and far made this influence widely felt."[12]

To fully appreciate Major Coker as an unstained businessman

and servant-leader, some concurrent national comparisons are in order. The economy of the victorious North grew very quickly in the post-war years. But corporate and political bosses in cities like New York, Chicago, and Philadelphia, introduced unprecedented levels of shameless and systematic greed into American business life. They exchanged contracts for bribes, overcharged customers, misrepresented products, and abused workers.

The most infamous may be William Tweed of Tammany Hall in New York who got elected paying people to vote several times. He then used fake stock certificates to take control of the Eerie Railroad and went on to award inflated contracts for public services, pocket the overages as kickbacks. He then cheated taxpayers out of 17 million dollars, equivalent to 525 million in 2020. He and cronies like Richard Croker created an entire business culture of deceit. In 2017, Jay Maeder of the New York Daily News reminded us of these times:

> Once upon a time, Tammany Hall had been purely a nest of thieves, for years presided over by the ravenous William Marcy Tweed, a man who plundered the city's coffers so openly that after a while it just seemed to be the natural order of things. By 1870, indeed, Tweed had engineered a new City Charter that effectively made it legal to steal.[13]

Many of the northern radicals and "carpetbaggers" Major Coker dealt with during Reconstruction brought these corrupt tactics with them when they tried to put the Major out of business. In *The Cokers of Carolina* Simpson writes that Darlington county was overrun by "carpetbaggers, scalawags, [and their recruits who] were responsible for 'outlawry'" and "influenced by improper pecuniary considerations."

In stark contrast, throughout Major Coker's litany of business successes, there was never a hint of corruption. He actually created the opposite kind of business culture – one based on the golden rule, "In everything, therefore, treat people the same way you want them to treat you" (Matthew 7:12). James's business practices reflect the description of genuine Christians in Philippians 2:15, "Children of God above reproach in the midst of a crooked and perverse generation, among whom you appear as lights in the world."

E. W. Sikes said: "In business, his word was his bond." Tom E. Goodson said of him:

> "Being a man of conservative business principles, he was opposed to any transactions which were highly speculative. Major Coker was the balance wheel in all his enterprises." Leon Coker, who worked with him in the Southern Novelty Company, added: "He had certain instructions there in the office that we would carry out – just office rules. His being so strict, you might say, in business methods showed his outstanding business ability and honesty in everything."[14]

His nephew Arthur Rogers, who worked with him in the general store, and later The Carolina Fiber Company, added this example:

> One thing that struck me about the Major was his fine sense of honor. I know on a good many occasions, for instance, in the railroad, there were many who had invested money with him. All the Coast Line wanted to do was to buy out the majority of the stock (just the Major's), so they would have control, but he would never do anything like that. They had to buy the whole thing so everybody would get the same price that he did. The same

thing happened in selling out the stock of the Darlington Cotton Mill. He insisted that others who invested along with him be bought out at the same time he was bought out. [15]

Confucius was on target when he said:

> One humane family can
> humanize a whole state;
> One courteous family can lift a
> whole state into courtesy;
> One grasping and perverse man
> can drive a nation into chaos. [16]

Another nephew, Paul Rogers, who helped lead The Carolina Fiber Company, wrote: I have always thought for many years that Major Coker did a great deal to uplift the standard of doing business. He had such high standards of right and wrong in business, and he demanded them of himself and those he dealt with. And his many connections near and far made this influence widely felt." [17]

Thomas M. McClellan, salesman for the Carolina Fiber Company, said: "He had no tricks in business. He was simply a strong business man and invariably made a success of any project he undertook. I have always thought he was the best business man I ever knew. To be as straight as he was it took extraordinary ability to make the success he invariably made." [18]

Hartsville's Presbyterian minister Rev. C. L. McDowell said: "May his great spirit burn warmly on the altar of other hearts charged with the conduct of large financial and industrial enterprises, that they may prove to the world that Christ can still do mighty works among the men of our day and generation." [19]

3. He Gave Back to the Church and Community

All too often, the wealthy shut up their hearts and their purses to the needs of others – only to end up lonely, isolated, and empty. Not so with the Major. He knew it was the Lord who had given him the power to succeed, and he wanted, in turn, share with and empower others. He often said that all of life was stewardship, and Tom E. Goodson wrote:

Major Coker ordered this bell for his First Baptist Church in 1896. It was shipped to his J. L. Coker & Company, then installed, which means he likely purchased it himself. By permission of Dr. Susan Reynolds, editor, *First Baptist Church Scrapbook*.

He told me more than once that he had prospered far beyond his expectations and that he felt that he didn't deserve all of the success that had been his. He believed in the principle of stewardship and realized to the fullest extent the responsibility of using rightly the means which were his.[20]

With increased prosperity, he gave proportionately more money to his church, to other Hartsville churches, to worthy causes such as the American Red Cross, and to schools. Besides endowing his college (see Chapter 12), he gave regularly to his Baptist church, donated the land for Saint Bartholomew's Episcopal Church in Hartsville,[21] and gave money for the building of the Wesley United Methodist Church in Hartsville and its gothic brick structure was completed in 1903.

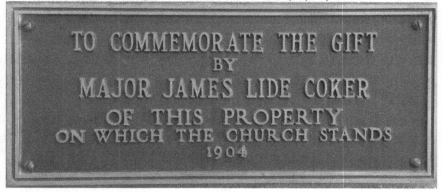

S. W. Garrett said: "He was loyal to the church. I was treasurer of the Baptist church for a number of years, and almost every Sunday, he made his regular contributions by merely putting his initials on a little slip of paper and dropping it the basket. The bank knew his habits so well that they gave the church credit even though no amount was specified. He also contributed heavily to Hartsville's community health causes. He often said: 'Tithing is not sufficient. We are stewards of 100 percent of our possessions.'"[22]

4. Delegation to Trustworthy People Whom He Mentored

As an effective leader, Major Coker was always on the lookout for good people whom he could train. He made it a practice to nurture and enable capable trainees, and to delegate responsibility and authority to them. He was conscious of investing his life in people so that his values would outlive him. His daughter Susan commented: "As time moved on and his business worries lightened, he was able to share the responsibility more and more with the competent executives he had trained."[23]

Twenty-first-century leadership author John C. Maxwell teaches that "A successful person finds the right place for himself. But a successful leader finds the right place for others."[24] The Major used these management principles in the 19th century, long before leadership studies and the term servant-leader became popular.

After the Major carefully picked his mentees, he was patient and exact with them. He groomed his nephew Paul Rogers to take over as secretary and treasurer of the Carolina Fiber Company in 1905. Rogers spoke of the Major's gentle but effective mentoring style:

> I always found him most considerate and concerned that I be able to take responsibilities that came to hand... When mistakes were made, and I made plenty of them, being inexperienced and a shy boy just out of college, he was very patient and never brought up a second time a mistake made. Some thought the Major demanded a good deal from those who worked for him, but my impression is that he was never demanding but that he inspired people to do their best, and they always wished to do so. He was exact but not demanding or critical.[25]

After mentees proved their character and had the necessary skills, Major Coker turned operations over while keeping a stake in ownership. For example, he delegated the operations of his farms to J. J. Lawton and, of his general stores to Arthur Rogers, Tom E. Goodson, A. L. M. Wiggins, and later to D. R. He had five partners in the Hartsville Railroad, especially J. J. Lawton. He eventually gave D. R. the entire management of the Pedigreed Seed Company and turned the management of the Hartsville Oil Mill over to J. J. Lawton.

In like manner, he depended upon the engineering skills

of his son James Jr. when founding the paper mill. And in starting the Southern Novelty Company, he called upon the expertise of his friend Wilbur T. Smith. In the early years, he trained his son Charles Westfield to become the first treasurer and the chief salesman of the Southern Novelty Company. Later, he groomed him replace him as CEO. Charles proved very capable in that position upon the Major's death in 1918, a testament to James's attentive training.

The Major could not have started Coker College without the collective efforts of himself, Pastor E. V. Baldy, J. J. Lawton, E.W. Sikes, S. W. Garrett, the Welsh Neck Baptist Association, and others. The Major's niece Mrs. Robert Lide said, "In later years, when Coker College was founded, he was congratulated on his magnificent contribution to education. He replied: 'Thank those who worked for me – not me.'"[26]

5. Openness to the Ideas of Others

Leon Coker, his co-worker in the Southern Novelty Company, wrote: "We used to have some mighty pleasant meetings of the directors up there at his house – this was in about 1909 or '10. He and Cousin Charlie, David [D. R.], and all of them were there. Mr. Lawton was there... He [Major Coker] was most agreeable and receptive to the ideas of others. He was willing to listen to new ideas and take to them and give them a chance."[27] As we'll see in the next chapter, it was the Major's openness to his son James's ideas that led to the founding of The Carolina Fiber Company.

6. Excellent Judgment

Major Coker was blessed with an extraordinary market sense. Tom E. Goodson said: "He had the best business judgment of any person I have ever been around. He was no speculator; he was just a good, sound businessman. He would always say the time to buy anything was when it was cheap and to sell when it was high, but it took a mighty good man to tell when anything was cheap or when anything was high."[28]

Goodson also commented on the Major's flexible business strategies: "I was credit man at Coker's [store]. I remember one thing he used to tell me. He'd always say if times were hard – 'Well, don't be too hard on our customers. They've been with us all these years, and we can afford to be lenient – reasonably lenient – with them.'"[29] The Major was no longer living during the Great Depression of 1929-1939, but his son D. R. and other successors helped Darlington County farmers to survive desperately hard times by following the Major's principles. They kept the general store and seed company prices down and stretched the credit a bit—adhering to his "leniency when needed" principle.

At the same time, the Major knew how to safeguard his bottom line. Goodson described the other side of extending credit as follows: "When it came to good times, he'd put the other light on it, saying, 'Well, now, you must be tight with them. What we've got here is ours, and we don't have to sell it on credit if we don't want to.'"[30]

Paul Rogers, an executive at the paper mill and later mayor of Hartsville, told of other aspects of his extraordinarily discerning mind:

> He seemed to have a sixth sense of just when to get out of any business interests with which he had no direct connections. For instance, he disposed of his stock in the old Darlington Trust Company a few months before it blew up in Darlington. Somehow, probably from their paying unjustified dividends, he realized that something was going wrong, and he wished not to have more to do with it. Whenever any phase of business that he sponsored failed to do well,

he did not hesitate to close it out without any regrets and give his attention to the others which were more promising.[31]

Major Coker's nephew Arthur Rogers, who worked in the store as bookkeeper, commented: "In his thinking, the Major was so clear. I can remember that on occasions at the store I would put up some problem to him – some problem we had to solve, and he might simply ask a question or say a word or two, and it would just open the whole thing up, and you'd see it all so clearly, either the fallacy or the solution."[32]

7. Thorough Planning and Quality Control

Leon Coker commented: "He was always very thorough in his planning of what he was going to do, and he didn't want anything to get started until he was sure it would go successfully. He was very particular about that."[33] A. L. M. Wiggins spent forty years with J. L. Coker and Company stores and was eventually head of The Coker Pedigreed Seed Company. He once said: "The seed company was an expensive experimental thing for a long time before it turned a corner."[34] In the 1880's and 90's, the Major and his son D. R. had success in seed experimentation. However, to guarantee quality, the Major would not let them go public as a business until they had absolutely perfected their early seed products in 1902. Similarly, though the Carolina Fiber Company was producing paper pulp in the mid 1890's he did not let them go public until all production problems were resolved in 1899.

8. Thrift

Major Coker saw all his resources as a trust from God and he never wasted anything. Will Coker said:

In my earliest days in our farm home and on the plantation itself, nothing was ever wasted. Father had a black oven built in the back yard near the barn with an iron pot sunk in the top of it and heated from below. This pot, as I remember, was about three and a half to four feet wide. Into this went all kinds of nutritious remnants – everything from the house that we would now call garbage except for big bones, and all the unusable vegetables from the garden, all scraps of corn, oats, etc. from the barns and bins, large quantities of turnips grown for the purpose, everything in fact that had nutritious value on the place. This was thoroughly boiled and fed every day to the hogs. Mother told me once that she never knew anybody that made every edge count like Father.[35]

W. C. Wilson, quoting his cousins Annie and Florrie, said: "I remember once when we were at Uncle James's someone threw an apple peeling in the fire. Uncle James gave a start. 'Never throw away anything any creature can eat,' he said." His habits of thrift paid off because he got the county's prize for the raising the biggest hog in 1859![36], and he saved thousands by building his railroad with perfectly good used rails.

Major Coker "made every edge count" in his other businesses as well. For example, in his younger years, excess cottonseed separated from the fiber by the cotton gin was discarded. One day the Major thought better of it. He realized he could extract oil from the seeds, and he founded the Hartsville Oil Mill for that purpose.

The Major was just as economical after he became wealthy as he was during the desolate times after the war. On more than one occasion, when riding in his buggy, if he spotted a stray ear of corn or two that had been dropped in the road, he was known to pick it up.[37] Carrie Lee Erwin Kalber tells this story of his careful frugality: "Somebody [from the college mail room] mailed Major Coker a letter and put a two-cent stamp on it. Then a two-cent stamp would go anywhere, and in town, only one cent was necessary, so he wrote them a letter telling them not to waste the penny." [38]

Major Coker's example of thrift is still relevant. Modern financial author and radio host Dave Ramsey wrote about a 2019 study on the thrift principles today's millionaires follow. They are similar to Major Coker's. For instance, the average millionaire today spends 30 percent less on groceries and 17 percent less on eating out than the average person.[39] The Major's basic business principles are simply timeless.

9. Gentlemanly Manners and Courtesy

One of James's pastors, the Reverend E.V. Baldy said: "He was a mirror of politeness, most courteous in conversation, deferential in manner, magnanimous in spirit."[40] Mrs. Katherine Coker Cannon said, "Grandfather was always courteous. When a lady came into the room, even when he was old and in the rolling chair, he would attempt to rise."[41]

10. Well-Dressed

Will Coker said, "He was very neat in dress and always made a good appearance. It was his habit to have two excellent suits of clothes a year, made of the best material, and by the best tailor in Charleston. He was a better dresser than any of his children."[42]

11. Self-Reliant

Though he delegated well, Major Coker also bore his own load. He wanted to stay on top of his affairs personally and was diligent in doing for himself. Ethel Laney Miller, his office administrative secretary, wrote: "He used to get up from his desk and walk to [the telephone] and do his own calling... He did many things – almost all of them – for himself without asking assistance of anyone. He was his own counsel, rarely ever calling in the services of an attorney. When he sold a piece of property, he would write the deed in longhand and draw a plat [plot] of the same at the bottom of it."[43]

12. Wise as a Serpent but Innocent as a Dove

The Major knew when he was not getting a deal. To ensure fair play and accountability, he preferred to do business on a person-to-person basis or through personal correspondence. Even when slighted, he played the gentleman and appealed to the nobler side of his vendor's character. For example, in October of 1913, he requested a conference with banker J. W. Perrin of Wilmington about his rates, anticipating a personal response. When Perrin sent sheets of interest rates instead— rates that the Major knew were too high—he wrote back to Perrin this wise letter on October 10, 1913:

> Dear Sir:
>
> Yours of October 8th was received on yesterday. I am very sorry that you did not allow us to confer with you before fixing the rates according to your type-written sheets showing the result of revision.

Going carefully over these sheets, I find a good many items that I feel sure you would have made more favorable to us if you had given us the opportunity to talk with you, but I will not try to go into details in a letter. I believe you will conclude yet to give us a fair showing by having a conference so that we may present our views before you issue these rates. I think we want only reasonable treatment, and I will still believe that you will not wish to treat us otherwise. Now, will you not accede to our request for a conference? I think it is to your interest to do so. Hoping to hear from you at once.

Yours very truly,
James L. Coker[44]

Note: For study groups, business classes, or mentoring, there are questions and further information on the Major's business principles at <u>https://www.willjoslin.com/major/questions/business</u>. Included are comparisons of Major Coker with Elon Musk, Steve Jobs, and Thomas Edison.

ENDNOTES FOR CHAPTER 7: THE MAJOR'S INHERENT BUSINESS QUALITIES THAT LED TO HIS SUCCESS

1   Ned L. Erwin, "Coker, James Lide, Sr.," on the South Encyclopedia of Fame website, op. cit.

2   J. W. Norwood, op. cit., p. 429.

3   254 E. W. Sikes, Ph.D. and then president of Clemson College, whose speech was recorded in the *Coker College Quarterly Bulletin*, "1937 Centennial Celebration of the Major," op. cit., p. 20.

4   Patrick Morley, *The Man in the Mirror*, Zondervan, 1997, p.74.

5   The Lord's Prayer, Matthew 6:10.

6   Karl Marx, *Das Kapital*, https://lawsdocbox.com/amp/102442052-Politics/Contemporary-european-philosophy-phil-314.html, accessed January 2021.

7   E. W. Sikes, in his talk *Major J.L. Coker, Leader in Education* given at Coker College from *Memorial Exercises*, subtitled *[Coker College] Founders Day, April 9, 1919*, op. cit., p. 40.

8   Susan Coker Watson, *Recollections*, p. 25.

9   Rogers and Nelson, *op. cit.*, p. 52

10 Editor, *The Hartsville Messenger*, "Worthy Citizen and Pioneer Passes," 1940's obituary (the exact date eluded my photocopy).

11 Tom E. Goodson, business associate of the Major at J.L. Coker and Co. and at The Carolina Fiber Company, speech "Leader in Business at the 1937 Centennial Celebration of the Major, op. cit., p. 13.

12 Paul Rogers, *Recollections*, pp. 23-24.

13 Jay Maeder, New York Daily News, August 14, 2017 article "Richard (The Boss) Croker: How the crooked Tammany Hall leader became 'Master of the City," https://www.nydailynews.com/new-york/crooked-richard-boss-croker-reigned-tammany-hall-article-1.803373 (accessed August 23, 2020).

14 Tom E. Goodson, *Centennial Celebration*, op. cit., p. 12.

15 Arthur Rogers, *Recollections*, p. 35.

16 Confucius, translated by Ezra Pound in *Confucius, The Great Digest; The Unwobbling Pivot; the Analects*, 59-61, quoted in Roger Lipsey's *Hammarskjold, A Life*, (University of Michigan Press, Ann Arbor, 2016), p. 132.

17 Paul Rogers, *Recollections*, pp. 23-24.

18 Thomas M. McClellan, Recollections, p. 31.

19 Rev. C. L. Dowell, Centennial Celebration, op. cit., p. 16.

20 Tom E. Goodson, op. cit., p. 13.

21 Edith Cook, *Recollections*, p. viii.

22 S. W. Garrett, op. cit., p. 2.

23 Susan Coker Watson, *Recollections*, p. 25.

24 See Peter Economy's website, op. cit.

25 Paul Rogers, *Recollections*, p. 23.

26 Mrs. Robert Lide, *Recollections*, p. 67.

27 Leon Coker, *Recollections*, p. 35.

28 Tom E. Goodson, *Recollections*, p. 33.

29 Ibid.

30 Ibid.

31 Paul Rogers, *Recollections*, p. 23. Note: Both Paul Rogers and Arthur Rogers were nephews of the Major.

32 Arthur Rogers, *Recollections*, p. 26.

33 Leon Coker, *Recollections.*, p. 36.

34 A. L. M. Wiggins, *Recollections*, p. 27.

35 Will Coker, *Recollections*, p. 4.

36 The Major's prize hog in 1860 is documented at the Darlington County Historical Commission. There I read the Darlington County Census of 1860, and the best memory serves me, I believes it was there that this record is documented.

37 George Lee Simpson, op. cit., p. 186.

38 Carrie Lee E. Kalber, *Recollections*, p. 70.

39 Editor, 2019 article "Millionaire Spending Habits That Will Surprise You," pp. 2-3, found at the blog site from Ramsey Solutions, https://www.daveramsey.com/blog/millionaire-spending-habits (accessed December 29, 2019).

40 Reverend E. V. Baldy, bulletin for Funeral Service of James Lide Coker, First Baptist Church, Hartsville, South Carolina, June 26,1918, p. 8. Courtesy of Coker College archives.

41 Katherine Canon Coker, *Recollections*, p. 126.

42 Ibid., p.74.

43 Ethel L. Miller, *Recollections*, p. 29.

44 Letter of James Lide Coker to J.W. Perrin, October 10,1913, from the James Lide Coker Collection, courtesy of South Caroliniana Library, University of South Carolina, Columbia, SC, File 3778-B.

CHAPTER 8

ON TO INDUSTRY: THE CAROLINA FIBER COMPANY AND THE SOUTHERN NOVELTY COMPANY

The Major's son James Lide Coker, Jr.
By permission of Coker College Press.

In 1889, the Major's oldest son, James Jr., came home after studying papermaking at Stevens Institute of Technology in New Jersey. He had a dream of turning some of the countless South Carolina pine trees into paper pulp and prodded his father to found a new company. The Major was skeptical. It would be a huge risk-reward gamble, because in the long history of papermaking, only hardwoods had been used, never pine. But on December 30th, 1889, the Major, wanting to encourage his son, agreed to give it a try on a

130

"small scale"[1] with a so-called "small investment." The Major's Civil War friend, C. J. Woodruff also became a partner.[2]

There were many setbacks during the first eight years. The pine sap was a problem because it produced paper too rough for anything but crude cardboard. Seeking experienced advice, James Jr. formed a partnership

South Carolina shortleaf pines. Picture courtesy of John Hardin, Southeastern Land Development Group.

with the American Sulphite Paper Company in New York, headed by W. H. Parsons. The agreement was that Parsons and his engineers would offer counsel and provide machine recommendations and papermaking patents in return for one-third of the Cokers' profits. Although James Jr. was a top-flight engineer, he was not the businessman his father was.[3] He left some things in the contract with Parsons unclear, including exactly how and when the patents would be transferred.

Continued Setbacks

The rough beginning continued when Mr. Parsons visited Hartsville in March of 1892 and was taken aback at how small the town was — a mere crossroads of only 300 people. Parsons was appalled that there were no electric lights, no paved streets, and no plumbing, and that the company's night work was done under kerosene lanterns hanging from the ceiling. When he saw that the Coker pulp machines were not yet producing as expected, he gave up on the Cokers and ran back to New York. Even though the Cokers had purchased his machines, he unilaterally broke the contract, refused them the patents, and ended the partnership.

This breach of contract completely derailed the Cokers because they still needed the undelivered patents. Up to this point, they planned to use Parsons' sulfite production method. Worse yet, their capital was gone, as they had already spent a fortune on the machines and consulting. To compensate, they were siphoning income from the Coker mills, stores, and farms, and the family wealth was all but used up.

The Carolina Fiber Co. turned wood to pulp in digesters like this one using sulphuric acid and heat. Before the Cokers, pine wood had never been used in this process and they found its acidic mxture ate through the bottom. James Junior rebuilt their digesters to make them self-sealing, a breakthrough invention that ensured success. By permission of alamy.com.

There was a serious problem with their method of making pulp. When the sulfite solution was pressure-heated with pine, it produced a sulfuric acid combination that was stronger than anything Parsons had experienced when pressure-heating hardwoods. The Cokers' acidic pine formula damaged the "digesters," which were the heating vats purchased from Parsons to follow his production method. Since he did not use pine trees, Parsons did not understand the problem.

The strong pine acid mixture ate holes in the concrete bottom linings of the digesters, the mixture leaked out. The Major and James Jr. became exhausted and discouraged. They had invested four times more in papermaking than planned, and the family was as close to poverty as they had been since the Civil War ended. But they could not turn back; their investment at this point was too significant to abandon it. As a result, they went for broke and fought on with more trial-and-error experiments.

The Eureka Moment

Finally, a real breakthrough came! In a show of true ingenuity, James Jr. devised a solution to the problem of the acid's destructive effect by replacing the concrete bottom linings of the digesters with a layer of bricks. Underneath the bricks, he added sand and a pressurized saline solution. With this new lining in place, the acid rarely ate through the bricks. But when it did, the acid instantly combined with the sand and the saline solution in a chemical reaction that produced a harmless solid,

The Carolina Fiber Company, viewed from the north side of Black Creek, c. 1905.
Permission granted by Sonoco Products.

simultaneously sealing up any damaged places in the lining. Through perseverance, trial, error, and brains, James Jr. had not only solved the immediate problem; he had invented a way to make their digesters self-sealing.[4] Will Coker wrote: "After a great deal of strain on Father's mind and even health, the business became successful – the first successful business in the manufacture of paper from pine in the world."

Based on this colossal step forward, James Jr. and the Major went on to make more of their own virtually leak-proof equipment. They ramped up their pulp production to ship pulp out to paper mills. However, they hit another snag when shipping costs proved prohibitive. The Major decided they would keep all of the pulp they produced and make more of their own paper. Their first product was butcher's paper for wrapping meat, but soon, they would make fine paper as well.

As he continued inventing upgrades for their pulp and papermaking machines, James Jr. also kept improving the way they managed the pine sap and resin. According Will Coker, James Jr. discovered that "If a pine tree was cut down and the log allowed to stay on the ground for one year, the resin underwent fermentation and disappeared. The solution was then to cut the tree a year before it was to be used."[5]

By the late 1890s, they had invented their own processes and their own machines and controlled their own papermaking destiny. In 1898, the Major dammed Black Creek in Hartsville to create Prestwood Lake and added an Edison Dynamo Generator at its waterfall. One of the first electric generators installed in South Carolina, it gave them the power to run the plant and to upgrade the town to electric lighting.[6] Another benefit was that Prestwood Lake "became one of the beauty spots of Hartsville and a destination for people to fish, swim, or boat."[7] It is still a popular place for recreation in Darlington County.

After the paper mill was running along well, on February 14, 1899, D. R. Coker wrote to his brother Will: "The mill is worth $100,000 more than it was two years ago."[8] It is also worth noting that from the outset, the mill employed both black and white workers,[9] and now they too would benefit from the company's growth.

The High Road to Success

Because the Cokers courageously chose to own and conquer their fiber company problems with gentlemanly integrity, they rose above Parsons' betrayal, and rendered his patents unnecessary. As production grew, they were more concerned about providing suitable and gainful employment for the community than being tied up on court. The New Yorker had greatly underestimated the Cokers, and Hartsville now became a model of the industrial power of the New South. With now reliable methods and products, the Major went public with The Carolina Fiber Company in 1899. Their two best customers were the Atlanta Paper Company and the Birmingham Paper Company.

That same year the Major led another breakthrough. He decided to merge his papermaking with his cotton mill production to make cardboard cotton-winding cones.

These could be used to wind cotton on his own weaving machines, or the cones could be sold unwound to other cotton manufacturers. This innovation caught the attention of Walter F. Smith, the engineer from New Bedford, Massachusetts. His interest in expanding the cone business led to a partnership and the formation of a new Coker industry, the Southern Novelty Company. Mr. Smith moved to Hartsville and provided consulting in exchange for partial ownership of the new company.

Southern Charm Saves the Day

Were it not for a good southern meal and the Major's quick thinking, the lucrative enterprises that ensued might never have happened. Like Parsons, when Mr. Smith saw Hartsville, he suddenly decided to quit. However, the Major was determined to rescue the relationship with Walter Smith and move forward with their plans. George Lee Simpson, Jr. elaborates:

Mr. Walter Smith, Secretary of Southern Novelty Co. Board of Directors, 1899-1912. From *A Century Plus* by Malcolm Doubles. Used by permission of Coker College Press.

Now Mr. Smith had not been to Hartsville when he agreed to the above arrangements. When he did come, he arrived at night. He was put off the train in the dark, in a cotton field in front of the Major's and James Jr.'s houses. The Major guided him to his home by lantern light, and before he crossed the threshold, Mr. Smith had made, and expressed to Major Coker, his decision to depart by first conveyance and never return... [After dinner] somewhat desperately, James took him forthwith to the paper mill on Black Creek. They did not return until the small hours of the morning, and they were absorbed in their talk and plans. The paper mill, in good operation, had convinced Mr. Smith that perhaps something, after all, could be made in Hartsville.[10] Operations were soon set up in an old tobacco warehouse.[11]

They succeeded in producing and selling cone-shaped paper yarn carriers for spooling and shipping cotton because their cones were cheaper and lighter than the wooden ones form other vendors. The Southern Novelty Company's products were soon in high demand by cotton manufacturers across the South.

Between the fiber mill and the novelty company, the Major could now sell all grades of paper and cardboard, bare cotton-winding cones, or cones fully wound with fiber from his cotton farms. And the Southern Novelty Company soon innovated many other kinds of cardboard tubing products for everything from concrete pouring molds to containers for shipping.

Family Atmosphere

The small town atmosphere in which the industry began carried forward as it grew. Quoting from Charles W. (Charlie) Coker Jr., president of Sonoco from 1970 to 1990: "You can just imagine the excitement as the community saw this job-creating opportunity come alive. Folks knew each other, cared about each other, and worked well together. You can see the seeds sprouting of a wonderful relationship between company and community."

Paul Rogers, who worked for The Carolina Fiber Company and Sonoco from 1905 to 1939, including a term as president, wrote of the friendly atmosphere the Major created: "The officers and workers were very much like a large family in those early days. There were only about seventy-five employees, and a little over half of them were on the day shift. Whenever any of these—superintendent or workers, black or white—came into the office, they usually went by the Major's office to have a friendly word or chat with him.[12]

**Carolina Fiber Co. employees chatting in Major Coker's Office.
Illustration by professional artist Dan Nelson.**

The family atmosphere continued after the Major's death when the colleagues he trained harnessed the momentum of the Major's fiber and novelty companies to form one of the greatest of all manufacturing businesses. We discover that remarkable story in the following chapter.

ENDNOTES FOR CHAPTER 8: ON TO INDUSTRY: THE CAROLINA FIBER COMPANY AND THE SOUTHERN NOVELTY COMPANY

1   W. C. (Will) Coker, *Recollections*, p. 20.
2   Editor, South Carolina Program of Archives and History, 2019, "South Carolina Historical Markers," https://scdah.sc.gov/sites/default/files/Documents/Historic%20Preservation%20(SHPO)/Programs/Programs/Historical%20Markers/SC%20Historical%20Marker%20Program%20Guidebook%20-%20Winter%202019%20(12-9-19).pdf, p. 185(accessed April 18, 2020).
3   George Lee Simpson, op. cit., p. 121.
4   Ibid.
5   W. C. Coker in *Recollections*, p.20.
6   Malcolm C. Doubles, *A Century Plus: A History of Sonoco Products Company*, op. cit., p. 15.
7   Ibid.
8   James A. Rogers and Larry E. Nelson, op. cit., p. 17.
9   Paul Rogers, *Recollections*, p. 22.
10   George Lee Simpson, op. cit., p. 130 as he quoted an account given by Mrs. Vivien Gay Coker, wife of James Lide Coker Jr.
11   James Lide Coker, *Hartsville — Its Early Settlers: The Growth of the Town with Sketches of Its Institutions and Enterprises*, op. cit., p. 36.
12   Paul Rogers, *Recollections*, p. 7

CHAPTER 9

THE BIRTH AND GROWTH OF SONOCO PRODUCTS

The Major's youngest son, Charles Westfield Coker, president of Sonoco Products from 1918-1931. Courtesy of Coker College Press.

The Major groomed his youngest son, Charles Westfield Coker (1879-1931), who had previously served with him as treasurer of the Eastern Carolina Silver Company, to replace him as CEO of The Southern Novelty Company. This was a wise decision. Charles, who assumed the reins in 1918, brought, according to Ned L. Irwin, "modern industrial and managerial practice…[and] established an industrial research and development program"[1] and continued to emphasize long-range planning. Charles was also one of our nation's pioneers in creating employee benefit packages for faithful workers.

The Related Companies Join Forces

In 1923, The Carolina Fiber Company merged with the Southern Novelty Company, and renamed the combination with the acronym Sonoco, the first two letters of each word in Southern Novelty Company. Thus Sonoco Products was born, a company that would eventually become one of the world's largest, most flexible, and most profitable companies. As of 2019, Sonoco has been listed as either a Fortune 500 or a Fortune 1000 Company for over sixty years. As of this writing, it's ranked Fortune 518.[2] The company claims 1899 as its founding year because that was the year the Major and James Jr. arose victoriously from the challenge of making paper from pine trees and founded The Carolina Fiber Company.

Sonoco's market edge took a huge leap when Gibson H. Kennedy, center, produced this superior cone-winding mandrel, which Sonoco patented in 1924. Used by permission of Sonoco.

The integration of the fiber company and the novelty company was cost-effective and productive. Sonoco soon employed many people of the Pee Dee region, allowing them to earn a much better

Sonoco's old and new logos. From Malcolm Doubles' book *A Century Plus: A History of Sonoco Products Company.* Used by permission of Coker College Press.

living than they could have made by tenant farming. Thanks to the inventions of superior yarn-winding mandrels by mechanical genius Gibson H. Kennedy, their operations became fully automated,[3] enabling them to mass-produce the finest cones for winding cotton available on the market.

Early Leadership in Recycling

In 1924, still under the Major's son Charles, Sonoco was one of the first companies to begin recycling cardboard. The company's effectiveness at repurposing materials has continued throughout its history. It has over thirty-nine full-service recycling centers in the U.S. and one

Sonoco employees boxing wound cones, c. 1925. Used by Permission of Sonoco.

in Britain. In my home city of Raleigh, North Carolina, all of our recycling goes to our local Sonoco Recycling Center. Sonoco is one of the largest recyclers in the U.S., annually collecting nearly 3 million tons of materials, much of which it uses as raw materials to make new sustainable packaging.[4] A 2019 Sonoco report states that "Sonoco recycles or causes to be recycled, the equivalent by weight of 65% of the product it places in the marketplace."[5]

World War II and the Modern Age

Sonoco continued to grow during World War II. The company contributed greatly to the cause, making tubes and containers for U.S. munitions, shells, and parachute flares.[6] And in the modern era, Sonoco has become the premier tube and package-making company in the world.

The Major's great grandson Charles W. (Charlie) Coker Jr. became president in 1970, continuing in that position until 1990. One of his favorite sayings is, "People build businesses." [7] Charlie once asked Sonoco's former senior vice president, Charles H. Campbell, whose Sonoco roots stretched back to the early days, how he would account for the continued success of the company. Campbell answered: "I believe it is the fact that the business principles laid down by old Major Coker have been followed implicitly by each succeeding president, which established continuity and credibility, [giving] all Sonoco people something to tie into."[8]

These brands represent just a fraction of the packaging products made by Sonoco. Permissions granted by Wigwam Corporation, Tree Top Inc., John B. Sanfilippo & Son, Inc., and Sonoco.

Sonoco also makes the enormous concrete form cylinders that are used to shape concrete for the huge vertical columns upholding highway bridges and for other construction projects. They are also the world's leader in carboard industrial packaging, protective packaging, and composite cans – i.e., cans with aluminum ends and sides made of cardboard. These products are used by some of the world's best known brands in food, clothing, cosmetics, and many other industries.

A Word from some Seasoned Old-Timers

On November 20, 2018, Roger Schrum, Vice President of Investor Relations and Corporate Affairs, graciously gave me a tour of the plant and the privilege of interviewing two veteran employees: Eugene Thompson and Walter Britt, both Hartsville natives.

Born to parents who were tenant farmers, Eugene Thompson has worked in a variety of capacities since he first came to work for Sonoco in 1965. Mr. Thompson made a point to tell me that he and his wife would not have been able to put his five children through college were it not for his job with Sonoco. Without hesitation, he named former CEO Charles Coker Jr., the Major's great-grandson, as the most influential person in his life. He had many stories to tell about the man. Perhaps the most touching concerned the gracious support Charles Jr. had shown to him when he was coaching the

Eugene Thompson, currently a mailroom employee, has worked for Sonoco since 1964. Picture taken by author during interview.

Sonoco All-Stars Little League baseball team in 1981 with his son Terrence, as a starter. At the State Championship in Charleston, there were three days of rain delays, and the team ran out of money. Eugene contacted Charles Jr., who promptly took care of all the expenses. It's good they stuck it out because once the weather cleared, the Sonoco All-Stars

Walter Britt has worked for Sonoco since 1962 in a variety of capacities and is currently a mailroom employee. Picture taken by author.

went on to win the state championship! Eugene is now of retirement age, and as Sonoco retirees have the option to continue to work in the mailroom, he is currently a mailroom employee.

Walter Britt also kindly granted me an interview. He said that after coming to Sonoco in 1962, he served in several capacities and worked his way up to sales and quality control. Now also working in retirement, he has joined Eugene in the mailroom. His story began with a father who sold insurance and a mother who worked in a grocery store. Keenly aware of his humble beginnings, Mr. Britt expressed deep gratitude for the life that he and his wife have been able to carve out for their family. He was quick to add that he could not have put their two sons through Clemson had he not worked for Sonoco.

Both men spoke warmly about the family culture they have found at Sonoco. While admitting that the company's focus on family is not quite as strong as it once was, Mr. Britt assured me that it is still strong. For example, the company still stages workplace picnics with games for the employees' children like putt-putt golf and ball-throwing, complete with prizes. It also sponsors a Christmas gathering and special meal for the whole Sonoco family at Lakeview Baptist Church every year. In addition, it actively sponsors the Lakeview Club, where employees can swim, play pool, and bowl.

This overview of Sonoco demonstrates that the small-town values possessed by the Major and his successors continue to define Sonoco.

Worldwide Operations and the Latest CEOs

As of 2019, Sonoco had 23,000 employees in more than 300 operations in 36 countries, serving more than 85 nations[9]—quite a far cry from its humble origins of 12 employees in a rented warehouse in 1899. After Charles Coker Jr. stepped down from being CEO in 1998, the last three CEOs have been Harris E. DeLoach, Jr., M. Jack Sanders, and Robert C. Tiede, elected in 2018. Since his life mission was to create a better life for others, it's likely that the Major would have been pleased with Sonoco's current motto: "Better Packaging. Better Life."

In April of 2019 Robert Tiede reaffirmed the Major's values, saying: "At Sonoco, we work to create a collaborative culture and family-centered work environment."[10] And leading financial news provider Barron's, in its January 8, 2020 article, "Sonoco Named One of America's Most Responsible Companies," quoted Tiede as saying: "It is truly our principle of People Build Businesses by Doing the Right Thing that guides our work."[11] Robert C. Tiede officially announced his retirement early in 2020 and Howard Coker, former CEO Charlie Coker's son, and the Major's great-great grandson, replaced him as Sonoco CEO on February 3, 2020.

Through company history, there have been many worthy CEOS without the Coker name. But a selective genealogy of CEOs in the direct family line from Major Coker to Howard Coker is as follows:

Major Coker

↓

Charles Westfield Coker

↓

Charles W. Coker – grandson

↓

Charles W. (Charlie) Coker – great grandson

↓

Howard Coker (today)– great-great grandson

**Howard Coker, the Major's great-great grandson,
became CEO of Sonoco on 2/3/2020.**

ENDNOTES FOR CHAPTER 9: THE BIRTH AND GROWTH OF SONOCO PRODUCTS

1   Ned L. Irwin, South Carolina Encyclopedia, April 15, 2016 article "Coker, Charles Westfield," http://www.scencyclopedia.org/sce/entries/coker-charles-westfield/ (accessed December 29, 2019).

2   Editor, *Fortune* web site, Fortune 500, "Sonoco Products," lists Sonoco at that time as Fortune # 518., https://fortune.com/fortune500/2019/sonoco-products/ (accessed February 17,2020).

3   Malcolm C. Doubles, op. cit., p. 28.

4   Editor, Sonoco Investor Relations 2018 News Release "Sonoco Introduces EnviroSense™ Sustainable Packaging Development Initiative," https://investor.sonoco.com/news-releases/news-release-details/sonoco-introduces-envirosensetm-sustainable-packaging, p. 1.

5   Editor, 2019 Sonoco Publication, "How Sonoco Reduces its Environmental Impact," provided to the author by Carolyn Johnson of Sonoco Corporate Communications.

6   Malcolm Doubles, *A Century Plus: A History of Sonoco Products Company*, op. cit., pp. 37-38.

7   Charles Westfield (Charlie)) Coker, in my interview with him at Sonoco on November 20, 2018.

8   Charles Westfield (Charlie) Coker, *The Story of Sonoco Products Company*, the Newcomen Society in North America, 1976, p. 22.

9   Editor, Barron's website, January 8, 2020 article "Sonoco Named One of America's Most Responsible Companies," https://www.barrons.com/articles/PR-CO-20200108-908361?tesla=y&tesla=y (accessed January 12, 2020)

10   Editor, Sonoco's website, article "Sonoco Named One of America's Best Large Employers 2019," summarizing recognitions given Sonoco by Forbes, https://investor.sonoco.com/news-releases/news-release-details/sonoco-named-one-americas-best-large-employers-2019, p.1 (accessed March 7, 2020).

11   Editor, Barron's website, op. cit.

PART IV

BEYOND BUSINESS: THE MAJOR'S WIDER CULTURAL VISION AND INFLUENCE

Major James Lide Coker, c. 1900.
Courtesy of Coker College Archives.

In commerce, Major Coker integrated his faith with the challenges of the marketplace as he raised the standards of the business culture in the South. But in the last 22 years of his life, he had more time for his broader passion and dream: to conquer educational and biblical ignorance in his state.

Major Coker had extraordinary intelligence along with a top notch education from Harvard and the Citadel. The Rev. R. E. Peele once said of him, "Major Coker is a wonder to me; he knows more things about a greater number of subjects than any man I've known."[1] James was awarded an honorary LL.D. (Doctor of Laws) by the University of South Carolina in 1910,[2] but he never even considered himself an "elitist." On the contrary, Angus Gainey's observation from 1873 in the Hartsville Sunday School was "When I first met the Major, I never will forget he made himself one of the boys. He wasn't the wonderful J. L. Coker – he was just another boy."[3]

English statesman Francis Bacon famously said: "Knowledge is power," but to Major Coker, knowledge was power to help others. His desire to uplift culture was simply a desire to upgrade the lives of the people of his state by creating an environment that brightened their wits, their opportunities, and their hopes for this life and the next.

As far as we know, the Major never wrote down his exact definition of Christian culture, but we can pretty well determine it from his life and his writings, including his writings in the founding documents of his schools, where he combined academic and spiritual ideals.

He said: "One cannot get too much education, if it is the right sort of education."[4] His view of the "right sort of education" was influenced by his belief in the divine inspiration of the Bible. In his farm journal, he said he wanted his thoughts and writings to be "in accordance with the teaching of the divine word."[5] He described God's Word as "the sweet promises of the One who is good."[6] Regarding the transcendent revelation of the Bible, he said, "He [God] is able to cause to occur by special interposition [into human history] those things which had been decreed."[7]

When we integrate James's passion for biblical revelation, higher learning, and down to earth service, the following is a fair definition of his ideals of culture: **As discerned by God's word, the acquisition of inspiring academic, spiritual, and business ideals, put to practical use to uplift the people of one's community."**

For a competing view of cultural foundations from that time, we need look no further than the Major's younger contemporary, attorney Clarence Darrow (1857-1938). Darrow spoke arrogantly of those who had a faith like the Major's, saying "I do not consider it an insult, but rather a compliment to be called an agnostic. I do not pretend to know where many ignorant men are sure of— that is all that agnosticism means."[8]

I think Darrow would have had a hard time convincing anyone that Major Coker, or those on his academic team like Dr. E. W. Sikes or Dr. E. V. Baldy were ignorant men. In an intellectual comparison, E. W. Sikes subtly commented that the Major was wiser than Darrow: "Darrow is intellectual, but his intellect is not well-tempered... Major Coker's intellect was such that it could convert knowledge into wisdom. There are many people who know many things, but they are not wise men. The Encyclopedias contain knowledge and facts but all of them together have to the wisdom of Solomon's proverbs" [9]

One of James's the workers on Coker farms, referring to his foresight, said "Major Coker is a long-headed man." Indeed, in carrying forward his ideals for culture, the Major was a visionary and far sighted leader whose spiritual legacy blessed many generations to come, including mine and beyond. In this section, we examine how he invested his cultural ideals in as many people as possible through the Sunday School, through Welsh Neck High School, and through Coker College.

ENDNOTES FOR OPENING COMMENTS TO PART IV: BEYOND BUSINESS: THE MAJOR'S WIDER CULTURAL VISION AND INFLUENCE

1   Rev. R. E. Peele, as quoted by Rev. C. L. Dowell, *Centennial Celebration,* op. cit., p. 16.
2   Cyclopedia of American Biography, op. cit., p. 22.
3   Angus Gainey, a Sunday School student of the Major's from 1873-1876, in the extract from Gainey's journal entitled *"Recollections of the Sunday School,"* South Caroliniana Library, University of South Carolina, Columbia, SC, p. 1 (not to be confused with the Hartsville Museum's book *Recollections of the Major).*
4   Rev. C. L. Dowell, whose speech was recorded in the Coker College Quarterly Bulletin, February, in "Centennial Celebration of Major James Lide Coker," op. cit.
5   James Lide Coker, January 28, 1859 entry in his *Farm Journal,* The South Caroliniana Library, University of South Carolina, Columbia, SC, p. 28.
6   George Lee Simpson, op. cit., p. 65.
7   James Lide Coker, Farm Journal, op. cit., p. 28.
8   Editor, goodreads, https://www.goodreads.com/author/quotes/31156. Clarence Darrow.
9   E. W. Sikes, president of Clemson College, speech at "1937 Centennial Celebration of the Major," op. cit., p. 21.

CHAPTER 10

THE MAJOR AND SUE'S SUNDAY SCHOOL MINISTRY

On one occasion, the Major told a neighbor, "Many feel they can worship God on the banks of the streams or in the fields as they turn the sod, and they can; but for me, nothing takes the place of worship in the House of God."[1]

James taught Sunday School to older elementary age children at First Baptist Church in Hartsville from c. 1857 to 1860, and again after the war from 1865 to c. 1905. The Major's daughter-in-law Vivien Coker said, "Mother taught the wee little children and the Major, the big ones. They had it every Sunday."[2] One of their students said "the Sunday School lessons were "written by Major Coker, planned in such a way to interest the students."[3] Many of the Sunday Schoolers were illiterate, so James and Sue also taught them out of Webster's *American Spelling Book*, 1824 edition, better known as the blue back speller. Counting earlier editions, this book was a standard text in U. S. public and private elementary education for over a hundred years, until the early 1900's. Webster often

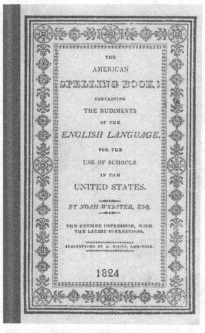

An Easy Standard of Pronunciation. 65

He that cov-er-eth his sins shall not pros-per, but he that con-fess-eth and for-sak-eth them shall find mer-cy.

IV.

The rod and re-proof give wis-dom; but a child left to him-self bring-eth his pa-rents to shame.
Cor-rect thy son, and he will give thee rest; yea, he will give de-light to thy soul.
A man's pride shall bring him low; but hon-or shall up-hold the hum-ble in spir-it.
The eye that mock-eth at his fath-er, and scorn-eth to o-bey his moth-er, the ra-vens of the val-ley shall pick it out, and the young ea-gles shall eat it.

V.

By the bless-ing of the up-right, the cit-y is ex-alt-ed, but it is o-ver-thrown by the mouth of the wick-ed.
Where no coun-sel is, the peo-ple fall; but in the midst of coun-sel-lors there is safe-ty.
The wis-dom of the pru-dent is to un-der-stand his way, but the fol-ly of fools is de-ceit.
A wise man fear-eth and de-part-eth from evil, but the fool rag-eth and is con-fi-dent.
Be not hast-y in thy spir-it to be an-gry; for an-ger rest-eth in the bo-som of fools.

TABLE XXIII.

Words of four syllables, accented on the first.

2	des pi ca ble	mis er a ble
Ad mi ra ble	el i gi ble	nav i ga ble
ac cu rate ly	es ti ma ble	pal li a tive
am i ca ble	ex pli ca tive	pit i a ble
ap pli ca ble	fig u ra tive	pref er a ble
ar ro gant ly	lam ent a ble	ref er a ble
cred it a ble	lit er a ture	rev o ca ble
crim in al ly	mar riage a ble	sump tu ous ly

Webster's blue back speller, cover & p. 65. Original publication is under public domain; this pictured reprint is courtesy of Applewood Books: Carlisle, MA. James & Sue used this book, plus their lessons, to teach children to read in their Sunday School classes.

used God's Word in his examples.[4] For instance, the pictured section on pronouncing two and three syllable words uses selected Proverbs, including Proverbs 28:13: "He that cov-er-eth his sins shall not pros-per, but he that con-fess-eth and for-sak-eth them shall find mer-cy."[5] The Cokers followed up the speller with the Bible's plan of salvation.

Taught Both Literacy and Bible

Robert W. Durrett, Dean of Coker College, added: "He was made superintendent of the Sunday School of the Baptist Church…. Along with the Bible, the three Rs were taught."[6]

Tom E. Goodson wrote:

Of course, I'd known the Major since I was a child. He was the pillar in the church, you know, and we were all members of the same church. His wife was my first Sunday School teacher. We learned our ABCs in Sunday School.

She was very devoted to her church. Of course, the Major was too.[7]

Dr. E. W. Sikes, First Baptist deacon, and president of Coker College from 1916 to 1926, wrote this about the Major's Sunday school ministry:

> He also believed in religious education and started and was superintendent of Sunday School here.... To me, there is no finer picture than this Harvard man, fresh from the command in the Confederate Army, printing Sunday School lessons for the children of his neighbors.[8]

When we consider all of his obligations running twenty-one businesses, it's an amazing testament to James's devotion to God and His will that he prioritized time to prepare lessons, teach children to read and make sure they heard the plan of salvation.

He Published the Sunday School Lessons

E. W. Sikes commented on how the Sunday School lessons were composed:

> Everyone was poor after the war, and it was difficult to obtain proper literature for Sunday School teachers and students. So Major Coker, Superintendent of the Sunday School, purchased a small hand printing press, and each week he and

First Baptist Church of Hartsville's first building, built in 1850 by its members who cut the log planks. The Major and Sue cheerfully taught Sunday School here and in rural areas from c. 1865 to 1900. This building later burnt. A new one was rebuilt on the same foundation, and the rebuilt one is the current church chapel. From the FBC scrapbook by church historian Dr. Susan Reynolds, 2011. Used by permission.

Sue prepared the lessons for the teachers and students. The Major and James Jr. printed the lessons on the small press. Many students who came to this early Sunday School were unable to read and write, so part of each period was devoted to teaching them these skills through simple passages from the lesson. For many years, there remained people in the Hartsville area who were taught by Mrs. Coker to read and write in the Sunday School hour of the Baptist Church.[9]

The Major as a Rural Missionary

James continued to follow his calling since childhood to remedy the spiritual and educational deprivations of rural South Carolinians, so he and Sue ministered in rural areas as well.[10] They would take their horse and wagon out to the country, pick up barefoot white and African American[11] children, and bring them to the church. First Baptist church member Miss Josephine Erwin, for whom a street in Hartsville is named, recalled:

> Major Coker was a very religious person, and my earliest recollection of the First Baptist Church of Hartsville was the pew on which he used to sit – there was always a pillow on that pew for him. I have often heard him tell stories about how he and his wife used to teach Sunday School to the children in the early days. They would bring them in wagons from across the creek [Black Creek].[12]

Vivien Coker once commented that the Major and Sue were known to hold Sunday school in their own kitchen:

About the days after the war, I know very little. I do know that they had a Sunday School here in the old kitchen, and it was fixed up. She had the children come over... so many people around here – [who now are] the old people – all the education they got was that one hour on Sunday. When I first came here, so many people would say, 'Oh, Miss Sue taught me to read. And only one hour on Sunday did they have to do it in.'"[13]

Miss Josephine Erwin commented regarding Mrs. Sue Coker:

About his wife, I know this was true. I lived at Mrs. Lawton's, and I've seen country people come in, and Mrs. Coker would take them in and play the piano for them and give them tea or lemonade and cakes; that was for poor country people."[14]

After teaching Sunday morning's class, they went out two Sunday afternoons a month[15] with their blue back spellers and Bibles to hold Sunday School a second time in small schoolrooms in the country.

Mrs. Robert Lide, the Major's niece, recalled:

When I was a child six or seven years old, we lived in Hartsville. My first impressions of Uncle James were as a Sunday School worker. He organized also a Sunday School out some miles among underprivileged children. Once when I was visiting Margie [Major Coker's daughter Margaret], he took us with him on Sunday afternoon to this school. Another recollection of these early years was something said by my mother about the second coming of Christ. [I remarked in response] – "Oh,

> Mother – don't you wish He would come? The
> flowers would bloom all around Him. And Uncle
> Jimmie [Major Coker] and the Sunday School
> children would all be there."[16]

Leland Segars Hungerpiller remembers how Major Coker also recruited adults from the surrounding farms to come to church:

> In teaching a Sunday School lesson on excuse-
> giving for not going to church, Prof. R. W. Durrett
> [assistant principal at Welsh Neck High School
> and later Dean of Coker College for twenty-one
> years] told the following story: Major went to visit
> a farmer to learn why he had not been coming to
> church. "You see these clothes I have on? Do you
> think they are good enough to wear to church?"
> asked the man. "Well," said the Major, looking
> him up and down, "I believe you are about my
> size. I'll send you a suit."[17]

This farmer kept the suit but never did come to church. Nevertheless, the incident reveals the Major's zeal for the residents of Darlington County to hear God's Word.

The Major and Sue Were "All In"

The Hartsville couple went beyond tithing; they often invested their personal funds into the Sunday School. James bought a printing press and supplies to publish their weekly lessons. Their nephew Frank R. Chambers gave additional insight into the Major's devotion to Christian education:

> When I was leaving for my youthful adventure in
> New York [in 1867], the Major handed me $20.00
> [worth $346.00 in 2019] to invest in books for his

Sunday School. At that time, and in his restricted circumstances, twenty dollars meant much, and bespoke his deep interest in the welfare of his people, intellectual and spiritual.[18]

Arthur Rogers recalled:

They had a large Sunday School at Hartsville, to which he gave a lot of his time and was very enthusiastic. One Sunday, a big rain came and caught the whole crowd at church. As they couldn't get home, the Major went into the store and got crackers and cheese, and I don't know what all, and they had a lunch at the church.[19]

Profile of God's work in a Sunday School Boy: Angus Gainey

Angus Gainey (1865-1951) was raised in the country near Hartsville before moving to nearby Darlington in 1876. From age eight to age eleven, he attended Major Coker's Sunday School class. He wrote:

In the Hartsville Sunday School was when I first met the Major, I never will forget he made himself one of the boys. He wasn't the wonderful J. L. Coker – he was just another boy. I always called him Mr. Coker.

… He'd make Jimmie [the Major's son, James Lide Coker Jr.] stand up and lead the singing…. The old Major knew a lot about music, too, and he taught the boys a lot of those songs. The Major would shake the stick [to lead the music]. At the time, I used to wonder what he was shaking that stick at. I never heard a group of children sing so well. They sang "Always Cheerful" quite often.[20]

Tom E. Goodson, speaking of the Major in a different context with no reference to the hymn, once wrote, "He was always cheerful, and I've never seen him when he was out of humor. He was always cheerful to me."[21] The hymn "Always Cheerful," to which Gainey referred, was written by blind Fanny Crosby (1820-1915), a contemporary of the Major, and was one of his favorites. I personally think that James, with his lame leg, identified with Miss Crosby's blindness, and was happy that they both still enjoyed transcendent cheerfulness. The hymn goes as follows:

> Let our hearts be always cheerful;
> Why should murm'ring enter there,
> When our kind and loving Father
> Makes us children of His care?

Refrain:

> Always cheerful, always cheerful,
> Sunshine all around we see;
> Full of beauty is the path of duty,
> Cheerful we may always be.

> With His gentle hand to lead us,
> Should the pow'rs of sin assail,
> He has promised grace to help us;
> Never can His promise fail.

> When we turn aside from duty,
> Comes the pain of doing wrong;
> And a shadow, creeping o'er us,
> Checks the rapture of our song.

Oh! the good are always happy,
And their path is ever bright;
Let us heed the blessed counsel,
Shun the wrong, and love the right.

Angus Gainey continued:

It was about 1874 when he [the Major] made the
offer of a prize to... the children if one would
attend Sunday School for a year and not miss
over three Sundays. And I lived five miles from
there and had to walk it most of the time. The
time came for him to give out the prizes. The
Major called out the different names for the
prizes – some were music [hymn] books, some
were picture books. And I hadn't learned to read
yet. "Well, Angus, which do you want – a music
book or a picture book?" I said, "A music book."
"Well, Angus, can you read?" "No, sir." "Well,
what do you want it for?" Well, I just want it" [the
Major later discovered that Angus was musically
inclined]. "Well," he said, "you can have it, but
I just wondered what you wanted if for if you
can't read."[22]

Before leaving Hartsville, he did learn to read via the
Sunday school. He said:

I carried a blue-back speller to that class... and
we learned to read in that way. We had that in
preference to the Sunday School lesson until we
learned to read, then we got the lesson papers.[23]

Gainey commented further on his experiences with the
Major:

He used to have picnics… usually around Christmas time, and I remember in particular [that] he insisted on serving the boys himself. He came around, and I was hesitating which piece of chicken to take. He said, "Oh, take a drumstick." "Which piece?" "A drumstick. That drumstick down there." "I don't see any drumstick." "Well, that leg down there." So I learned what a drumstick was.[24]

After moving to Darlington, Angus, at the age of thirteen, fell in with the wrong company and became a heavy drinker. Walking the streets of Darlington, he heard a band playing melodiously in an upper room. He knocked on the door at street level to inquire, was invited in, and was allowed to play in their band. In God's providence, it turned out to be a temperance society! He soon became sober and remained so the rest of his life.[25]

In 1915, Gainey helped found Darlington's Central Baptist Church as a charter member.[26] The spiritual, musical, and literary training Angus received from the Major stayed with him for life. He walked in the Major's footsteps by

Angus Gainey as an adult. C/o Darlington Co. Historical Commission.

investing in young people through his own Sunday school. Darlington's *News and Press* also reported: "Angus was a factor in the music in the Sunday School of the church.'" [27] One of the songs he taught the children in both Sunday School and in the public schools (it was allowed) was "The Old Rugged Cross."[28]

So time showed that there was something in Angus's DNA that cried out to Major Coker for that music book! From those beginnings in Major Coker's Sunday School class, he went on to become an accomplished musician and music teacher.

According to the Darlington's *News and Press*, he "organized one of the first high school orchestras in the entire South in 1918, and reputedly the first in the state of South Carolina. The orchestra later came to be known as St. John's High School Orchestra, and won… the top award in the state."[29]

So we see that the Major and Sue weren't just "in it for kicks." They were intentional about teaching and mentoring young people like Angus, patiently loving them, teaching them to read, and showing them the way of salvation. Many, like Angus, became future Christian leaders. Let's look further at Major Coker's devotion to training up church leaders.

Passing the Torch to J. J. Lawton

Major Coker remained a deacon for life and continued teaching Sunday school until at least 1905.[30] However, in 1888, he passed the torch of Sunday School superintendence to Joseph James (J. J.) Lawton. In the true spirit of love and discipleship, it is clear that Major Coker valued the opportunity to mentor younger men, such as Lawton and Angus Gainey.

Joseph James (J.J.) Lawton.
By permission of Coker College.

A little background on J. J. Lawton (1861-1941) is needed. He was three years old when Sherman's men terrorized his hometown of Allendale, South Carolina and torched his home. His family fled for their lives and became refugees. Lawton was trying to eke out a living as a worker in cotton fields when, at his daughter Margaret's bidding, the Major noticed him in the early 1880's, and had pity on him. He took him under his wing, soon made him his farm manager, and mentored him for the next thirty years.

Twenty-four years his junior, Lawton patterned his life after the Major. In 2020, J. J.'s grandson, Edgar H. Lawton Jr. of Hartsville, said that "both J. J. and the Major were intensely religious."[31] Lawton married James's daughter Margaret and became a partner in the store a year later."[32] Lawton became one of the original members on the board of the Southern Novelty Company and partnered with James in many other business enterprises, including the Hartsville Railroad, J. L. Coker General Store, the Hartsville Oil Mill, and Coker's Pedigreed Seed Company.

First Baptist Church's men's Sunday School class taught by J.J. Lawton (front center), c. 1918. Major Coker modelled Christian leadership to Lawton in church and business. The Major followed the Apostle Paul's succession principle: "The things which you heard from me... entrust to faithful men, who will be able to teach others also." Photo by permission of Dr. Susan Reynolds of FBC.

Like the Major, Lawton was elected a lifelong deacon and proved to be an outstanding lay leader in the First Baptist Church for well over thirty years. Following the Major's precedent, he devoted himself to Christian education and gave around 35 years of outstanding service as a Sunday school teacher. In 1938, the church's then-new Sunday School building, a sizeable facility, was named for J. J. Lawton in appreciation of his zealous and very capable service.[33]

Lawton also integrated his faith into academics. He was a

founding board member of Welsh Neck High School and Coker College and went on to serve on the boards of the Southern Baptist Theological Seminary and Furman [Baptist] University.[34]

First Baptist Church chapel with J.J. Lawton Sun. Sch. Building in background, c. 1955. By permission of Dr. Susan D. Reynolds, editor, First Baptist scrapbook.

According to my mother Mary Coker Joslin, in her book *Growing Up in the Brown House*, J. J. Lawton had a grand sense of humor. She wrote that he was a favorite among children, often buying them candy at the Coker store.[35] It is no wonder that he boosted the growth of the church.

The Major's Influence on Coker College Student Josephine Erwin

Josephine Erwin, Coker College Class of 1909 and Coker College honorary doctorate recipient. From Malcolm Doubles' *In Quest of Excellence* and used by permission of Coker College Press.

Josephine Erwin, Coker College class of 1909 and later assistant to all the Coker College presidents until 1958,[36] also caught the Major's vision for ministry and mentoring. Perhaps on the country carriage rides for Coker College young women (detailed in Chapter 12), he even talked to her about investing her life for Christ. In any case, she followed in his footsteps by teaching Sunday School at First Baptist for five decades.

Miss Erwin also had a spiritual influence on my mother, who wrote: "When we graduated from the Junior Department, then directed by Miss Josephine Erwin… we received a gift of our own Bible and were expected to stay for the adult service. This seemed like an important rite of passage."[37]

Josephine wrote the letter pictured below to two young

people whom she taught at the First Baptist Church. She commended them for giving their lives to Christ.[38] It reflects the fact that the Major and Sue's Christian influence on the college staff outlived them.

COKER COLLEGE
HARTSVILLE, SOUTH CAROLINA

October 6, 1954

Dear Elizabeth and Curtis-

I went to the Methodist Church last Sunday, as the Pilots were observing Founder's Day, but I was delighted to hear that you went forward at the church service and said by doing that you wanted to live your lives for Christ. This is the most important step you will ever take in your life, and the one that will bring you the greatest joy and happiness. You will not find it always easy to live the Christian life. You will meet with temptations on every hand, but with the help of God and your fine Christian parents you can.

I pray that God's richest blessings may rest upon you now and always.

Sincerely yours,

Josephine Erwin

Josephine Erwin
Supt. Junior 11 Department

1958 letter from Coker College Alumni Director Josephine Erwin encourgaing two young people for giving their lives to Christ. From the Hartsville First Baptist Baptist Church scrapbook. Used by permisson of scrapbook author Susan Reynolds.

Through his Sunday school (and later his high school and college), the Major not only uplifted Christ, but began a river of succeeding Christian leadership that continued to change lives through others such as Angus Gainey, Josephine Erwin, and J.J. Lawton.

He Considered Teaching Sunday School
A High Calling

Dr. Henry N. Snyder, Methodist educator and author, then president of Wofford College, remarked that the Major's ministry was symmetrically integrated into his entire life's work: "He was a Christian gentleman who, in gracious and appealing ways, kept faith with the high duties that life brought to him in respect to his family, his community, his church, and his state." [39]

ENDNOTES FOR CHAPTER 10: THE MAJOR AND SUE'S SUNDAY SCHOOL MINISTRY

1   Reverend Davis M. Sanders, DD, pastor of Hartsville First Baptist Church, in his speech on Coker College Founder's Day, April 27, 1960, p. 7. Courtesy of Coker College archives.
2   Vivien Coker, Recollections, p. 60.
3   Mrs. J. F. Ousley, *Recollections*, p. 41.
4   Editor, Noah Webster College site, remarks re Blue-Back Speller, http://www.nwebstercollege.com/736949, accessed 11/2/2020.
5   Noah Webster, *The American Spelling Book*, (Holbrook and Fessenden: Brattleborough, VT), 1824.
6   Robert W. Durrett, MA, Dean of Coker College, "A Good and Great Man," as quoted in the Coker College publication of the Centennial of the Major's birth, op. cit., p.36.
7   Tom E. Goodson, *Recollections*, p. 61.
8   E. W. Sikes, "Major James L. Coker" Founder's Day Speech, Coker College, April 28, 1928, as cited by Malcolm Doubles in *In Quest of Excellence: A History of Coker College on its Centennial*, Coker College Press, Hartsville, 2008, p. 6.
9   Ibid, p. 125.
10 Mrs. Robert Lide, *Recollections*, p. 66.
11 Miss Jane Lide, op. cit., p. 5.
12 Josephine Erwin, *Recollections*, p. 60.
13 Vivien Coker, *Recollections*, p. 60.
14 Mrs. Josephine Lawton Patterson, *Recollections*, p. 102.
15 Kate Chambers, op. cit., p. 78.
16 Mrs. Robert Lide, niece of James Lide Coker, *Recollections*, p. 66.
17 Leland Segars Hungerpiller, quoted in April 1941 article of *The Hartsville Messenger,* in *Recollections*, pp. 55-56.
18 Frank R. Chambers in his talk "Major J. L. Coker, Christian and Philanthropist," Coker College Founders Day, April 9, 1919, op. cit., p. 57.
19 Arthur Rogers, *Recollections*, p. 63.
20 Angus Gainey, a Sunday School student of the Major's from 1873-1876, in the extract from Gainey's journal entitled *"Recollections of the Sunday School,"* South Caroliniana Library, University of South Carolina, Columbia, SC, p. 1 (not to be confused with the Hartsville Museum's book *Recollections of the Major).*
21 Tom E. Goodson, *Recollections*, p. 129.
22 Angus Gainey, op. cit., pp. 1-2.

23   Angus Gainey, op. cit., p. 3.

24   Angus Gainey, op. cit., pp. 2-3

25   Angus Gainey, *Angus Gainey's Journal*, written c. 1950, provided to me by Brian Gandy of the Darlington County Historical Society, pp. 53-54.

26   Darlington's *News and Press*, article "Central Baptist Church celebrates 100 years," Wednesday March 18, 2015, http://www.newsandpress.net/central-baptist-church-celebrates-100-years/ (accessed December 29, 2019).

27   *News and Press*, obituary of Angus Gainey, op. cit.

28   Angus Gainey, Angus Gainey's Journal, op. cit., pp. 57-59.

29   Editor, Darlington's newspaper, *News and Press*, in Angus Gainey's obituary on April 19, 1951, "Angus Gainey of Darlington Dies at 85." Obtained from Darlington County Historical Commission.

30   Mrs. J. F. Ousley in *Recollections*, p. 41, describes the Major composing and teaching Sunday School lessons to the Welsh Neck High School students on Thursday nights, then taking the leftover papers and teaching again at First Baptist on Sunday morning. This would have occurred during the time frame of Welsh Neck High School, 1896 to 1908.

31   Edgar H. Lawton, Jr. I was privileged to have a phone interview with Edgar H. Lawton, Jr., J. J. Lawton's grandson, on March 27, 2020.

32   Malcolm C. Doubles, *A Century Plus: A History of Sonoco Products Company*, op. cit., p. 9.

33   Dr. Susan D. Reynolds, op. cit., p. 185.

34   From *One Hundred Years of Service, 1850-1950, A Brief History of the First Baptist Church, Hartsville, SC*, published by the church itself on their centennial anniversary, pp. 188-193.

35   Mary Coker Joslin, *Growing Up in the Brown House*, Coker College Press, Hartsville, 2008, p. 46.

36   Malcolm Doubles, op. cit., p. 29.

37   Mary Roper Coker Joslin, op. cit., p. 113.

38   Dr. Susan D. Reynolds, op. cit., p. 61.

39   Dr. Henry N. Snyder, president of Wofford College, whose speech was recorded in the *Coker College Quarterly Bulletin*, "1937 Centennial Celebration of the Major," op. cit., p. 27.

CHAPTER 11

THE WELSH NECK HIGH SCHOOL

E. W. Sikes said that after the war, Major Coker was disturbed to find "many indigent children of Confederate soldiers without educational opportunities."[1] Years earlier, with the war winding down in late 1864, for two years he served briefly as a representative

Welsh Neck High School, c. 1899, not including dormitory buildings. Coker College was later built on the same locaton off Home Avenue in Hartsville. Major Coker gave weekly chapel messages here, then used the same lessons in his First Baptist Sunday School. Permission from Coker College Press.

to the South Carolina General Assembly. He and Dr. James H. Carlisle, president of Wofford College from 1850 to 1904,[2] introduced the first bill to build public schools for all the children in South Carolina, both African American and white.[3] Unfortunately, this bill, ahead of its time, was defeated.

Major Coker was not interested in remaining in political

office, and went back to his businesses and community service, but he never lost his vision for education. It would materialize first in the form of the Welsh Neck High School in Hartsville in 1894. He made it coeducational and included military training for boys under principal Major Gaines.[4] Arthur Rogers described its formation:

> At the Welsh Neck [Baptist] Association, meeting on that occasion at Black Creek Church. He was trying to put over the Welsh Neck High School. I remember his talk was an enthusiastic one before the Association for the establishment of the school.... You see, he really put up most of the money for it, but he wanted the Association to be cooperative and to give what they could give and then give it their interest. He was determined to have it. He gave the land and buildings.[5]

Major Coker asked the ever-capable J. J. Lawton to be on the board, and he helped significantly with the operation of the school. [6] Drawing from well beyond Hartsville, they had a peak enrollment of 256 students,[7] quite a bit for a small town of 300 people.

Military Training and Football Success

Apparently, the Major thought the relatively newly-invented game of football could help build his high school boys into men, because he wanted his school to have a team. The combination of this military and football training kept the boys in shape. An amazing but true story from 1907 is that the Welsh Neck High football team actually beat the University of South Carolina![8]

Philosophy of Education

The Major believed education should address learning, faith, and character. Ethel Laney Miller said: "Major Coker was diligent in his business, but I think he found the greatest pleasure in the promotion of Christian education."[9]

The Major wanted the high school, and later Coker College, be faith-based in purpose, but not sectarian. In the section on "Religion," the Welsh Neck High School manual says:

> Devotional exercises will be held in the High School daily. There is preaching in the village every Sunday by ministers of different Protestant denominations. Pupils will be required to attend, under such restrictions as the principal may deem advisable, the churches being designated by their parents. While the High School is the property of the Baptist denomination and conducted under their auspices, it is in no sense sectarian. No attempt whatever to influence pupils in their denominational preferences will be made or tolerated.[10]

Welsh Neck High graduate Mrs. J. F. Ousley recalls how personally the Major related to each of the students at Welsh Neck High School, and how they recognized his genuine faith:

> At the age of twelve, I, along with three other members of the Rhodes family, entered Welsh Neck High School – thus having occasion to come into personal contact with Major Coker through Chapel exercises, his observation visits to the school, and the study of Sunday School lessons each week on Thursday nights.[11]

She added:

> During my five years as a boarding student at Welsh Neck High School, I had occasion for personal contact [with the Major and Sue] through invitations to dinner and regular practice on his piano daily for some years... Always I had that feeling of nearness and generosity, felt only when among genuine Christian friends.[12]

The Major's Personal Touch

Mrs. J. F. Ousley continued:

> When the time for graduation was drawing near, we were requested to go to his private office in his home to secure his signature on our diplomas. He received us privately, one by one, and gave a personal word of encouragement, counsel, and assurance of continued interest in our welfare and success in future years. His presence with us was truly a benediction and comfort and brought forth the highest respect and reverence.
>
> As long as he lived, his attitude toward me seemed the same – always glad to see me and to greet me with that same handclasp and word of approach, "Daughter." To me, Major Coker will always seem a kind, generous, considerate, helpful, never tiring, unselfish father to those in need of him.[13]

Sue Coker's Leadership

Sue Coker modelled the school's ideal of Christian service by training others to provide for the poor. Mrs. Ousley detailed Sue's work:

> Mrs. Coker would plan a sewing bee where she would furnish material, letting the girls help to make garments for needy families. Then she would let the girls take turns about to accompany her to visit and present garments to these families.[14] Indeed, her Christianity was both deep and practical. She gave herself in love to all who needed her. The school's flower garden was under her own special care, and the fragrance that arose from it was the fragrance of Sue's life.[15]

End of the High School, but...

In 1908, South Carolina began to provide public high school education, rendering the Welsh Neck school less necessary. After fourteen years of service, the school was closed. But in a sense, it never closed, for at age seventy-seven, the Major had already set new sites on a women's college. Tom E. Goodson said, "He came to doubt the good of the mixed school and later converted it to a girl's school."[16]

ENDNOTES FOR CHAPTER 11: THE WELSH NECK HIGH SCHOOL

1 E. W. Sikes, 1919 Founder's Day Commemoration, op. cit., p. 40.
2 Editor, website of Knowitall.org, "James H. Carlisle History of SC Slide Collection," https://www.knowitall.org/photo/james-h-carlisle-history-sc-slide-collection (accessed December 29, 2019).
3 E. W. Sikes, *Centennial Celebration*, op. cit., pp. 19, 22
4 Nan Lawton, paper given to Thursday Study Club, 2020, p.5, drawn as she wrote, from boxes of Lawton papers.
5 Arthur Rogers, *Recollections*, p. 39.
6 George Lee Simpson, op. cit., p. 175, and *The Cotton Oil Press*, obituary on J. J. Lawton, June 21, 1941.
7 E. W. Sikes, Founder's Day Speech at Coker College on April 9,1919., op. cit., p. 44.
8 Nan Lawton, op. cit., p. 6.
9 Ethel Laney Miller, *Recollections*, p. 44.
10 Welsh Neck High School Manual, c. 1888, section on "Religion." The actual text is below.

> Religion   Devotional exercises will be held in the High School daily. There is preaching in the village every Sunday by ministers of different Protestant denominations. Pupils *will be required to attend*, under such restrictions as the principal may deem advisable, the churches designated by their parents.
>
> While the High School is the property of the Baptist denomination and conducted under their auspices, it is in no sense sectarian. No attempt whatever to influence pupils in their denominational preferences will be made or tolerated.

Welsh Neck High School Manual, c. 1904. Used by permission of Coker College Press.

11 Mrs. J. F. Ousley, *Recollections*, p. 40.
12 Ibid., p. 43.
13 Ibid.
14 Mrs. J.F. Ousley, *Recollections*, p. 43.
15 Evelyn Snider, Coker College Class of 1928, in her 1939 speech entitled "From Coker Backstage," Box 2 of the James Lide Coker Collection, courtesy of South Caroliniana Library, University of South Carolina, Columbia, SC, pp. 1-3.
16 Tom E. Goodson, *Recollections*, p. 47.

CHAPTER 12

COKER COLLEGE

This chapter on Coker College is not intended to be comprehensive. I will present Major's founding principles for the school, and using comments from some key personalities, trace those principles through the decades. For a more thorough history of Coker College from 1908 to 2008, I recommend Malcolm C. Doubles' fine book, In Quest of Excellence: A History of Coker College at Its Centennial, *Coker College Press, Hartsville, 2008.*

Foundations for Coker College

Major Coker and early classes of Coker College girls, whose names, unfortunately, were not included in the picture, c. 1916. Left of The Major is Samuel W. Garrett, Dean of Faculty. To the right is E.W. Sikes, college president, 1916-1925. Picture courtesy of Coker University, Administration Building.

There is no question that Hannah, the Major's mother, influenced his vision for Coker College. She not only positively influenced his views on education, but were it not for her courage, he would have died in the Civil War. To him, she represented Christian womanhood at its best. Surely, he had his mother in mind when he said:

> The members of our Board believe in education for all, but especially for the potential mothers of the land whose influence will soon be the most powerful of all influences for good to those who come after us... We confidently launch our new enterprise with great hope for its future usefulness and asking the favor of God and the goodwill of our fellow men.[1]

In the Coker College magazine, *Euterpean,* he stated in the section "Spirit and Purpose:" "It is the prime purpose of Coker College to afford, under the inspiration of Christian influences, such thorough and broad educational opportunities as may result in the production of the highest type of Christian womanhood."[2] That quote, from the 1912 edition, was repeated in many early editions of the magazine.

Major Coker also said, "Women should be good scientists, for they are close observers."[3] He was also in favor of women's suffrage, and the

Early copy of Coker's Euterpean magazine, including course descriptions.

Nineteenth Amendment, which passed Congress in 1920, giving women the right to vote.

In 1908, there were very few female colleges in the state of South Carolina. There could have been more, but in my research I only found two, so in any case, women's higher education was a rarity.

Hartsville farmer and prosperous businessman McIver Williamson thought Major Coker was too idealistic and that the largesse of his generosity toward young women was foolish. He told James it would be more worthwhile to make sausage than to educate women – exclaiming: "Putting in a female plant! You'd better put in a packing plant and buy these farmers' hogs."[4] But the Major had seen enough pigs, and his vision was to invest in young women.

Original Coker College structure built by Major Coker. He nicknamed it "great buildings in a row." They are, from left to right, Memorial Hall, Belk Residence Hall, Susan G. Linville Dining Hall, and Robert and Lois Coker Residence Hall. Picture taken c. 1916. By permission of Coker College.

Regarding the post-Civil War plight of Southern women, early Coker College student Mrs. Charles Kupfer commented:

> [When people] read *Gone with the Wind*, they... realize not only the lack of educational advantages [for] women in this great devastated South.... The hardships that women [had to] endure would have undermined much that was lovely and feminine, but by culture, that feminineness has been preserved [and] their character only enhanced in all of its beauty.... How farsighted was the Major when he gave us a college.[5]

Major Coker did not want the college to be named after Him, but J. J. Lawton, E. V. Baldy, and his board would accept no other name than Coker College.[6] The college was founded on the same property as the high school.

Shortly after the Major's death, Mattie Baker, class of 1914 and first president of the alumni association, wrote a poem as a memorial toast to the Major. It summarizes his reasons for founding the college. I will give two stanzas:

> In gratitude, we thank the man who
> opened life's doors with his hand.
> This man, with vision keen and strong,
> saw the mistakes of days bygone,
> That through the selfishness of man, few
> schools for southern girls were planned.
> Sharing the mind of Christ, whose love
> lifted woman far above her former state,
> He freely gave, the women of the
> state to save, from ignorance.
>
> Life's true foundation is based
> on Christian education.
> A noble man, with vision rare, he saw
> the need, his wealth did share,
> To train young women of our land to
> live and serve as God has planned.
> And thus uplift humanity, and
> build for all posterity.[7]

The Major prescribed that the college, like the high school, be distinctly Christian, but denominationally inclusive.[8] He established the college board of five, composed of two Baptist ministers and three ministers from other denominations.[9]

James's Generosity to the College

The Major's quiet liberality is illustrated in the following incident. Samuel W. Garrett observed: "When we made our first fiscal report, we found ourselves in debt to the extent of $9,000. Major Coker came over to the office, gave me a check for this amount, and asked that I not tell even the members of the Board of Trustees who paid off the account. Later he made many and generous gifts to the college in the same way."[10]

On one occasion, he gave $150,000,[11] to endow the college. This amount is the equivalent of just under 4.2 million dollars in 2020. It is not possible to know how much money the Major actually invested in the college, for he covered many deficits and made other gifts. But his most remarkable donations were the thought, love, and time he gave to the students.

Integrating Faith and Academics

The Major's vision was to provide the girls with a foundation of Christianity and a classical education. He was more educationally broad than some of his Baptist friends, and had a wider comfort zone regarding the acquisition and usefulness of so-called "secular" knowledge. He could think in many dimensions, and saw reason as an asset, rather than an adversary, to faith. Then, as now, some Christians tended to have a defensive posture when it came to alternate perspectives, even for the sake of study and growth. The Major met intellectual challenges head on and sifted out verifiable truth from abstract speculation. For example, with his scientific mind, he sifted through Darwin's *Origin of Species,* accepted the part about variations within a species, as demonstrated by the finches of the Galapagos, but James saw no reason to accept Darwin's larger conjectures of macroevolution across species. For more detail on his thoughts on this subject, see Appendix 5 (p. 283).

Mrs. Charles Kupfer, an early Coker College student, said: "He was well-read in many fields, including the ancient classics, biographies, Christianity and the Bible, science, history, music, poetry, and politics. He read one French book every year and could pick up a French newspaper and easily read it."[12] Throughout his life, the Major could also recite chemical formulas with exactness.

Reflecting the Major's vigorous mind, Coker College's academics were first-rate. His prescribed comprehensive curriculum ranged from the classic Greek philosophers to observational science in the laboratory, from trigonometry to advanced French and German, and from the study of the English novel to a robust classical music department of renown.

As a young man Major Coker had enjoyed vigorous intellectual development as president of the Polytechnic literary debate society at The Citadel. When he founded the college, he saw to it that the young women had similar opportunities to work out their minds in the arena of competing viewpoints. The Major founded dueling debate societies, the Phi Mu and Zeta Alpha, and he enjoyed watching their spirited debates.[13]

Under the Major's direction, the college catalogue and magazine, *The Euterpean*, prescribed the study of other

religions, yet wrote of the preeminence of Christ among them. The required comparative religion class was described as "a candid study of the non-Christian religions of the world—their origin, progress, influence, and elements of value. In contrast, the superior merits of Christianity will be pointed out."[14] Old

Major Coker in his garden, c. 1900. From Malcolm Doubles' book on Sonoco called *A Century Plus.* Used by permission.

and New Testament classes were also taught by believing professors, such as the Rev. E. V. Baldy, Dean of Faculty Samuel W. Garrett, and by Dr. E. W. Sikes, and these Bible classes were required for graduation.[15]

A statement printed after he died, which perfectly captures Major Coker's heart to integrate learning and faith, is found in the 1934 Coker College catalog. "[The college] insists not only that no incompatibility exists between learning and piety, but that in theory and practice, they cannot be disunited."[16]

He Left Students' Responses in God's Hands

As a student of history, the Major knew the tragedies of religious intolerance. It is clear that he intended for his students to hear the gospel of Christ, but it is equally clear he never tried to forcefully convert them. He left their responses to the gospel in God's hands, and in God's timing. He also left them free to choose their own religious denomination.

Knowledge and Truth

Unlike the agnostics of his day, the Major did not believe that truth is unknowable, elusive, or situational. In his farm journal, he wrote of the "truth" of "Adam's fall and punishment, in the history of Noah and the flood, in the lives of Abram and Isaac and Jacob, of Moses, and all the prophets and kings mentioned in the Bible."[17]

Religious Life

While not sectarian, a positive Christian influence will prevail. Daily devotional exercises will be held. Students will be required to attend church on Sunday. There are two Baptist churches, one Presbyterian, and one Methodist. The Episcopalians have a preaching service regularly twice a month, and contemplate the erection of a house of worship. Students will be allowed to attend the church of their choice, under suitable restrictions. Local pastors and visiting ministers of the various denominations will be frequently invited to take part in the chapel service and address the student-body thus assembled. It is expected that the

12	*Coker College for Women,*

students themselves will organize a Y. W. C. A. or some such society for Christian fellowship and service.

Coker College manual for 1909-1910, pages 11-12. Used by permission of Coker College.

He spoke confidently of objective truth, and the need to reach others with it: "Coker College does not exist for itself. It does not wish to confine its influence for good within the limits of its own walls, but rather to *hold the torch of truth* so high that its benignant light may shine afar into many a home and many a community."[18]

When the college's third president, Dr. Howard Lee Jones, suddenly died, the Major again referred to objective truth. Setting up a scholarship fund in Jones's name, he praised Lee's sound biblical leadership: "Good influences gain strength as they move into the currents of society. Otherwise, we might safely predict that the world will grow worse with the lapse of time, whereas we are confident that *truth is mighty and will prevail*"[emphasis in the original].[19] in life, Dr. Jones himself taught the primacy of biblical truth, saying, "It is wonderful how all the words of Jesus are contemporaneous. How all the words of invention are still led by the words of Jesus after two thousand years."[20]

The Major made sure that his Coker College seal, pictured here, declared the Christian foundations of the school. A symbol of his values, the seal graced the college class rings for forty-six years. At Major Coker's memorial service in 1937, held on the centennial of his birth, Mrs. Charles Kupfer said: "To us, Major Coker is a mighty bulwark for the three great C's: Character,

Original Coker College seal with the thee "Cs." From *A History of Coker College on its Centennial.* Used by permission of Coker College Press.

Christian service, and Culture, emblazoned on our college seal; and we will see that mighty bulwark like an Egyptian pyramid standing in the community."[21]

"Truth is Mighty and Will Prevail" in an Age of Agnosticism

The Major's sustained belief in the objective truth of Christianity and his full intention to found Coker College on the faith is all the more noteworthy considering he founded the college when skepticism was on the rise. At Harvard, James had been exposed to nascent Darwinian ideas in his botany classes with Professor Asa Gray, who became a theistic evolutionist.[22] James agreed with *Origin of Species* as far as microevolution within a given species, which Darwin had demonstrated with the various finch beaks in the Galapagos Islands. But when it came to Darwin's wider inferences of macroevolution from one species to another, James wrote his own answer to macroevolution in his Farm Journal, detailed in Appendix 5.

Darwin's idea that all reality is ultimately natural or material goes under several names: "macroevolution," "philosophical naturalism," "ontological naturalism," "anti-supernaturalism," "logical positivism," and sometimes simply "materialism." But whatever the Darwinian philosophy is called, let's not confuse it with natural history. In its pure form, natural history is the study of organisms, including animals, and plants, and fungi, apart from philosophy. This distinction is important because Major Coker enjoyed natural history, but was never a philosophical or ontological naturalist.

From about 1870 on, agnostic and atheistic "evangelists" – such as "Darwin's bulldog," Britain's Thomas Henry Huxley (1825-1895), "the great agnostic," New York's Robert Ingersoll (1833-1899), British academic atheist Bertrand Russell (1872-1970), and American lawyer Clarence Darrow (1857-1938) seized Darwin's theory as an opportunity try and impose the militant irreligion of the French Revolution and the radical side of the European Enlightenment onto Americans. They taught that humankind had "come of age," and that people were now too intelligent to accept "ignorant" ideas like original sin and the need for a Savior, and that Christianity should be abandoned.

Major Coker did not give credence to these agnostic intellectual fads as he founded his Christian schools. He understood eternal verities, and he understood his own times. They were attacking his God, his church, and his educational philosophy. James, confident in his God, did not become embittered, but as the leader he was, neither did he sit back and leave the self-appointed prophets of meaningless and despair unanswered.

William Jennings Bryan Speaks at Coker College

Major Coker and Dean of Faculty Samuel W. Garrett opened the door for William Jennings Bryan to speak on campus on June 19, 1911, as part of celebrating the completion of the college's new administration building, Davidson Hall[23]. Bryan was a leading Christian figure in the creation/evolution debate of the time. He was also a notable Democratic Congressman, and Secretary of State under Woodrow Wilson from 1913-1915.

Bryan gave his speech, "The Prince of Peace," to the crowded auditorium. This was one of the traveling lectures Bryan delivered at many educational gatherings around the world from 1904 to 1924.[24]

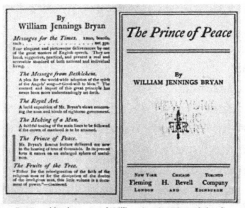

Front and back covers of William Jennings Bryan's book, *Prince of Peace* published by Revell, 1909, containing his "Prince of Speech" he gave worldwide, including at Coker College. Permission from Baker Publishing Group.

Among other things, Bryan said this about macroevolution (Darwin's "amoeba to Reba" theory):

"When the follower of Darwin has traced the germ of life back to the lowest form in which it appears – and to follow him, one must exercise more faith than religion calls for – he finds that scientists differ. Those who reject the idea of creation are divided into two schools, some believing the first germ of life came from another planet and others holding that it was the result of spontaneous generation. Each school answers the arguments advanced by the other, and as they cannot agree with each other, I am not compelled to agree with either."[25]

When he spoke at Coker College in 1911, Bryan still had his powers. When defending creation at the Scopes Monkey Trial in 1925, he did not, and he died just five days after that trial.

The First Four College Presidents

Major Coker knew the first four college presidents. E. V. Baldy, the scholarly minister of the First Baptist Church in Hartsville, served as the first president from 1908 to 1910. He put heart and soul into it; however, he was pastoring at the same time, and the double load became unsustainable. Seeing the need to search for a new president, he and the Major wrote "Qualifications for the President of Coker College." These qualifications, given in part below, describe the Major's desire for the school to integrate lively faith with real scholarship:

- Scholarship, culture, refinement, dignity, and pleasing address.
- Teaching ability and fondness for educational work.
- A positive religious conviction without narrowness or bigotry.
- An educational ideal and an educational program suited to a Christian college.
- Readiness to consecrate his very life for the cause of the college and Christian culture.

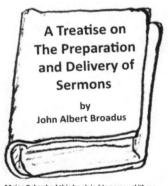

A Treatise on The Preparation and Delivery of Sermons

by
John Albert Broadus

The second college president, Dr. Arthur Jackson Hall, served from June 1911 to 1914 and wrote the school's first alma mater. The third, Dr. Howard Lee Jones, who previously pastored the Citadel

Major Coker had this book in his personal library and sometimes gave Coker College chapel messages.

Square Baptist Church in Charleston, took office in 1914. Some of the 1915 messages at Spivey Chapel in Memorial Hall from Dr. Jones' tenure are preserved in the Coker College archives, where dates for each message are given but not the name of the speaker. However, it is reasonable to assume that they were given by either President Jones or by Major Coker, who also gave chapel messages. Referring to the Major, the school's Dean, Samuel W. Garret said, "Both students and faculty always looked forward to his chapel talks."[26]

It is worth noting that the Major had a copy of John A. Broadus' *Preparation and Delivery of Sermons*.[27] Whether by President Jones or Major Coker, we do not know, but two extant chapel messages from 1915 are given in condensed form below.

COKER COLLEGE CHAPEL MESSAGES, 1915

January 8, 1915, entitled "Prayer"

Will God answer prayer? ...The thing is not whether God will hear us, but whether or not we will hear God. I want to say sincerely that you have never prayed unless you have in prayer heard God speak.... We leave no place for the voice of God. You remember Samuel in the stillness of the night he heard the voice of God calling, and Eli said to him, "And it shall be if He calls you, that you shall say, 'Speak, Lord, for Your servant is listening'" [1 Samuel 3:9]. Let me say that this conception of prayer gives a far more exalting idea of prayer.

If I should suddenly open that door and say that President Woodrow Wilson is going to come and say a word to you, all of you would be breathless and would listen with delight to what he said. Then think of having a God to listen to!

March 12, 1915, on Saul's Conversion and Life's Essentials

It begins with "Read Acts: 9ᵗʰ Chapter, 1-21." For brevity, only Acts 9:3-7 and 19 are given here:

"As he [Saul] was traveling, it happened that he was approaching Damascus, and suddenly a light from heaven flashed around him; and he fell to the ground and heard a voice saying to him, 'Saul, Saul, why are you persecuting Me?' And he said, 'Who are You, Lord?' And He said, 'I am Jesus whom you are persecuting, but get up and enter the city, and it will be told you what you must do.'

"Now for several days, he was with the disciples who were at Damascus, and immediately he began to proclaim Jesus in the synagogues, saying, 'He is the Son of God.'"

The speaker said: "I suppose if most of us were called upon to

Spivey Chapel, c. 1940. By permission of Coker College Archives.

talk about Saul, we would talk about the miraculous voice and the blindness, and the restoring of his sight. Those are the most obvious ones to us – those things which show changes in Saul's life...

"What was it that went all the way through Saul's life with him? What was it that was responsible for changing the standard of his living? Two things. One was that it made no difference whether or not the light

was little or big. 'Who are thou, Lord?' 'I am Jesus, whom you are persecuting...'

"The other thing was that Saul became conscious – he had a revelation to righteousness. You remember he said, 'What, Lord, wilt thou have me to do?'... We are not Christ, but Christ's. If I can do the thing God wants me to do, this is the thing that will transform my life. May God grant that all of us may find these essential things in life, rightly to direct our paths and ambitions and desires."[28]

Succeeding Jones after his untimely death, the fourth president, the Major's longtime friend, Dr. E.W. Sikes, provided stable academic and Christian leadership. Sikes was president of the college until 1925, and afterward, was president of Clemson from 1925-1940.[29]

Fun, Physical Fitness, Canoe Racing, and the Great Outdoors

Major Coker wanted his girls to have fun and to stay fit. He kept himself in shape by walking vigorously with his crutch. Samuel W. Garrett recalled how he wanted his girls to be well-rounded. "He

Canoeing on Black Creek, c. 1916.

gave the girls three beautiful little canoes to be used on Black Creek Lake. He built an indoor swimming pool, and otherwise encouraged physical sports."[30]

In 1919, the college girls organized a spirited intra-college canoe race, which has become a century-old tradition. They pitted a team from the freshman-junior classes against one from the sophomore-senior classes.[31] A similar race is still enthusiastically held on Prestwood Lake annually to this day.[32]

Former Coker history professor Robert R. Simpson likely referred to Coker College's canoeing team in the early decades when he wrote: "Miss Evelyn Snider, '28 recalled that during canoe season the crews would go to the lake every daybreak, practice for an hour or so, then return hungry and exhilarated to breakfast, which on Mondays meant bacon and apples."[33]

Carriage Rides, Picnic Lunches, and Botany Lessons

Nov. 7, 1914.

Miss Taylor McBride
    Hartsville, S. C.

Dear Miss McBride:·

        If you find it convenient I would like
to have a party consisting of one teacher and six
girls to go to ride this afternoon at three
o'clock. Please phone my residence (number 21)
about one o'clock whether this is agreeable to
you or not.

        Yours sincerely,

Note from Major Coker scheduling an afternoon buggy ride with Coker College girls.
C/o South Caroliniana Library, University of South Carolina, Columbia, SC.
The library's carbon copy was retyped by the author.

Carrie Lee Erwin Kalber, one of the early students, said that in her day, there were at least 150 students at the college, and the Major knew them all by name.[34] She fondly recalled how the Major took the college girls on picnics: "He would have his carriage and these wonderful lunches fixed. We didn't have sandwiches back in those days. He would have wonderful picnics with biscuits and ham—good things like that. He always

191

had a wonderful lunch and one of the places—always the favorite place—was the Cathedral of Pines over here across the creek..."[35]

In all his dealings with the women on the staff and the students, the Major followed 2 Timothy 5:2: "[Treat] the younger women as sisters, in all purity." Samuel W. Garrett said: "We all admired him for his sincerity, absolute honesty, and purity of thought and speech."[36]

Miss Josephine Erwin, Coker College class of 1909, also wrote of these outings: "About twice a week, Major Coker would take the college girls, in relays, out riding. He had a big carriage with three or four seats... Usually a faculty member went along too (the faculty wanted to go as much as the girls). Major Coker would drive out to some nice cool spot in the country. Then everybody would get out and have the best lunch that anybody ever had... This was one of the highlights of the year – to go to ride with the Major."[37]

The Major became a folk hero! Carrie Lee Erwin Kalber wrote: "The girls didn't get out much as they do now, and they always looked forward to getting out with him. He used to tell us stories about nature and birds.

Major Coker and his staff took Coker College girls on country picnic rides in his three seated "big buggy." Courtesy of Raleigh, NC professional artist Dan Nelson.

Everybody just listened to him with the greatest of interest. I have a song [called "To the Major"]... we used to sing on Founder's Day:

"To the Major," sung to the tune of "Bonnie Blue Flag." Written by Miss Lucy Dickerson, early Coker College English Teacher:

There was a little college that
said, "I believe I will grow;
I would really like to stretch myself—I
am too cramped up, you know.
And so it stretched until it filled
great buildings in a row;
Because you see, that college had
the Major help it grow.

Chorus:

A cheer, a cheer, the Major now we cheer!
For one and all, we're here to
state the Major is a dear.
Who takes us out on Monday,
for picnics and a drive?
Who built a great white swimming
pool where we can swim and dive?
And who has given us a chance
to paddle our own canoe?
Why, what do all these colleges that have no
Major do?[38]

Elsie Ellison of the Class of 1915 said of the picnics: "Major Coker busied himself helping the girls into the carriage while each of them peeped mischievously into the well-filled picnic basket."[39] Mrs. Josephine

The trailing arbutus, also known as the mayflower, which Major Coker loved. Permission granted by istockphoto.com.

Lawton Patterson remembered that "the Major used to take us out Sunday afternoons—there were just a few families here, and he'd father all the young people and take them out to the creek (now the lake), and he would explain the different flowers and the trailing arbutus [also known as the mayflower], and we'd have all these beautiful walks..."[40]

Major Coker's desire to teach others about nature was universal. Even his nurse, Lucy Drakeford Timmons, spoke of it: "I can recall his interest in nature, his love of birds that seemed to find a sanctuary in his garden. He made many efforts to teach me to recognize the different birds in their songs."[41]

In his desire to open up the wonders of creation, the Major annexed for the college Kalmia Gardens, the home and gardens once owned by early Hartsville planter Captain Thomas Edward Hart.[42] The Major's son D. R. Coker and his wife "Miss May" took great interest in it, and cultivated for the benefit of the college and the public, and it remains a beautiful spot to visit.

The College's Musical Emphasis

Major Coker was interested in the musical development of the young ladies. During 1918, his last year, Lucy Drakeford Timmons wrote: "I remember at least twice during this time that when recitals were given at the college, they were repeated at the Major's home. A girl would get through her part in the college auditorium, then be carried straight to repeat the performance for the Major. When one girl finished playing, another would be waiting, while all this time, the Major would be sitting there, perfectly delighted with his private performance."[43]

Sue Coker's Contributions, by Evelyn Snider

Evelyn Snider from Conway, SC, Coker class of 1928, who went on to become an English professor at Campbell College,[44] gave a speech at Coker in 1939 called "Coker Backstage." She elaborated on James's wife Sue's Christian foundations of the school and the college gardens:

> He [James and Sue's son Will Coker] told me of her practical Christianity that gave itself in sympathy, love, and help to all who needed her; her simplicity of life; of her love for flowers, the flower garden being her own special care while she left the vegetable garden to [the tending of] Major Coker. I understood then, the quiet fragrance that gave itself in all the Coker gardens—it was the breath of a Christian woman who had given herself in service.
>
> It is perhaps then due to Susan Stout Coker, the gardener, that we owe our Coker [College]… No mere words then are they that we bear on our fingers; it is not a happen[stance] that "Christian Service" should be written on our college seal at the very base of the administrative building. For Coker was founded on and for CHRISTIAN SERVICE [emphasis in original]. What a glorious heritage it is that Coker has never had to apologize for Christian service. Her faculty have been proud to represent Christian culture, to teach all truth as sacred, and to live the truth they teach. This, then, is Coker's backstage: the quiet, powerful Christian Service that is her heritage. [45]

Evelyn Snider's Warning

Snider believed that without its foundation built upon faith, Coker College would no longer thrive. She concluded her speech as follows:

> ... Can we then afford to compromise her tradition, to live for less than that purpose of Christian service for which she was conceived and nurtured, for which calling costly sacrifice has been made?
>
> Too much sacrifice has been made, too many hearts have been broken, too great a dream is being fulfilled, too significant a future unrolls for [those] who love the meaning of Coker to compromise her heritage and cut her roots. Cut flowers give charm and color and fragrance to a banquet table, but soon they are dead, leaving behind no life to beget life. Coker's roots are sacred; and unless we alumnae, the product of those roots, keep them growing, Coker will soon have an abundance of cut flowers, pretty, showy, colorful, fragrant, graceful transient things, then—nothing.[46]

Beautiful Brown House Gardens, c. 1929, reflective of the quality of Coker College Gardens. Here the returning bluebirds saluted the Major a week before he died. Joslin family archives.

Evelyn Snider's Warning Realized

In 1944, the college board removed the requirement that a majority of its board members be Baptists, but Coker continued to be a basically Christian school for a few more years. However, from 1947 to 1971, in spite of the objections of many, Evelyn Snider's warning was realized. Part of the responsibility for the slide belongs to the Christians, who, unlike Major Coker, failed to understand the times, failed to defend the faith intelligently, and failed to show how Christ was still relevant to all Americans as the country became more pluralistic.

The next crop of Coker College administrators did not align with the Christian purpose that the Major and the founders intended. They removed Major Coker's thoughtfully inscribed "Christian Service, Character, Culture" from most appearances of the college seal, eliminated campus chapel services, discontinued required Bible classes, and neglected Christian service. This happened in spite of what Major Coker had written on "The Mission of Coker College" in the very first volume of the *Euterpean*, on May 12, 1912:

> To render the most efficient service, it must never be forgotten that this college is for the education that is in harmony with *religion* [emphasized in the original]. All the Faculty will combine in efforts to advance this great feature of our college work. They will encourage and assist the students in the Young Women's Christian Association work and in other proper activities that pertain to the Christian life.[47]

Neglect of the college's Christian mission was no longer in doubt when Dr. Gus Turbeville became president from 1969 to 1974. He chose to embrace the rebellion, and even the anarchy, of the '60s and '70s and gave it prominence at the school. In its

October 18, 1969 article "Changes at Coker," Charleston's *News and Courier* commented on Turbeville's agenda:

> Dr. Gus Turbeville has announced that he will throw out the college's grading system, replacing it with an adaption of the pass-fail method... In an era of strict academic standards, when many students seek graduate degrees, it seems to us unwise to adopt a grading system favored in old-style "progressive" schools.
>
> Dr. Turbeville also expressed dissatisfaction with the conventional academic curriculum. He said Coker will make an effort to offer any field of study that the students desire: "Hindu spiritualism or the effects of smoking marijuana."[48]

Turbeville also removed all dress codes and all regulations on chaperones, sexual conduct, and alcohol. He also failed to speak out against student dissidents, even when they destroyed property.[49]

Contrast Turbeville's ideas with what the Major included as the college's "Spirit and Purpose" in the 1912 catalog: "There must be an emphasis on the refinement of the emotions, the formation of good habits, and the cultivation of high ideals. Culture, character, and Christian service are prominent among the educational ideals of Coker College." Also, compare Coker College during this period with Major Coker's words under "Religious Life" in the 1912 *Euterpean* magazine: "Nothing is left undone in order to make the atmosphere of the College morally wholesome and spiritually uplifting."[50]

Although not official until a few years later, the school also became coeducational in 1969. Mixed education is not a bad idea, but considering the rebellious tenor of this confusing period, perhaps the timing of this change was not the best. Things became so chaotic that on the Student Liaison Committee, many students felt the new administration had caused the chaos and wrote a long letter to the board. While commending a few of the changes, they complained about the immoral standards of conduct, the lack of academic standards, and the conflicts that existed between the newly adopted standards and the very values that had led them to attend the college in the first place.

The committee leader, Susan Weathers, herself a student, specifically lamented "the problem of men spending the night in the dormitory rooms of female students and the embarrassment of 'flagrant displays of intimate affection on campus in broad daylight' in the presence of elementary students attending the Junior School of Music."[51]

That same year, 1969, was the year that the Rolling Stones' song "Sympathy for the Devil" was playing on American rock stations, and among the lyrics: "I've been around for a long, long year, stole many a man's soul to waste."[52]

During the late sixties and early seventies, the college also removed all direct references to Christianity. Under "Character and Control," the 1971 catalog removed the word "Christian" and now stated: "Coker College is a small, independent, nonsectarian women's college of liberal arts." However, the catalog continued its new Christ-less description with a non-sequitur, "dedicated to the ideals of its founder, Major James Lide Coker."

Coker College Moves on to Greener Pastures

The 1970s are now behind us. Most people who admired the Major's faith and principles were glad to see the school move past this unsteady period. The college returned to stability under the next two presidents. Dr. C. Hilburn Womble

(1975-1980) brought in steadfast leadership with new hires, including Mr. Frank Bush from the College of Charleston, who served as admissions director for over 30 years, and Dr. Malcolm C.

Dr. Malcolm C. Doubles, Provost and Dean of Faculty, 1976-1997. C/o Coker College Archives.

Doubles, biblical scholar and author with a Ph.D. from Saint Andrews University in Scotland. Doubles served as Provost and Dean of Faculty from 1976 to 1997 and is now Provost Emeritus. Following Womble, Dr. James D. Daniels, with a Ph.D. from UNC, was president for twenty-one years (1981-2002), the longest term of any Coker president. James D. Daniels' daughter, Dr. Susan Daniels Henderson, is presently serving as Coker's Provost and Dean of the Faculty. Following the tenure of James D. Daniels, Dr. B. James Dawson (2002-2009) and Dr. Robert L. Wyatt (2009-2019) presided over the school until 2019.

Today, many of the current Coker faculty, staff, and alumni continue to respect the Major's principles and do their part to preserve his intentions and legacy. The university has academic freedom, freedom of religion, and freedom of speech across campus for those of any persuasion. Local churches, such as Saint Bartholomew's Anglican (to whom Major Coker donated the land in 1904) and Saint Mary's Catholic, continue to have a presence on campus. Christian groups such as the Baptist Collegiate Ministry, the Fellowship of Christian Athletes, Because Christ Matters, Greater Grace, The Gospel Choir, and others freely meet on campus.

Coker Recognized as a High-Value School

For decades, *U.S. News & World Report* has consistently rated Coker College as one of the top educational values. In 2018, *The Princeton Review* and *Washington Monthly* joined *U.S. News and World Report* in naming Coker as one of the Southeast's "best bang for the buck" colleges.[53]

The School's Business Emphasis Goes Back to Major Coker

In the *U.S. News* article, under the school's most popular majors, the first ones listed are Business Administration and Management and General Business/Commerce.[54] This successful business legacy draws upon a deep well, going back to Major Coker himself, and for further study and growth, I have included Questions on the Major and Business / Economics in the discussion question sets at www. willjoslin.com/major/questions/business. Perhaps they can supplement business studies.

Today Coker also offers a variety of internships ranging from business management to criminology to physical education and more. Graduates often secure jobs with top companies. On a tour of Sonoco Products in 2018, I met a young man who, after studying graphic design at Coker, had had no trouble landing a design job at Sonoco, one of the world's best places to work.

Coker College Becomes Coker University

Coker offered its first graduate program in May 2012, and the graduate school has grown steadily, offering at least five master's degrees, including: MS in College Athletic Administration, M.Ed. in Literacy Studies, M.Ed. in

Curriculum and Instructional Technology, MS in Criminal and Social Justice Policy, and MS in Management and Leadership.

As of the summer of 2019, the college upgraded its name to Coker University, but is still a private institution. In December of 2018, ABC News did a piece on Coker's transition from college to university. In an interview with then-president, Dr. Robert Wyatt, he made it clear that the intention was still to keep the college's small-town feel that it had in the Major's day. "Although we are updating our name to reflect… new graduate degrees and our significant online presence, we are committed to retaining the essence of the close-knit community we have always been, [one] that has led to our national recognition as a leading innovation institution in the Southeast."[55]

Coker University's New President as of June 2020

As of June 1, 2020, Dr. Natalie Harder, formerly Chancellor of South Louisiana Community College (SLCC), was chosen as Coker's new president. Dr. Harder is Coker's first female president. She has served in numerous leadership positions in support of higher education and economic development, and is committed to expanding

Dr. Natalie Harder, Coker University President as of June 1, 2020.

student opportunity and success at Coker. She prioritizes building a culture of excellence and integrity with community engagement.[56] Dr. Harder said: "I look forward to honoring Coker's many traditions while moving the university to new levels of innovation and success."[57]

ENDNOTES FOR CHAPTER 12: COKER COLLEGE

1 Malcolm C. Doubles, op. cit., pp. 20-21, as he quotes from the Coker College archives.

2 *Euterpean*, Series Two, Number One, January 1912, p. 8.

3 Mrs. Charles. Kupfer, *Centennial Celebration*, p. 30.

4 Tom E. Goodson, *Recollections*, p. 48.

5 Mrs. Charles Kupfer, *Centennial Celebration*, p. 31.

6 Miss Josephine Erwin, *Recollections*, p. 48.

7 Mattie Baker, Coker College class of 1914, became the first president of the Coker College Alumnae Association in 1915. The exact date of the toast given by her was unclear in the Coker College Archive files, but it was probably given at the reception at the college on *Founder's Day, April 9, 1919*, the first Founder's Day after Major Coker's death.

8 George Lee Simpson, op. cit., p. 178, as he quoted Major Coker's letter to A. J. Hall, April 25, 1914 (R.G. Coker).

9 Malcolm C. Doubles, op. cit., p. 22.

10 Samuel W. Garrett, op. cit., p. 1

11 Coker College Balance Sheet, June 1912, found in Coker family files, courtesy of South Caroliniana Library, University of South Carolina, Columbia, SC.

12 Mrs. Charles Kupfer, *Centennial Celebration*, op. cit., p. 30, and see also Susan Coker Watson, quoting J. W. Norwood in *Recollections*, p. 94.

13 Josephine Erwin wrote of the Coker College debating societies in, *Recollections*, p. 57. Thomas Law wrote of those at the Citadel in his Citadel Journal as that was reprinted by John Adder Law, op. cit., p.41.

14 Elma Stith, editor in chief, Coker College's magazine, *Euterpean*, Series Two, Number Two, June 1912, op. cit. p. 50.

15 Ibid, pp. 30: "Bible Studies are provided for in the requirements of graduation," and pp. 44-46 list Bible literature classes, including New Testament, the Old Testament, and the Hebrew Poets.

16 Coker College Catalog, Office of Academic Records, Hartsville, SC, 1934, under section on "Spirit and Control." The same statement is also found in the 1935 and 1936 catalogs.

17 James Lide Coker, Farm Journal, op. cit., pp. 28-29.

18 Coker College Catalog, 1913, p. 35

19 Major Coker's Personal Papers, The Caroliniana archives storage system. Courtesy of South Caroliniana Library, University of South Carolina, Columbia, SC.

20 Chapel Messages of Coker College, found in the Coker College archives. Though the extant copy does not have Dr. Howard Lee Jones'

name attached to it, the message is dated February 26, 1915 when Jones was President, and in the same message, he mentions having his office on campus.

21 Mrs. Charles. Kupfer, op. cit., p. 33.

22 Editors, Brittanica.com, 1998, 2020 article "Asa Gray, American Botanist," https://www.britannica.com/topic/Hall-of-Fame-for-Great-Americans.

23 Editor, Bishopville, SC's *Leader and Vindicator* newspaper, "Local Items," Thursday, June 11, 1911, Vol. 10, No. 1 p. 1.

24 William Jennings Bryan, "The Prince of Peace" speech at http://trisagionseraph.tripod.com/Texts/Prince.html (accessed December 29, 2019), and the *Prince of Peace* book cover graphic at https://archive.org/details/princeofpeace00brya/page/n8 (accessed December 29, 2019).

25 Ibid.

26 Samuel W. Garrett, Dean of Coker College and Professor of Math, Education, and other subjects, in papers from the early days of Coker College, courtesy of South Caroliniana Library, University of South Carolina, Columbia, SC, Letter 2, p. 4.

27 See list of the Major's books in Appendix 2 (p.259).

28 From the Charles W. and Joan S. Coker Library-Information Technology Center, archives box on James Lide Coker containing some of the chapel messages from 1915, Coker College, Hartsville, SC.

29 Editor, ClemsonWiki, November 12 2013 article "List of Presidents of Clemson," https://clemsonwiki.com/wiki/List_of_Presidents_of_Clemson (accessed December 29, 2019).

30 Samuel W. Garrett, Coker Files at the South Caroliniana Library, University of South Carolina, Columbia, South Carolina, from his second letter, p. 3.

31 Robert R. Simpson, A Century of Education: *Welsh Neck High School and Coker College*, (Coker College and R. L. Bryan presses: Hartsville, SC), 1994, p. 14.

32 Coker University website, "Hazel Keith Sory Clubhouse and Boathouse," https://www.coker.edu/offices-services/campus-grounds/facilities/campus-life/clubhouse-boathouse/ (accessed December 29, 2019).

33 Robert R. Simpson, op. cit., p. 14.

34 Carrie Lee Erwin Kalber, *Recollections*, p. 46.

35 Ibid., pp. 44-45.

36 S. W. Garrett, Dean of Coker College and professor of Math, Education, and other subjects, letter in papers from the early days of Coker College, op cit., p. 4.

37 Miss Josephine Erwin, *Recollections*, p. 53.

38 Carrie Lee Erwin Kalber, Ibid., pp. 45-46.

39 Mrs. Elsie Ellison, Coker College class of 1915, in her talk "Major Coker Eulogized" at the Alumnae Luncheon of Coker College, June 1, 1936, p. 1. Courtesy of Coker College archives.

40 Mrs. Josephine Lawton Patterson, *Recollections*, p. 102.

41 His nurse Lucy Drakeford Timmons, *Recollections*, p. 135.

42 John Britton Boney, profile manager, WikiTree, 2018 article (updated 2019), "Thomas Edward Hart (1796-1842)," https://www.wikitree.com/wiki/Hart-10755 (accessed December 29, 2019).

43 Ibid, p. 133.

44 See Coastal Carolina University's 2020 article "Evelyn Mayo Snider" at https://www.coastal.edu/aboutccu/historytraditions/founders/honorees/evelynsnider/ (accessed December 29, 2019).

45 Evelyn Snider, Coker College Class of 1928, in her 1939 speech entitled "From Coker Backstage," Box 2 of the James Lide Coker Collection, courtesy of South Caroliniana Library, University of South Carolina, Columbia, SC, pp. 1-3.

46 Ibid., pp. 2-3.

47 Under "The Mission of Coker College," *Euterpean*, Vol. 1, No. 1, May 1912, p. 3.

48 "Changes at Coker," News and Courier, October 18,1969, p. A-10, as quoted in Malcom C. Doubles' book, A Century of Excellence, op. cit., p. 97.

49 Ibid.

50 Under the introductory section, "Religious Life," *Euterpean*, May 1912, pages in this section were not numbered.

51 Ibid., p. 98.

52 The Rolling Stones, "Sympathy for the Devil," *Beggars' Banquet* album, Olympic, London, 1968.

53 Editor, Coker University's site referring to recent review at https://www.Coker.edu/?s=princeton.

54 Editor, US News, 2018 article "Best Colleges, US News Rankings," Coker College, Coker College Academics, https://www.usnews.com/best-colleges/coker-college-3427/academics (accessed December 29, 2019).

55 Tonya Brown, ABC15NEWS, 2018 article "Coker College Has a New Name," https://wpde.com/news/local/Coker-college-has-a-new-name (accessed December 29, 2019).

56 Summarized from an announcement by Angie Stanland, chairman of Coker University Board of Trustees, May 7, 2020

Coker University web article, "Coker University names Dr. Natalie Harder as its 17th President," http://blogs.coker.edu/news-stories/coker-university-names-dr.-natalie-harder-as-its-17th-president.

57 Ibid, quoting from Dr. Harder.

CHAPTER 13

CONFEDERATE SOLDIER REUNIONS, SOUTHERN HISTORY AND SOUTHERN HOSPITALITY

James fervently loved his Hartsville Civil War compatriots, for they had been, almost literally, through hell and back together. The managers of his general store knew that "there was always credit beyond the usual limits for members of Company E."[1]

E. W. Sikes observed: "Major Coker loved the Bonnie Blue Flag [the unofficial banner of the Confederate States, with one white star on a blue background] and preserved his company's flag in a casket. He loved his comrades who fought with him, but his spirit was too magnanimous to cherish rancor."[2]

Confederate Soldiers' Reunion Dinner at the Major's House, c. 1909.

First row left to right: James Culpepper, Nelson Stucky, John C. McIntosh, D. Durant, J.E. Polson, Capt. E.W. Cannon, Major James Lide Coker, H.E.C. Fountain, J. Brock King, E.W. Boswell, John H. Kelly, Capt. Zimmerman.

Second Row left to right: McLeod, Thomas G. McLeod, James L. Coker, Jr., Rev. A.T. Dunlap, David R. Coker, Col. Rhames, Rev. Thomas Henderson, H. Lide Law, Robert Wiley, R.T. Howle, Joe Brunson, J.F. Howle. Picture from *Recollections* book, permission of Hartsville Museum.

On the last page of his 1899 book, *History of Company G and E,* Major Coker said: "It cannot be expected that we old Confederates will ever cease to love the Starry Cross of the South under which we fought, or that we will ever rejoice at our failure to establish the Confederate States of America. It is enough to require of us, that having suffered the destruction of our dearest hopes, we shall henceforth loyally support the Government of the United States, and shall honestly assist in whatever promises to promote the nation's usefulness and greatness.... There is one great result of the War Between the States for which we are truly thankful: *Slavery is abolished.*"[3]

With help from James Jr.'s energetic and socially oriented wife Vivien, the Major and Sue hosted regular Confederate reunions. Beyond the reunions, Vivien said that Major Coker wanted his home to be a "social center."[4] Miss Josephine Erwin, Coker College class of 1909, added: "Major Coker was always the life of the party and was always so interested in everybody."[5]

Adaptive Hospitality

James bent over backwards to make his guests feel welcome. He made sure his gatherings were about user-friendly, if imprecise, hospitality. For example, Mrs. J. L. Harrison wrote:

Home of Major James Lide and Susan Coker on East Home Ave. Unfortunately, it burned in 1922. By permission of Hartsivlle Museum.

It seems that Major Coker, about once a year, would entertain some of the friends of his Company at a dinner or luncheon at his home there at Hartsville. At this particular time, finger bowls [meant for rinsing the hands after dessert] were in use. One old fellow from out of somewhere – not used to finger bowls – picked up his and drank out of it. And Major Coker in his sweet way, not wanting to hurt anyone, took up his and drank out of it, too.[6]

Mrs. Lucile Segars Kerfoot commented, "Later someone asked him why he did that and he said that in his mind, the greatest of all the arts of entertaining was to make a person feel at home."

Regarding another Confederate reunion, Mrs. William Egleston recalled a light moment:

> Vivien Coker said that every year about June, the Major would tell her he wanted his old soldiers to come and have dinner with them. Just as long as he lived, he would collect these people and have them for dinner.
>
> Mrs. Coker said she had run out of anything to have and didn't know what to have for dessert. She decided to play a trick on him. You know, he was against any form of liquor. She had blackberry cobbler and stand-up sauce on which she poured a generous amount of homemade wine... So the stand-up sauce lived up to its name – it really stood up! She said that the old men sent that plate back for the second helping – every one of them.[7]

After dinner, the Major said, "Vivien, that was a delicious dessert you had today. I would like to know how you made it." She told him just how she made it – only left out the wine ingredient, so he was very well pleased with it and didn't know he'd had a joke played on him.[8] Interestingly, the Major's daughter Susan Coker Watson added: "Father was no teetotaler! He was very temperate, and we always had wine in our house."[9] However, it must be stated that Major

Major Coker on the veranda of his home, c. 1904. From here he saw York return. From *Recollections of the Major,* permission of Hartsville Museum.

Coker drew the line when it came to hard liquor and did not partake of it. He also saw to it that the city charter stated that strong liquor could not be sold in Hartsville.[10] This was the law until well after he died.

Historian and Author

James genuinely enjoyed the fun at social gatherings, but to him, the reunions represented more than good times with old friends. His interest in the history of his region ran deep.

Letterhead of the Pee Dee Historical Assoc. indicating that James Lide Coker was then president. From Coker College Archives. Used by permission.

The Major was an author and published *Hartsville and its early Settlers,* along with *History of Company G and E,* the adventures of his Pee Dee company during the Civil War. He was also a member of the Southern Historical Association, the American Historical Association, and the American Institute of Civics.[11] In 1903, he and local businessman Bright Williamson founded the Pee Dee Historical Association[12] (today called the Pee Dee Historical Society), of which the Major was president for many years.

The Most Remarkable Reunion

In about 1913, another reunion occurred during a moment when the Major and his son Will Coker were enjoying a leisurely moment on the Major's veranda. Will told the story as follows:

> Suddenly, Father looked up with interest to the entrance gate and said: "Why, William, I believe that is old York coming in there!" [He had not seen York since the Battle at Lookout Mountain in 1863.] We sat quietly watching old York ambling slowly up the 75 or 100 yards that separated us from the road. He came to the steps and leaned against the post. Looking up at Father, he said, "Marse James, you remember me, don't you?"

After 50 years, York returns to James, who gladly gave him employment.
Picture by Raleigh, NC artist Dan Nelson. Used by permission.

Father said, "Yes, I remember you very well. You are York." "Well, Marse James, you remember how we promised each other to always take care of each other as long as we lived?" Father said, "Yes, York, I remember very well, and if you need my help, I'll take care of you now."

From that time forth, York was a member of our group. Father gave him a place to live and fed him from our kitchen. The only duty he had to perform was to be down at the paper mill about a mile away and hitch Father's horse for him in the mornings. York after a while became such a nuisance around the kitchen that one of the servants asked Father to please do something about it. Father then sent him to Society Hill, where he kept his promise by supporting him for the rest of his life.[13]

At the national archives, I sought out more information on York, such as his full name and family records – as well as what happened to him between becoming a freedman in 1863 until his reunion with the Major in 1915 – but was unable to discover anything further. If the reader has additional information on York, please contact me through WestBow Press.

ENDNOTES FOR CHAPTER 13: CONFEDERATE SOLDIER REUNIONS, SOUTHERN HISTORY AND SOUTHERN HOSPITALITY

1 Simpson, op. cit., p. 183.
2 E. W. Sikes, *Centennial Celebration,* op. cit., p. 18.
3 James Lide Coker, *History of Company G and E,* op. cit., p. 210.
4 Vivien Coker, *Recollections,* pp. 105-106.
5 Josephine Erwin, *Recollections,* p. 103.
6 Mrs. J. L. Harrison, *Recollections,* p.100.
7 Mrs. William Egleston, *Recollections,* p. 100.
8 Ibid.
9 Susan Coker Watson's footnote to the anecdote on the "stand-up sauce," courtesy of South Caroliniana Library, University of South Carolina, Columbia, SC.
10 Leon Coker, *Recollections,* p. 36.
11 Editor, *The National Cyclopedia of Biography,* vol. 17, op. cit., p. 22.
12 See Appendix 2 of this book, which lists Major Coker's personal library, including dozens of works on Southern and United States history. The Major was also a member of the Darlington County Historical Society.
13 W. C. Coker, *Recollections,* p.11.

PART V

BROADCASTING HIS IMPACT:
PASSING ON HIS PRINCIPLES

CHAPTER 14

SUE AND THE MAJOR'S FINAL YEARS

A Tribute to Sue

Kate Chambers spoke of her Aunt Sue Coker's genuine and winsome qualities:

Susan (Sue) Armstrong Stout Coker, James's wife. Picture is in the public domain.

Her frankness, her deep piety, generosity, hospitality, and cheerfulness were all bound together by love, which was her watchword all through life... The music of the piano and her birdlike voice, which she gave generously to her neighbors, friends, her family—and above all, to her beloved husband—was like a clear mountain stream that ran refreshingly through all of her life... Her lovely voice was heard in the Sabbath School, where she had a class, and in the little country church, with its meetings only twice a month, and I have often wondered how many hearts have been uplifted and rested by this gift of hers.[1]

Like her husband, Sue was passionately helped others learn to read and learn the Bible basics. Up until about 1985, many in Hartsville still remembered her fondly as the one who taught them to read in Sunday school class.[2]

Sue's two great joys in life were God's work and the sweet relationship she had with the husband she so admired. Frank R. Chambers remembered:

The greatest influence for good in [the Major's] life was that of his devoted Christian wife. Her estimate of his character was expressed when once asked what was her ideal of earthly happiness, she replied, "To have spent forty years with James." [In the end, they were married 44 years.][3]

Kate Chambers also told of her conscientious care for the needy as Hartsville grew:

With increasing industries and increasing business came many new people. It was her mission to minister to the sick and the afflicted, the poor, the needy, and the lonely, and with frank sincerity, she counseled, admonished, and reproved those who needed her help. Her aim was to win precious souls to Christ. As her health failed, much of her work was given into the capable hands of... her daughter, but her patience and Christian fortitude and her desire for the welfare and betterment of those about her never slackened.

All through those years, her steadfast faith in Christ, her deep practical interest in everything good, was an inspiration and support to her husband. The time came in the summer of 1904 that she went to receive her reward from her beloved Master.

During her last several years, she had a heart problem and frequent headaches. The Major remained very considerate and attentive to her. Toward the end, her daughter Jennie and their daughter-in-law Vivien maintained her household affairs and filled in the area of hospitality. In this way, Coker College gatherings were able to continue in the Major's home for many years.

Sue's Departure

Jennie wrote this ode at her mother's death in 1904:

> You beautiful Mother, if I might only put some of your charm into stories, your humor and above all, your love of people, your self-effacing interest in all with whom you come in contact, your genuine good will, common sense, and a merriness that made use of the slightest pretext to scatter about your whole soul, and your irresistible laughter. [4]

A few years after her death, Major Coker dedicated Memorial Hall at Coker College to Sue. J. E. Norment of the *News and Courier* wrote:

There is one feature [of Coker College] that had a tender and holy meaning for this man whose love and thoughtfulness was exemplified always. Memorial Hall, one of the most elaborate and artistically built of the college appointments, is a memorial to his wife, Susan Stout Coker. This noble woman was all that a mother and wife could be, sharing in all things the full life lived in this household, and while her memory lives in all that he wrought, it has its own beauty and lasting remembrance dedicated entirely to her lovely life in this artistic and imposing building.[5]

After the dedication, Major Coker told Kate Chambers, "All that is best in my life, I owe to her influence."[6]

Evelyn Snider summed up Sue's fragrant life as follows:

A woman worked with God on her knees, and her garden grew, filling the world with the fragrance of roses, kalmias, and sweet olive. A woman prayed, and a college was born whose spirit was strong to teach young women how to live. And like the garden, the roots of the college go deep, down to the eternal verity of: "Whosoever would become great among you shall be your minister; and whosoever would be first among you shall be your servant..."[7]

Discussion questions for women drawn from Sue Coker's legacy may be found at https://willjoslin.com/major/questions/women.

The Major's Last Years and Departure

When Sue died in 1904, Major Coker was 67. He was aware he was getting older but continued to work hard with the college and in leading and advising his various companies. Simpson wrote, "There was no evident falling off in his capacity to do several jobs well."[8] In 1910, James said, "Whatever we old folks find in our hearts to contribute must be attended to without delay."[9] He was conscious of the need to continue to pass the baton of business, academic, and church leadership, which he did.

James Jr. was appointed chief engineer, Paul Rogers, secretary and treasurer, and Charles Westfield Coker, his youngest son, was assigned the position of CEO. Charles served very capably in this position from 1918 to 1931.[10] Simpson added, "These things took several years, and the Major was quite active in the affairs of these companies until he was well past his seventy-fifth birthday."[11]

A few years later, he began having a series of strokes, but was still articulate. Mary Lucia Mobley, Coker College's student body president, wrote that on Major Coker's 81st birthday, "The student body went over as a whole to his home... and presented him with American Beauty roses on his birthday. It was a beautiful sight to see him in front of his home with the students gathered around to wish him well. How happy he was – I can see him now, and how he responded."[12]

During his last couple of years, Major Coker got around in his "rolling chair." Photo from *Recollections of the Major.*

The Major remained active in business and church until his final stroke and illness. Nurse Lucy Drakeford Simmons said, "As long as Major Coker was physically equal to it, he was always faithful in his church attendance." He had a cheery, happy disposition, and even as he grew weaker, he never complained. He was not confined to his bed except during the last few weeks.[13]

At the Centennial Celebration of Major Coker's birthday in 1937, Howard Reaves, pastor of Hartsville's First Baptist Church, read 2 Timothy 4:7-8 to describe his life: "I have fought the good fight, I have finished the course, I have kept the faith; henceforth there is laid up for me the crown of righteousness, which the Lord, the righteous judge, shall give to me at that day; and not to me only, but also to all who have loved His appearing."[14]

Shortly after Major Coker died, the following was recorded in the church minutes:

> The First Baptist Church of Hartsville wishes to record on its records its appreciation of the services of Major James Lide Coker whose death occurred on June 25, 1918. From the early days of this church, he was actively connected with it as superintendent of Sunday School and as a deacon. He was deeply interested in the affairs of the church and in all its kingdom activities. This church was blessed by his noble, upright life, his willing service, and his gentle, devout spirit.[15]

These minutes were signed by E. W. Sikes, church deacon and president of Coker College, Pastor E. V. Baldy, and church clerk J. W. McIntosh.

The Major's thoughts often turned toward heaven, his true home. One of his favorite hymns about going to heaven was "On Jordan's Stormy Banks." On Sunday evenings, he could often be heard singing it on the porch of his home while visiting with his sons and his friends.[16]

On Jordan's stormy banks I stand
And cast a wishful eye
To Canaan's fair and happy land,
Where my possessions lie.

All over those wide extended plains,
Shines one eternal day;
There God the Son forever reigns
And scatters night away.

Chorus: I am bound (I am bound)
I am bound for the promised land;
I am bound (I am bound)
I am bound for the promised land.

Bluebirds Salute Major Coker at His Departure

The winters of 1915 to 1917 in Darlington County were unusually cold. The Major had not seen his friend the bluebird in three years and was afraid they would never return. In June 1918, his last trip outdoors was to cross the street in his rolling chair to inspect an old bluebird nest.[17] Mrs. D. R. (May) Coker recalled the wonder of it: "I remember the last time

The bluebird returned to Hartsville after a three year absence to salute Major Coker a week before his departure from this life. Permission granted by istock photo.com.

he ever came into our garden. There had been some severe snowstorms for several winters, and the bluebirds had not come for several years, for they had been killed out by these exceptionally long periods of cold weather. The second year after we had moved into this house, a bluebird made a nest in a rotten tree down in the garden. David excitedly went over to tell his father that a bluebird's nest was in the garden. Right after lunch, even before he had had his nap, the Major came over to rejoice over the return of the bluebirds… We all sat quite a while and were fortunate enough to see the birds work on the new nest."[18]

That's the kind of tender heart the Major had. It's as if the only thing on his "bucket list" was to see the bluebirds return to Hartsville. About a week after his gratification at their return, Major Coker went home to be with the Lord on June 25, 1918. He was buried next to Sue in the cemetery of First Baptist Church.

The Funeral

In *A Century Plus*, Malcolm Doubles recorded that the Major's funeral was attended by "one of the most distinguished assemblies of that size in the Carolinas."[19] Among those who joined his family were leading businessmen, scientists, college professors, and government leaders of the early twentieth century.

Pastor E. V. Baldy said at the funeral: "He was a mirror of politeness, most courteous in conversation, deferential in manner, magnanimous in spirit. He also delighted in the law of the Lord and so was 'like a tree planted by the rivers of water that bringeth forth his fruit in his season' [Psalm 1: 2-3]. For on this spiritual tree might be seen the ever-ripening fruits of the Spirit of God."[20]

In the *Cyclopedia of American Biography*, we find this tribute:

> Major Coker's career was one to command admiration and respect. Emerging from a Federal prison lamed for life and penniless, by dint of perseverance, wisdom, and integrity, he became a notable figure in the state. He was characterized

by energy, promptness, dignity, reverence, tolerance, and charity, discharging fully every obligation, adhering rigidly to principle, he was unmoved by personal danger. He spoke evil of no one, noted the best in everyone, and of everyone, expected the best; he was self-sufficient and a tower of strength, yet he was neither opinionated, self-assertive, nor dictatorial. He was kind to animals, gentle to his servants, loved birds and flowers, and was profoundly interested in many scientific subjects.[21]

Dr. W. L. Byerly of Hartsville once said: "This town [Hartsville] grew under the observation and influence of a man trained in science, a lover of nature and things beautiful, a businessman and a Christian man... We have, because of the beautiful character and high standards of its founder, a town of culture and of happy people."[22]

The day after the Major died, B. Pressley Smith of Southern Baptist Theological Seminary in Louisville, Kentucky, wrote this letter of condolence to J. J. Lawton:

Dear Mr. Lawton:

It is with much sadness that I learn of the departure of our friend, Major Coker.... We shall miss him much, and we cannot but join with John the Seer, as he writes: 'Happy are the dead who die in the Lord henceforth; yea, says the Spirit, that they may rest from their labors, for their works follow with them' [Revelation 14:13, KJV].

Sincerely Yours, B. Pressly Smith[23]

ENDNOTES FOR CHAPTER 14: SUE AND THE MAJOR'S FINAL YEARS

1   Kate Chambers, op. cit., p. 78.
2   Vivien Coker, *Recollections*, p. 60.
3   Frank R. Chambers, op. cit., p. 60, and Kate Chambers, op. cit., p. 79.
4   Susanne Gay Linville, *Jennie: A Biography of Jennie Coker Gay* (no publisher is named), 1983, p. 13.
5   J. E. Norment, *News and Courier*, June 30, 1918, found in Coker College archives.
6   Kate Chambers, op. cit., p. 141.
7   Evelyn Snider, Coker College Class of 1928, in her 1939 speech entitled "From Coker Backstage," Box 2 of the James Lide Coker Collection, courtesy of South Caroliniana Library, University of South Carolina, Columbia, SC, p. 3.
8   Simpson, op. cit., p. 173, as he quotes from Major Coker to Major J. J. Lucas, January 12, 1910.
9   Ibid.
10 Ibid., p. 174
11 Ibid.
12 Mary Lucia Mobley (Mrs. T. E. McAlpine), *Recollections*, p. 58.
13 His nurse Lucy Drakeford Timmons, *Recollections*, p. 135.
14 Coker College Quarterly Bulletin, op. cit., p. 8
15 E. W. Sikes, who signed the first of three signatures, First Baptist Church of Hartsville, Minutes, for September 15, 1918, as found on microfilm from the Baptist archives at Furman University.
16 Paul Rogers, *Recollections*, p.105.
17 Mabel Montgomery, op. cit.
18 Miss May Coker, *Recollections*, p. 125.
19 Malcolm Doubles, *A Century Plus*, op. cit., p. 8.
20 Pastor E. V. Baldy, Funeral Service of James Lide Coker, First Baptist Church, op. cit.
21 *The Cyclopedia of American Biography*, op. cit., p. 22.
22 Dr. W. L. Byerly, *Centennial Celebration*, op. cit., p. 11.
23 Coker College archives. This letter of sympathy regarding the Major's death from B. Pressley Smith of the Southern Baptist Theological Seminary to J. J. Lawton was added in as the last page of the memorial speeches given on Founder's Day, April 9, 1919, concerning Major James Lide Coker. The letter is dated June 26, 1918.

CHAPTER 15

THE MAJOR'S PERSONAL CHARACTER QUALITIES CONSIDERED

The Major's Shortcomings

In this final chapter, we will sum up the characteristics of this astonishing man. But before we describe his exemplary qualities, a bit of realism is in order. Like any human, he fell short in some areas.

He Owned Slaves for Eight Years

For eight years James made use of ten or twelve slaves, which his father gave him, and though I believe he reluctantly received them from his father, this was plainly wrong. Whether from the pressure of his father's expectations, or for whatever reason, James Lide Coker made use them on his Hartsville farm for four years before he went to the Civil

War, and four more years if we count his time away at war. Aside from that aberration, the entirety of his life shows that James was not a harsh, abusive, or prejudiced man. In fact, as a racial progressive, he was just the opposite, and <u>Appendix 4</u> (p. 269) on <u>How Major Coker Grew Beyond the Mindset of the Old South</u>, covers his rapid and progressive growth in detail, with documentation.

He Taught His Children by Example, but was too Sparse with Instruction

Major Coker fell short in the area of teaching in his home. While he was glad to verbally instruct his Sunday School students, he was too subtle in his household, and his children lamented that he chose to teach them almost entirely by modeling. Will Coker said" "Father himself never talked to us about religion."[1] This verbal reticence is peculiar, but I think the most probable explanation is that the Major and Sue bore their children between 1861 and 1879, which means part of each child's growing up years was while their father wrestled with his period of doubt, c. 1879-1894. Still, his reticence to advise them seems to be a significant shortcoming.

George Lee Simpson, Jr. described it this way: "It was a matter of occasional exasperation to the children that he taught them almost wholly by example."[2]

Susan wrote, "When it became time for us to go off to college, Father refused to advise us. He agreed readily to send us to whatever college we ourselves selected. I often wished for much more advice from my father than he was willing to give me."[3]

His son D. R. put it this way:

> Major Coker was not a man who taught by precept. Scarcely at all would he lecture to his children or those who worked for him or with him. He felt that right-minded persons should, by right observations and their own inner knowledge, know how to behave and how to act. I cannot remember that my father ever gave me a lecture. That may surprise some of you, but the nearest he ever came to giving me a lecture was when I stepped into the buggy to go to college. And all he said then was, "Son, always remember that you are a gentleman."[4]

The reader is to be commended if, without checking this endnote,[5] he or she can recall, from earlier in the book, who spoke those same words decades before and to whom!

Did Youthful Pride Get the Best of James at The Citadel?

Though he was not guilty in a judicial sense, James might have been more gracious in seeking reconciliation with Professor Capers of The Citadel when the professor insulted him by accusing him of plagiarism, as described in Chapter 2. Though Capers' subsequent apology to James fell short of taking full ownership for his fault, James could have considered broader relational issues than just defending his own honor, and he could have found a way to allow Capers to save face. He may have been a fault for not trying harder to negotiate a middle ground. Then, instead of having to leave, he might have been able to receive the degree he had in fact earned at The Citadel.

I acknowledge that there is more than one way to look at the incident. For example, respected author Malcolm C.

Doubles and others are of the opinion that James was all the more honorable for not apologizing, as it showed "strength of character."[6] In any case, it seems that The Citadel incident had no adverse effect on his military relationships, his promotion to his eventual rank of Major, or on his ability to maintain close friends for the rest of his life.

The Major's Positive Qualities

These descriptions of the Major's positive personal qualities complement the Major's twelve winning business attributes already described in Chapter 7. The two lists, taken together, read like a manual for "How to Earn the Friendship and Respect of Others," "How to be Successful in Business," "How to Keep Your Integrity for Your Entire Life," "How to Live a Productive Life," or "How to Have an Impact Serving the Lord."

We will look at 18 of Major Coker's positive character qualities, followed by documented descriptions of each one. All of us probably will not succeed on this earth to the extent this rarely talented man did, but as we apply these principles, we will experience benefits.

> Humility
> Sense of Humor
> Uncorrupted Integrity in His Personal Life
> Vigorous Masculinity and Authentic Manhood
> Leadership
> Modesty
> Like Jesus in Unselfish Concern
> Suffered for Others
> Actively Involved in Public Health
> A Lover of Music and Hymns
> Friendliness and Winsomeness
> Redeemed the Time and Finished His Race Well

<u>Nobility with Humility</u>
<u>Disciplined</u>
<u>Stewardship of All of Life</u>
<u>Generosity and Care for the Less Fortunate</u>
<u>Love for Nature and Beauty</u>
<u>A Family Man</u>

Humility

The Reverend B. A. McIlhany, his younger contemporary and pastor of Hartsville Presbyterian Church, said that the Major lived "without his philanthropy being heralded, quietly, modestly, humbly, with faith quite as simple as a little child's."[7] Mrs. Charles Kupfer, President of the Coker College Alumnae Association, said: "The most remarkable trait in the Major's personality was his realization of the need of God."[8]

Sense of Humor

The Major's granddaughter, Miss Hannah Coker, said: "Often we visited grandfather in his bedroom. One day when I was a little girl, I was sitting with him in front of an open fire in his room. I decided that it was time I learned something from him of our forbearers. Looking up at him, I said, 'Grandfather, please tell me something about my descendants.' I can still remember the twinkle in his eye as he replied, "I too would like to know something about your descendants, but I cannot foretell the future."[9]

Coker College student Lucile Segars Kerfoot said, "The most beautiful thing about him was the twinkle in his eye that was like a star in the blue sky of night as it came and went."[10] Similarly, Mrs. Chas Kupfer observed: "There was a laughter in the blue of his eyes and a twinkle like the stars as they come peeping through the darkness at eventide...."[11]

The Major like to laugh. Arthur Rogers recalled "At the

Baptist Church one Sunday—Laura was the organist—and the Major was there. They were singing a hymn and trying to fit it to a certain tune; they were singing and singing, and when they came to the end of a certain line, they had to give a jump to make it fit. After trying the first two verses, they decided they would have to give it up. The choir was in confusion. The Major just laughed and laughed about that. The Major was full of fun. A good joke he certainly laughed at."[12]

Uncorrupted Integrity in His Personal Life

Major Coker had right motives, right manners, and right morals. His life was an open book. Samuel W. Garrett said, "We all admired him for his sincerity, absolute honesty, and purity of thought and speech."[13]

As an example of his financial integrity, the Major did not want to profit personally from Coker College. Mr. Samuel W. Garrett said: "The college was to be operated for the students, not for profit, nor for any commercial advantage to J. L. Coker and Company. He always advised me, as buyer for the college, not to buy from his store if I could do as well elsewhere."[14]

J. W. Norwood told this story of his exceptional integrity in the business culture: "On one occasion while he was president of the National Bank of Darlington, a customer of the bank who had not been in Darlington long paused to pass the compliments of the day with Major Coker, and in the course of his conversation, by way of making himself entertaining, told Major Coker a vulgar anecdote. The Major neither smiled nor made any comment, and the visitor awkwardly withdrew, feeling more embarrassed than if he had been rebuked by a bishop."[15]

J. E. Norment summed up his uncorrupted integrity as follows:

> The arena of life was broad and inviting to this rarely gifted man. He entered its struggles and opportunities with a brave heart, with broad vision, and with clean hands. He was a victor in his striving; he came from the struggle with heart and hands clean and unstained, having ever borne himself as the high-minded, lofty-souled Christian gentleman.[16]

Vigorous Masculinity and Authentic Manhood

Today, there are those opposed to real manhood (and for that matter, opposed to real womanhood). These would castrate America. Early in January 2019, the American Psychology Association issued a report on men and boys saying that "traditional masculinity—marked by stoicism, competitiveness, dominance, and aggression—is, on the whole, harmful."[17] The report regards masculinity as an evil to be tamed rather than a blessing to be utilized for the good of all. In response, in *The Wall Street Journal* on January 17, 2019, Erica Komisar, a female author and psychoanalyst, said that the report amounted to a denial of biology. She wrote:

> The truth is that masculine traits such as aggression, competitiveness, and protective vigilance not only can be positive but also have a biological basis. Boys and men produce far more testosterone, which is associated with increased aggression

and competitiveness, [both] biologically and behaviorally. They also produce more vasopressin, a hormone originating in the brain that makes men aggressively protective of their loved ones.[18]

The Major certainly did not allow psychologists to confuse his identity or tame his masculinity. An editorial from the *New York Times* from 1908, describing the Major's remarkable comeback from the war, used the term "manly struggle" and added that men like him "are ready to come to aid all who need aid and will take it."[19]

More examples of his masculinity are not hard to find. Through ongoing pain, he did not allow his lame leg to prevent him from keeping his body in the best possible physical condition and with his crutch, he exercised vigorously, pacing back and forth on his porch to stay healthy. Ethel Laney Miller remarked: "If he came in using only his stick, I felt that his leg was not hurting him, but if he came on his crutches, I thought he must be suffering some. However, I never heard him complain once, and we took his being crippled as much a part of him as we did his beard and cutaway coat. The Major was a striking-looking gentleman, tall, of decided military bearing, never allowing his short leg to weaken his spine in the slightest. And I might say here that he did not permit anything or anyone else to weaken that spine either!"[20]

His manly courage is not hard to document. He saw to it that the town charter did not allow strong liquor in Hartsville, and he stared down bootleggers in order to enforce it. Near bankruptcy after nine years of failed risks and setbacks starting The Carolina Fiber Company, he doggedly triumphed over them all to create one of the world's greatest companies. When he succeeded, he cemented his place in history as one of the world's great businessmen. In the end, his tenacity resulted in the provision of gainful employment to thousands during his time, and as Sonoco has grown, to the employment of tens of thousands around the world in our time. That's a legacy of gutsy manhood. Built from his legacy, discussion questions on masculine expression in the church, family, and workplace are found at http://www.willjoslin.com/major/questions/men.

Leadership

Twenty-first-century motivational speaker and leadership expert John C. Maxwell says, "Everything rises and falls on leadership."[21] The Reverend C. L. McDowell, a contemporary of the Major, said: "The people recognized his ability and fitness for leadership, and naturally yielded the position of leadership to him... The people trusted him as a Christian worthy of their confidence and cooperation."[22]

James Lide Coker rose above of the trappings of this world to be Darlington County's transcendent leader, problem-solver, and spiritual model during what was arguably the roughest patch of South Carolina history. John C. Maxwell wrote: "Leaders are meant to help others become the people God wants them to be."[23] The Major did just that - changed lives, and helped others fulfill their potential.

Major Coker was not interested in how far he could advance himself, but in how high he could lift others. Dr. Patterson Wardlaw, Professor of Education at the University of South Carolina, said:

> Major Coker was one of the really great South Carolinians, not merely of his own day, but of the entire lifetime of the state. His nobility of character was guided by a vision exceptionally high, broad, and progressive, yet sanely conservative, and he made the vision work.[24]

Mrs. Kupfer added, "A man may be endowed with intellect, but unable to lead or influence others. Major's beliefs and traditions led many."[25] The Major led many women, rural people, and African Americans up from extremely limited opportunities into a better life. Dr. Henry Snyder of Wofford College said of his leadership:

> He sought to develop the economic resources of the State as the fundamental basis for the prosperity and happiness of its people, and also to preserve and advance their abiding spiritual needs. Farmer, merchant, manufacturer, he was a sincere and loyal churchman and educator who saw a richer future for his state by means of a finer training for the youth of today.[26]

Never a detached armchair executive or pompous autocrat, the Major earned the right to lead others because they knew he was genuinely concerned for their well-being and protection. He knew and loved the people and shared life with them through church, his general store, assistance with their farming, at his banks, and through relationships with the workers in his industries. The respect earned through the bonds he forged made it natural for others to trust him. If we would influence and lead others, we would do well to build credibility as Major Coker did by building grass roots relationships, and working together for the common good.

Another aspect of the Major's leadership was in the realm of politics. Though he had no ambition for public office, out of leadership necessity and duty, he periodically served in the government of his state. In late 1864, he served briefly as a representative to the South Carolina General Assembly, valiantly attempting to start public schools in his state.[27] During Reconstruction, he was a leader in the racially progressive Union Reform Party, which put at least one black candidate on every ticket.

In 1908, Charleston mayor R.G. Rhett and three other South

Carolina business, educational, and religious leaders declared their trust in the Major's leadership by strongly recommending him to run for the United States Senate. This suggestion won the backing of the South Carolina General Assembly, where the speaker officially nominated him, concluding with the following statement:

> Major Coker has never sought political preferment, nor does he seek it now; but his friends, in the interest of South Carolina, ask it for him, in the full confidence that, if he be elected, his official career will add luster to the name of the state.[28]

The petition was signed by 20 other leading South Carolina business, government, and religious pacesetters, including, Furman University president Harvard Toliver Cook. Major Coker declined, feeling that his calling remained in Hartsville to his family, his businesses, his church, his church, and to Coker College.

Sometimes I wish there had been two Major Cokers, one to do exactly what he did with his life, and another called to use the brains and character he had to positively influence government. Mark Twain remarked: "An honest man in politics shines more there than he would elsewhere."[29] If you, my reader, have a similar life foundation of character, and vision, perhaps you may be called to carry forward the Major's leadership legacy into politics today, where it is sorely needed. For challenging discussion questions on our current need for people with leadership integrity like the Major's to lead in politics today, see https://www.willjoslin.com/major/ questions/politics.

Modesty

Many leaders who rise quickly become egotistical, and pride is their undoing. English Prime Minister Margaret Thatcher's quest for excessive power caused her to be ousted from her own party in 1990.[30] Oil drilling and aircraft entrepreneur Howard Hughes lost millions in the 1930s when he was too prideful to listen to his advisors.

The Major was just the opposite. He saw himself as a servant and a worker, even though he was a Harvard graduate and the wealthiest man in his state. He simply had no need for self-importance as he faithfully taught children in the Sunday school, sought the welfare of Coker College young women, and uplifted the underprivileged of Darlington County.

He was never showy about his wealth, good deeds, or generosity. Miss Josephine Erwin wrote:

> Major Coker was very, very modest. In fact, I think that one word describes him better than almost any other I can think of. He never wanted his right hand to know what his left hand was about. He did so many, many things for the college, and for people that never have been known.[31]

Regarding his distaste for gaudiness, Will Coker wrote: "[Father was] averse to the slightest show of display of prosperity. He believed in the essentials of good living but with none of the frills that so strongly attract smaller minds."[32]

Like Jesus in Unselfish Concern

Katherine Coker Cannon, D. R.'s daughter through his first wife Jessie Richardson, said: "All of us adored our grandfather, and not meaning to be sacrilegious, he was my idea of the kind of person that Jesus was. He was so gentle and kind to little children and patient in telling us about nature, the birds, and taking us on rides to see the first wildflowers in bloom.[33]

The Major's shattered leg did not allow him to swim, yet by giving a large donation, he arranged for Coker College to have a pool so the college women could stay fit. He could not play basketball or volleyball, but by making a large contribution to the local YWCA, he created those opportunities for the women of the Pee Dee.

Suffered for Others

James endured pain beyond measure with his shattered femur, his tortuous odyssey behind enemy lines, lifelong physical weakness, and facing the brink of bankruptcy twice, just after the war, and again in the early tribulations of the Carolina Fiber Company. Yet with his tender heart, suffering served only to enlarge his soul. Unlike many high born, early on he knew the raw fragility of the human condition, and in this knowledge, he fully identified with the plight of the distressed, and so lived to better their lives.

He suffered in other ways as well. He knew emotional pain as he bore the brunt of malicious spite from the destruction of his farm, from the near murder of his wife, and for a decade and a half after the war when carpetbaggers tried to put him out of business. And in Darwin's heyday, when many were ridiculing the Christian faith, James stood firm and maintained his belief in Christ, and continued to lead and teach the First Baptist Sunday School.

Dr. E. W. Sikes said: "From the lips of Major Coker fell no words of vituperation or hate. He reviled not. You will search in vain to find in him carping criticism or fault-finding. His spirit was too wholesome to harbor hatred... Magnanimity is the mark of a great Christian. Stephen, like Christ, prayed 'Father forgive them; they know not what they do.' When a Yankee soldier crippled him for life in the war, it was just not in him to become bitter. He moved on with contentment and trust that God was in control and would use it all for good in the end."[34]

At Hartsville's centennial celebration of the Major's birth, Rev. B. A. McIlhany prayed: "We thank Thee that his heart was filled with love like unto Christ's love and that he bore the burden of the weak, the oppressed, and the sorrowing."[35]

At first glance, the Major and Dr. Martin Luther King, Jr., from two generations later, might seem to have little in common. But both men willingly suffered for the benefit of others. Having suffered greatly themselves, both acutely felt the pain of others. And just as the Major intentionally freed many whites and African Americans in Darlington County from stifling poverty and biblical and academic illiteracy, Dr. Martin Luther King Jr. freed African Americans from abuse, poverty, and limited opportunities. In October of 1960, Dr. King was locked up in Reidsville State Prison in Tattnall County, Georgia, for calmly but firmly defending racial equality. It was during that period in his life that he wrote these words, which could apply to both men:

> The cross we bear precedes the crown we wear. To be a Christian, one must take up his cross, with all of its difficulties and agonizing and tension-packed content, and carry it until that very cross leaves its mark upon us and redeems us to that more excellent way, which comes only through suffering.[36]

Both men carried that cross so the benefits of their suffering would reach others. Hudson Taylor, the 19th century British missionary to China, said: "It is doubtful that God can use a man greatly until He has hurt him deeply."

Actively Involved in Public Health

Major Coker was interested in all aspects of social welfare. Since colonial days, malaria had been a huge problem in the Pee Dee. His cousin Miss Jane Lide, in her Coker College Founder's Day speech of 1956, said: "The plantation lands along the Pee Dee were infested with malaria, costing the health and in some cases the lives of the field hands. No one knew how to eradicate malaria."[37]

Will Coker studied public health at Johns Hopkins University, and informed his father around 1913 that flies and mosquitoes, which thrived in the stagnant tributaries of the Pee Dee River and Black Creek, "carried the germs, malaria, and infectious diseases." Major Coker also bought books on both malaria and mosquitoes and did his own studies on the problem. Simpson elaborates: "Convinced, the Major began to take direct action. He went to considerable trouble and expense to see that his own properties were drained and cleaned up. That screens were put in and that all measures thought to be necessary were taken. He was equally insistent in regard to the whole town."[38] Hartsville's Dr. W. L. Byerly, the beloved medical doctor for whom Hartsville's Byerly Hospital (now called Carolina Pines Regional Medical Center) wrote that, due to Major Coker, "We have a clean town, the first in the United States to be made malaria-free."[39] Major Coker was also a member of the American Red Cross.[40]

Dr. W. L. Byerly commented further: "He had organized the Hartsville Board of Health, was its chairman, and maintained an active interest in community health problems until his final illness. [His] simplicity, his friendliness, his interest in me, his understanding of social and health problems gave me a delightful evening. I left his home convinced that the great man is great not because he has accumulated wealth, but because he has a knowledge of the problems of his fellow man and gives to them a sympathetic, intelligent, and unselfish understanding and help."[41]

As I am finishing up this book, America is locked down with a public health pandemic, the coronavirus. Given his passion for public health and his practical conscientiousness, I can't help but think that if this pandemic had occurred during his lifetime, the Major and perhaps Will and/or D. R., with their biological knowledge and the Major's chemistry set, would be working on an vaccine, probably in conjunction with the American Red Cross.

Leon Coker recollected on how the Major was ahead of his time regarding the dangers of cigarettes to health: "They never sold cigarettes in the Coker Store because James Lide 'just didn't believe in the cigarette business—he didn't want to influence the young people to smoke.'"[42]

After describing Major Coker's business successes in Darlington County, an editorial in *the New York Times* written in 1908 stated: "[Due to] the application of the same high intelligence and public spirit to other than purely material aims... it seems that sanitation, education, and religion prosper there in the same way as cotton and pulp and paper."[43]

A Lover of Music and Hymns

The Major loved to sing. He attended recitals at Coker College and hosted musical gatherings in his home. May Coker, D. R.'s second wife, recalled: "On Sunday evenings we would often take the children [to the Major's house] and the whole group would sing hymns. The Major would 'line them out,' and that was the first time I had heard 'On Jordan's Stormy Banks, I Stand.' He knew every word of many hymns. He sang very well."[44] Of the same gatherings, James's nephew Paul Rogers wrote, "Occasionally, Cousin James [James Lide Jr.] played his guitar, and he and Cousin David [D. R.] sang or whistled. Cousin David could whistle two parts at once."

The Major's granddaughter, Mrs. George Ruth Wilds described the singing at Christmas this way: "They would all be whistling different hymns, and they would sing these hymns and songs and Christmas carols. You know all of those men had such good voices and liked to sing. Uncle James would play the guitar, and grandfather loved to sing and would join in that—and then many of the grandchildren played the piano.[45]

Friendliness and Winsomeness

Artist's retouch of a photograph of Major Coker, c. 1900. Used by permission from Charles W. Coker of Sonoco.

His nurse Lucy Drakeford Timmons wrote: "Major Coker had many interests, but above everything else, he loved people. Until the last, he displayed a very active interest in all with whom he came in contact."[46] D. R. commented on his father's friendliness, summarizing what he taught him: "You have to go out from yourself just a little more than halfway; a smile will take you a long way in this world."[47] Mrs. Ousley once said: "I would say that the Major had a striking personality – one of kindness and a keen personal interest in the individual which became a growing personality as [he] revealed a fatherly feeling towards students."[48]

He made everyone feel that they were somebody important. Miss Caroline Reaves, Coker College professor for about thirty years, said: "He had such an inspiring effect that he made you feel even better satisfied with yourself. I always felt when I was with him that he was glad to see me."[49] Mrs. Elise Ellison, Coker College Class of 1915, said: "Every girl in the college approached him with the most ease because there were no barriers to let down."[50]

In all of his enterprises, the Major was good to his employees, and they reflected love back to him. Malcolm C. Doubles, the author of *A Century Plus: A History of Sonoco Products Company*, relates the story of how Carolina Fiber Company employee

Henry Alexander Gandy did not want the Major to worry too much in the 1890's while the plant was struggling. Employee and CEO were such devoted friends that Mr. Gandy felt compelled to look out for his CEO. In the words of La Verne Vickery, Gandy's grandson: "The old Major was walking down the aisle with his lantern one cold winter night, and so Mr. Gandy said, "Now Major, you go home and take your rest. I'm not going to let this mill freeze.""[51]

Redeemed the Time and Finished His Race Well

Major Coker never grew lazy. He made every day count. At about age 70 he said: "Whatever might reasonably be accomplished, ought to be accomplished."[52] While many today talk of early retirement so they can spend it on their pleasures, the Major, though wealthy, never retired. He saw his life mission as a permanent, earnest duty, and continued to serve God and others until the end. Mrs. William Eggleston said: "I always took note of it when he passed by on his way to church. He held out just as long as he was able to walk up those steps."[53]

Nobility with Humility

His daughter Susie remarked:

> The breadth, tolerance, and stability of Father's nature reminded one of Robert E. Lee, who had, of course, a tremendous influence on his life and character... Much has been said and written about Father's character and personality – chiefly the grandeur and nobility of the man. Just here, I will quote from certain pronouncements of Mr. Norwood [J. W. Norwood, son of Major Coker's lifelong friend George Norwood] and others. Mr. Norwood has told me that he considered Father

> not only the greatest man in the state (then he
> went into details to prove that men like John C.
> Calhoun couldn't hold a candle to him) but also
> the greatest man, without exception, that ever
> lived.[54]

We will not exalt the Major inappropriately, for like any human, he had his shortcomings, some of which we listed at the beginning of this chapter. But Norwood's superlative statement of his nobility does show the immense respect he earned. And while nobility earned him respect, his humility kept him approachable, loved and trusted by all who knew him. Questions for a general audience comparing James with other notable Americans are found at https://willjoslin.com/major/questions/notableamericans.

Disciplined

When he started over from nothing after Sherman had wreaked havoc on South Carolina, the Major demonstrated his iron will of discipline. Store and Seed Company business partner A. L. M. (Lee) Wiggins commented on Major Coker's personal discipline: "One thing about him was taking this cold bath every morning. He would get up and take a cold bath until his last years when he wasn't able to. In some respects, he reminds me of what you read about Robert E. Lee. He disciplined himself more than anyone else."[55] Once, he lost an umbrella and did not replace it until the time he calculated that the umbrella's useful life would have been over.[56] Later in life, according to his daughter Susie, he was able to lighten up a bit: "As time moved on and his business worries lightened, and as he was able to share the responsibility more and more with the competent executives he had trained, his mood, of course, became lighter, and he had more time for the human things of life."[57]

Stewardship of All of Life

Major Coker's exponentially productive life parallels the parable of the talents in Matthew 25:14-30, where different amounts of money are given to three different people to see how well each would redeem what he received. For the sake of illustration, let's say that James, with his inherited land and farming skills, had five talents before the Civil War, and after the war crippled and plundered him, was down to just one talent.

Then, with his crutch and hoe, he took that one talent and worked the fields, started his store, and built one success upon another, not just for himself but for the entire Pee Dee area. Thus, it could be said he acquired thousands of talents, which he then reinvested in a compounding chain of bounty and benefit. His life is summed up concisely in Luke 16:10: "He who is faithful in a very little thing is faithful also in much." The Major was faithful when he had little, and he was just as faithful when he had much.

Regarding the principle of stewardship in the Major's whole life, Florence attorney Fred L. Wilcox spoke at Coker College's centennial memorial service of Major Coker's birthday, saying: "He seems to me to have possessed that quality which the greatest of all teachers had in mind when He said: 'For whosoever will save his life shall lose it; and whosoever will lose his life for My sake shall find it.'"[58]

Generosity and Care for the Less Fortunate

Part of his generosity was looking out for the poor in the Hartsville area. Maum Delphi Chapman, an African American woman who worked as servant and cook for the Major and Sue, said: "They were honest people and good people. When there was a hard winter, Major Coker would send wood around to all the poor people's houses. Way back—he used to do that often—for widowed women and those that had children too."[59] She added, "People at the paper mill—the Major used to give them all turkeys at Christmas."

Vivien Coker wrote around 1930: "Father's [affectionate term for Father in law's] relationship [with African Americans] was always very good indeed. He was honored and revered by all of them, and I think upon hearing anyone speak of the Major today, any colored person would rise to the name, and even a later generation would have heard about him through someone."[60] I ask that the reader to please not object to the archaic term "colored people" quoted above, as I am quoting from those who lived in an earlier era.

One of the last things Major Coker did was to donate part of his land near the end of Sixth Street to be used for a school for African Americans. Due to his donation, in 1920, the original building was replaced with a large-frame school building on 6th Street far superior to anything previously constructed[61] and was called The Darlington County Training School, then Butler High School[62]. As was the nationwide custom of that time, the school was separate from white schools. Looking back, we may frown on this separation, but for the Major's time, we must realize he was way ahead of almost all white Americans in his concern for African American advancement.

Author Malcolm C. Doubles has pointed out that the very earliest pavements (c. 1910) in Hartsville were wheelchair accessible, and that Hartsville was one of the first places in the country to offer this accommodation for the handicapped. In his later years, the Major needed to get around Hartsville in his "rolling chair."[63] The decision to make the pavements wheelchair accessible was probably his idea when he served as mayor of Hartsville from 1893 to 1894,[64] and if not then, the city of Hartsville did it afterward to honor him.

Love for Nature and Beauty

Fascinated by the beauties of creation, Major Coker had great interest in the plant and animal kingdoms, from foliage to crops to bluebirds. He gave tours through his gardens to his grandchildren, pointing out the names and characteristics of each tree and flower. His nurse wrote this about the last days of his life: "I can recall his interest in nature, his love of birds that seemed to find sanctuary in his garden. He made many efforts to teach me to recognize birds in their songs."[65] Mabel Montgomery of South Carolina's *The State* newspaper wrote, "[The Major was] a lover of nature; few happenings in the natural world escaped his keen observation."

A Family Man

James was a kind and devoted husband, who, during Sue's prolonged period of decline, looked after her tenderly. He was an attentive father who walked with his children in the snow, instructed them in the ways of nature, and later invited them into his businesses. With the exception of the complaint mentioned earlier in this chapter that he did not teach them enough by precept, he and Sue were warm and successful parents who raised seven honorable children, all of whom ended up being active in commerce, the church, or academics.

ENDNOTES FOR CHAPTER 15: THE MAJOR'S PERSONAL CHARACTER QUALITIES CONSIDERED

1   Will Coker, *Recollections*, p. 67.
2   Simpson, op. cit., p. 185.
3   Susan Coker Watson in the section on "Generosity to the Family," *Recollections*, p.75.
4   David R. Coker, *Recollections*, p. 1.
5   Near the beginning of Chapter 2 of this book, James's mother Hannah spoke those exact words to him when he was at The Citadel.
6   Malcolm C. Doubles, *A Century Plus: A History of Sonoco Products Company*, op. cit., pp. 6-7.
7   Rev. B. A. McIlhany, *Centennial Celebration*, op cit., p. 7.
8   Mrs. Chas Kupfer, *Centennial Celebration*, p. 33.
9   Miss Hannah Coker, *Recollections*, p. 122.
10 Lucille Segars Kerfoot, *Recollections*, p. 57.
11 Mrs. Chas Kupfer, *Centennial Celebration*, p. 32.
12 Arthur Rogers, *Recollections*, p.62.
13 S. W. Garrett, Dean of Coker College and professor of Math, Education, and other subjects, letter in papers from the early days of Coker College, op cit., p. 4.
14 S. W. Garrett, op. cit., p. 2.
15 J. W. Norwood, op. cit., p. 430.
16 J. E. Norment, op. cit.
17 Stephanie Papas, American Psychological Association, 2019 article "APA issues first-ever guidelines for practice with men and boys," Volume 50, No. 1, p. 2, https://www.apa.org/monitor/2019/01/ce-corner (accessed December 29, 2019). The link works if you copy and paste it into your browser.
18 Erica Komisar, 2019 Wall Street Journal article *"Masculinity Isn't a Sickness,"* from the American Psychological Association's new report on men and boys at https://www.wsj.com/articles/masculinity-isnt-a-sickness-11547682809 (accessed December 29, 2019).
19 Kate Chambers, op. cit., in her Appendix, p. 175.
20 Ethel Laney Miller, *Recollections*, p. 28.
21 See Peter Economy's website, op. cit.
22 Rev. C. L. McDowell, *Centennial Celebration*, op. cit., p. 14.
23 John C. Maxwell, *Leadership Promises for Every Day*, op. cit., back cover.
24 Dr. Patterson J. Wardlaw, University of South Carolina Professor of Education, in *Centennial Speeches,* op cit., p. 27.

25 Mrs. Charles. Kupfer, President of the Coker College Alumnae Association, whose speech was recorded in the "1937 Centennial Celebration of the Major," op. cit., p. 33.

26 Dr. Henry N. Snyder, President of Wofford College, "1937 Centennial Celebration of the Major," op cit., p. 27.

27 E. W. Sikes, Centennial Celebration, op. cit., pp. 19, 22

28 Kate Chambers, quoting from the speaker of the South Carolina General Assembly, op. cit., p. 173

29 Daniel Kurtzman, Liveaboutdotcom, May 26, 2019 article "Mark Twain Quotes," https://www.liveabout.com/mark-twain-quotes-2734314#:~:text=%22An%20honest%20man%20in%20politics,there%20than%20he%20would%20elsewhere.%22

30 John Baldoni, February 2, 2012 article from Inc. website called "Leadership Lessons from *The Iron Lady*,"https://www.inc.com/john-baldoni/the-pride-and-peril-of-the-iron-lady-margaret-thatcher-leadership-lesson.html (accessed December 29, 2019).

31 Josephine Erwin, *Recollections*, p.79.

32 Will C. Coker, *Recollections*, p.73.

33 Katherine Coker Cannon, *Recollections*, p. 119.

34 Dr. Enoch W. Sikes, then president of Clemson University, from his address *James Lide Coker—The Man* at "1937 Centennial Celebration of the Major," op. cit., p. 18.

35 Coker College Quarterly Bulletin, February 1937, "1937 Centennial Celebration of the Major," op. cit., p. 7.

36 Dr. Martin Luther King Jr., in David J. Garrow's book, *Bearing the Cross*, Vintage Books, 1988, page preceding table of contents.

37 Miss Jane Lide, op. cit., p. 1.

38 Simpson, op. cit., p. 181.

39 Dr. W. L. Byerly, *Centennial Celebration*, op. cit., p. 11

40 The National Cyclopedia of Biography, vol. 17, op. cit., p.22

41 W. L. Byerly, MD, in Coker College Quarterly Bulletin, op. cit., p. 9.

42 Leon Coker, *Recollections*, p. 36.

43 Kate Chambers, op. cit., from the editorial from the *New York Times*..

44 Mary Coker, *Recollections*, p.105.

45 Mrs. Ruth Wilds, *Recollections*, op. cit., p.116.

46 His nurse Lucy Drakeford Timmons, *Recollections*, p. 135

47 David R. Coker, *Major James Lide Coker: A Son's Tribute*, a speech given at Coker College at "1937 Centennial Celebration of the Major," op. cit., p. 5.

48 Mrs. J. F. Ousley, *Recollections*, p. 42.

49 Miss Caroline Reaves, *Recollections*, p. 80.

50 Mrs. Elsie Ellison, op.cit., p. 1.

51 Malcom C. Doubles, *A Century Plus: A History of Sonoco Products Company*, op. cit., pp. 15-16.

52 Simpson, op. cit., p. 184.

53 Mrs. William Eggleston, *Recollections*, p. 62

54 Susan Coker Watson, quoting George Norwood in *Recollections*, p. 68.

55 A. L. Wiggins, *Recollections*, p. 69.

56 George Lee Simpson, op. cit., p. 186.

57 Susan Coker Watson, *Recollections*, p. 25.

58 Fred L. Wilcox, Ibid., p. 42.

59 Maum Delphi, Major and Sue Coker's cook and household helper, *Recollections*, p. 90.

60 Vivien Gay Coker, *Recollections*, p. 91.

61 Lucille Boswell Neely, op. cit., p. 37. Also documented by Frank R. Chambers, op. cit., p. 59.

62 Editor, "Butler School," SC Picture project web site, 2012, https://www.scpictureproject.org/darlington-county/butler-school.html.

63 The Major's pioneering work in handicapped sidewalk access related by Hartsville expert Malcom C. Doubles, who wrote me: "My comment was based on observation of photos showing the Major occasionally in or standing beside a wheelchair, and noting that the earliest pavements in Hartsville are wheelchair accessible, from which I drew the conclusion that such had to be so that the Major could be easily transported to downtown meetings, offices, etc. I think it an obvious conclusion, but would not want to suggest any documentary evidence for such."

64 Lucille Boswell Neely, op. cit., p. 258.

65 Lucy Drakeford Thompson, *Recollections*, p. 135.

Conclusion

THE MAJOR'S TORCH
SHINES ON

Major Coker ascended from the ashes of financial ruin and permanent injury to become perhaps the greatest multi-dimensional leader in American history. He never sought fame, power, or coveted riches, but became spectacularly successful because he surrendered his remarkable talents to God. The Major saw struggling people, and helped them thrive. He had the power to conquer, but stooped to help the weak, and lifted them up to join in his victories. His inspiring life continues to shine undimmed after more than a century.

His life helped give light to me when, at age 40, I had to admit that doing what I loved no longer adequately supported my wife and children. At that defining juncture, I knew I should make a career change, but wondered if I could. I remembered how Major Coker overcame greater crises than mine, and uplifted thousands in the process. His bravery in crisis inspired me to learn what I needed to begin a new career, and a few years later, to start my own business. His example helped me persevere until restored to productive service. Whatever problems you, your family, your business, or your community may be facing, I believe Major Coker's life can also help inspire you to transcend the challenges.

Mrs. Chas. Kupfer superbly summed up Major Coker's radiant life as follows: "He was a man of unbelievable ability, and yet he allowed God to draw him out of time to live and shine for the riches of eternity. We know there was a blessing in the life of this man not only to our state but like the waters in their galloping haste to the sea, the influence of him will go on and on to the end of time."[1]

If you want to extend Major Coker's encouraging influence, you might give this book to a friend, recommend it to your study club, history or business class, or suggest it to a church group. Another idea is using the book to mentor and inspire young people, and to help them to find their life purpose.

ENDNOTE FOR CONCLUSION: THE MAJOR'S TORCH SHINES ON

1   Mrs. Charles. Kupfer, *Centennial Celebration*, p. 34.

APPENDICES

APPENDIX 1

ADDITIONAL PICTURES

Gardens bordering Brown House & Coker College grounds, c. 1930. Joslin family archives.

Mrs. D.R. Coker, D.R.'s 2nd wife, and the author's grand-mother. She was affectionately known as "Miss May." The Major was with her and D.R. when he witnessed the return of the bluebirds a week before his death. Miss May attended First Baptist and lived until 1975.
Used by permission of Coker College.

Enduring J.L. Coker Store sign on the exterior of what is now the Hartsville YMCA building, a previous location of the store. Picture taken by author.

**Coker Farms National Historic Landmark
on 4th Street in Hartsville.**
Public property photographed by the author.

Coker Farms National Historic Landmark on S. Fourth St. in Hartsville. Picture taken by author.

THE GUARANTEE OF QUALITY

HARTSVILLE, S.C.

May 5, 1947

Mr. Robert H. Garrison
In Charge of Seed Certification
Clemson College, S. C.

Dear Bob:

Many thanks for your nice letter of May 2nd.

Not handing out bouquets at all, but it was unanimously agreed by those who attended your recent organization meeting in Columbia that more was accomplished in the same length of time at this meeting than at any other meeting previously attended. I want to congratulate you on your thorough planning and efficient execution. We were all well pleased with the meeting, in its entirety, and were only too glad to take part and contribute as we were able.

Rest assured that we are behind you 100% and want you to call on us whenever we can be of assistance in any way. Don't forget that we are counting on having you spend some time with us in our small grain experiments. We want to have the South Carolina Seedsmen's Association here one day. The date has not yet been decided but will write you and hope that you can arrange to come at same time.

Looking forward to seeing you and with appreciation and best wishes,

Sincerely,

George J. Wilds, President

GJW:R

A 1947 letter from Geroge J. Wilds, then Coker Pedigreed Seed Co. president, to Clemson College about co-operative grain experiments. Permission of Clemson Univ. Experiment Station.

The Author and his late mother, Mary Coker Joslin in 1998. Mrs. Joslin wrote two books based on her Hartsville roots, *Growing Up in the Brown House* and *Essays on William Chambers Coker, A Passionate Botanist.*

Author Will Joslin's family. Left to right: me, my wife Becky, our son Andrew, his bride Amy, our dauther Lydia, and our son Joel. Picture date September 21, 2019.

APPENDIX 2

BOOKS IN MAJOR COKER'S PERSONAL LIBRARY

This is the list of books in the Major's personal collection. I found it in the Coker College archives in the Coker Box, and it was dated November 4, 1919, seventeen months after Major Coker's death.

The list is at least partially incomplete. Probably some of it was lost or auctioned off before the college made this record of his library. For example, in *Recollections of the Major: James Lide Coker, 1837-1918*, p. 116, Mrs. Ruth Wilds mentioned that Major Coker had a copy of Dickens' *A Christmas Carol;* that work is not listed here. Similarly, Will Coker wrote "Father had a good library of excellent quality, containing many of the best classics such as Dickens, Scott, Emerson, Macaulay, Ruskin, the New England poets, etc. He never mentioned Darwin's *Origin of Species* to me, but I found it on the shelves when I was about sixteen or seventeen years old."[1] But Scott, Emerson, Macaulay, Ruskin, and Darwin's *The Origin of Species* are not on this list. Similarly, the King James Bible that his mother Hannah gave him in 1860 is also not listed. Even so, what remained on this list does lend a good bit of insight into Major Coker's interests.

Christianity

Babcock, M. D.	*Thoughts of Everyday Living*
Benson, A. C.	*Paul the Minstrel*
Boyd, R.	*Moody and Sankey*
Broadus, John A.	*A Treatise on the Preparation and Delivery of Sermons*
Broadus, John A.	*Sermons and Addresses*
Brown, L. F.	*Baptist and Fifth Monarchy Men*
Drummond, Henry	*A Life for a Life* (A Tribute to D. L. Moody)
Bushnell, H.	*The Character of Jesus*
Dossey, W.	*The Choice* (hymnbook)
Earle, A. B.	*Bringing in the Sheaves*
Fisher, George. P.	*Manual of Christian Evidences*
Forrester, E. J.	*The Baptist Position*
Gardner, C. S.	*Ethics of Jesus*
Gordon, A. J.	*In Christ*
Jervey, T. D.	*Christian Principle in Little Things*
Jervey, T. D.	*The Elder Brother*
Jones, J. W.	*Christ in the Camp*
Knight, W. A.	*The Song of our Syrian Guest* (musings on Psalm23)
Meyer, F. B.	*Christian Living*
Newman, A. H.	*A Century of Baptist Achievement*
Paley, William	*Evidences of Christianity*
Russell, H. H.	*A Lawyer's Examination of the Bible*
Spencer, I. S.	*A Pastor's Sketches*
Trumbull, H. C.	*Prayer, Its Nature and Scope*
Van Dyke, H.	*The Mansion*
Wells, Amos H.	*Cheer Book*
Wilkinson, W. C.	*Paul, and the Revolt against Him*
Wayland, F.	*A Memoir of the Life and Labors of the Rev. Adoniram Judson*
Young, J.	*Christ of History*

History / Biography

Agassiz, E. C.	*Louis Agassiz, His Life and Letters*
Armes, W. D., ed.	*Autobiography of Joseph LeConte*
Alexander, Edward P.	*Military Memoirs of a Confederate Soldier*
Burdette, R. J.	*Chimes from a Jester's Bell*
Callahan, C. H.	*Memoirs of Captain H. Vicars*
Callahan, C. H.	*Washington, the Man and the Mason*
Carroll, B. R.	*Historical Collections of South Carolina,* 2 volumes
Cave, R. C.	*The Men in Gray*
Clayton, W. F.	*Narrative of the Confederate States Navy*
Coker, F. W.	*Readings in Political Philosophy*
Cooke, J.	*The Occident*
Cooke, J. E.	*Life of General Robert E. Lee*
Coolidge, A. C.	*Three Peace Congresses of the 19th Century*
Craven, J. J.	*Prison Life of Jefferson Davis*
Creel, G.	*Wilson and the Issues*
Cuyler, T. L.	*Recollections of a Long Life*
De Quincey, T.	*Biographical Essays*
Dickert, D. A.	*The History of Kershaw's Brigade*
Cooke, H. T.	*Education in SC under Baptist Control*
Dowd, C.	*Life of Zebulon B. Vance*
Dubose, John W.	*General Wheeler and the Army of Tennessee*
Evans, C. A.	*Confederate Military History,* 12 volumes
French, S. G.	*Two Wars*
Gracie, A.	*The Truth about Chickamauga*
Greg, P.	*History of the United States*
Hagood, J.	*Memoirs of the War of Secession*
Hatcher, E. B.	*William F. Hatcher*
Hatcher, W. E.	*Along the Trail of Friendly Years*
Hewat, A.	*Account of the Rise and Progress of the Colonies of South Carolina and Georgia,* 2 volumes
Humphrey	*My Grandparents*
Irving, W.	*Life of George Washington,* 5 volumes
Jones, J. W.	*Life, and Letters of R. E. Lee*
King, W. L.	*Newspaper Press of Charleston, SC*

LeNormand, M. A.	*Empress Josephine*
Lea, H.	*The Valor of Ignorance*
Lee, F.	*General Lee*
Longstreet, James	*From Manassas to Appomattox*
Maffitt, E. M.	*Life and Service of J. N. Maffitt*
McCants, E. C.	*One of the Grayjackets*
McClellan, H. B.	*Life and Campaigns of J. E. B. Stuart*
McCrady, E.	*Eminent and Representative Men of the Carolinas*
McGill, S. D.	*Reminiscences of Williamsburg County*
Mills, R.	*South Carolina*
Morgan, W. H.	*Personal Reminiscences of the War*
O'Neall, J. B.	*Bench and Bar of SC*, 2 volumes
O'Neall, J. B.	*Annals of Newberry, South Carolina*
Page, T. N.	*Gordon Keith*
Pierson, D. L.	*Northfield Yearbook*
Pryor, R. A.	*Reminiscences of Peace and War*
Ramsay, D.	*History of South Carolina*
Ravenel, Mrs. St. Julien	*Life and Times of William Lowdness*
Ridpath, J. C.	*History of the U.S.A.*
Schurz, C.	*Reminiscences*, 3 volumes
Steele, M. F.	*American Campaigns*, 2 volumes
Steele, M. F.	*Reports of American Historical Association*, 4 volumes
Stiles, R.	*Four Years Under Marse Robert*
Taylor, C. E.	*Story of Yates*
Taylor, R.	*Destruction and Reconstruction*
Thompson, H. S.	*South Carolina – Resources and Population*
Walker, C. I.	*Romance of Lower Carolina*
Wallace, D. D.	*Life of Henry Laurens*
Worth, N.	*The Southerner*
Wyeth, J. A.	*Autobiography of John Stuart Mill*
Wyeth, J. A.	*Life of General N. B. Forrest*
Yonge, C. M.	*Chaplet of Pearls*

Miscellaneous

Blaine, M. E.	*Games for All Occasions*
Celli, A.	*Malaria*
De Quincey, T.	*Essays on the Poets*
Drummond, Henry	*Drummond's Yearbook*
Goldsmith, O.	*Vicar of Wakefield*
Greenwood, G.	*Stories from Famous Ballads*
Howard, L. O.	*Mosquitoes*
Spencer, H.	*Education*
Wayne, A. T.	*Birds of South Carolina*

Politics

Barron, C. W.	*The Mexican Problem*
Blane, J. G.	*Twenty Years of Congress*
Locke, J.	*Essays*
Powell, E. A.	*Socialized Germany*

Science / Theoretical Science

Chapman, F. M.	*Bird Life*
Darwin, Charles	*The Descent of Man*
Garner, R. L.	*Apes and Monkeys*
LeConte, J.	*Religion and Science*
Miller, H.	*The Cruise of the Betsey*
Pouchet, F. A.	*The Universe*
Saleeby, C. W.	*The Cycle of Life*
Toumey, M.	*Geology of South Carolina*

ENDNOTES FOR APPENDIX 2: BOOKS IN MAJOR COKER'S PERSONAL LIBRARY

1 Will Coker, *Recollections*, op. cit., p. 67.

APPENDIX 3

FAMILY TREES OF MAJOR
AND SUE COKER

Family Tree A

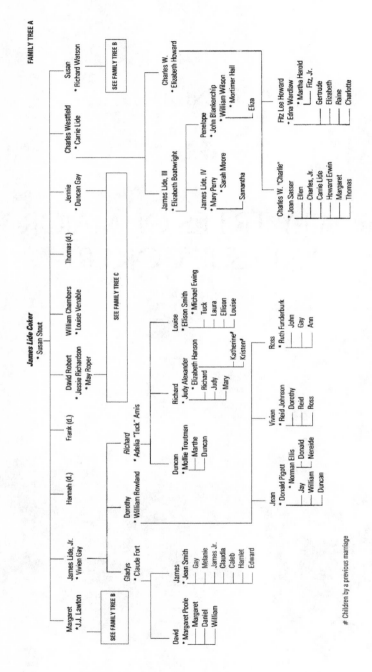

Children by a previous marriage

The three pages of this family tree were originally published in Dr. Malcolm Doubles' book, *A Century Plus, A History of Sonoco Products*, Coker College Press, 2005, pp. 18-20. Reprinted here with a few typesetting changes and additions. *Used by permission.*

Family Tree B

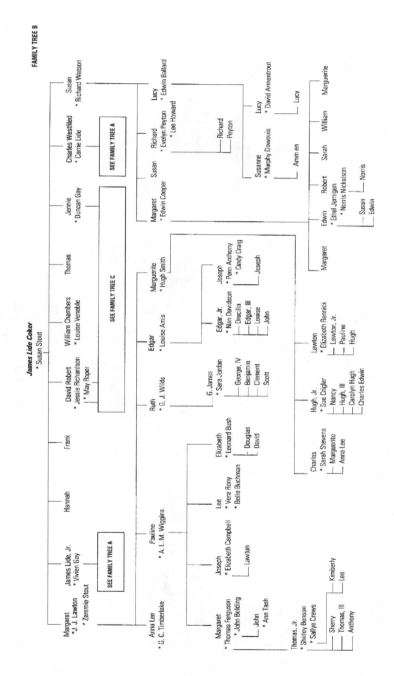

Family Tree C

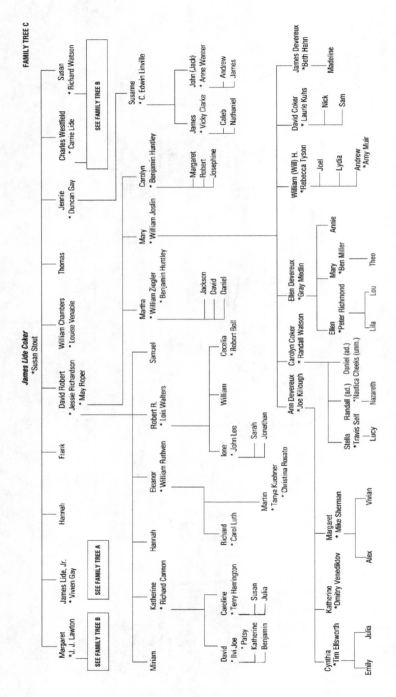

On this page, the author has extended Major Coker's descendents through William and Mary Coker Joslin two more generations.

APPENDIX 4

HOW MAJOR COKER GREW BEYOND THE MINDSET OF THE OLD SOUTH

In this appendix, we gather up the evidence from James' entire life to demonstrate in a focused way that, in spite of making use of ten slaves given to him by his father, for eight years, James became a champion of civil rights for more than half a century.

Major Coker's Progression

By jumps and starts, Major Coker went from being a 20 year old scientific farmer who vocally disagreed with slavery and chose not to purchase slaves, into eight year descension when, whether from family influence or self-interest, he received ten of his father's slaves. After eight years, in full repentance, he clearly ascended from this lapse to become an active and courageous civil rights advocate for the last 53 years of his life.

He underwent a maturation process to come into the full courage of his convictions. Psychologists, including Jean Piaget and Lawrence Kohlberg, allow for several stages of human moral and ethical development, lasting well into adulthood.[1] Also, from the Christian viewpoint, as God superintends the growth of His children into Christlikeness, a bumpy road is pretty much the usual Christian experience (Philippians 1:6, 2:12). So if God, human psychology, and Rev. Caldwell, all allow Major Coker time to grow beyond the mindset of the Old South, it seems that we should as well.

If one wants to blame Major Coker for a bumpy eight year journey from slave owner to civil rights champion, we must also blame Abraham Lincoln for taking 11 years to mature in his attitudes on race. In 1854, Lincoln said that his first predisposition was "to free all the slaves, and send them to Liberia."[2] And at his first inaugural address on March 4, 1861, he promised he "had no intention to change slavery in the South."[3] It was not until 1863 that he made his Emancipation Proclamation, two years into the Civil War, and only two years before Major Coker freed his slaves. People take a little time to grow.

James and York grew up to be best friends.
Drawn by professonal artist Dan Nelson.

After 50 years, York returns to James, who gladly gave him employment.
Picture by Raleigh, NC artist Dan Nelson. Used by permission.

Why Major Coker Grew Beyond Racial Prejudice

James's life purpose took root when he was a youngster. His calling was to provide better economic, educational, and spiritual opportunities for his fellow South Carolinians, both white and African American. Despite his father's slave ownership, James was never comfortable with slavery, and his best friend in boyhood was an African American boy named York. York gained freedom during the war, but 50 years afterward, he still respected Major Coker as a man and as a friend. After half a century he returned from the north to James and to Hartsville, and Major Coker embraced him.

James's alliance with the Confederate cause in the Civil War was not because of prejudice. James volunteered to defend his home state from northern invaders because he believed it was his duty. Also, he, like most southerners, were frustrated at over 30 years of economic exploitation from the North due to The Tariff of 1828. As described in detail at the beginning of Chapter 4, the war started not just over slavery, but also because of this economic exploitation of the south.

J. W. Norwood, son of James's boyhood friend George Norwood, commented: "[James] did not believe in slavery, but he did believe that the tariff laws operated against the best interest of the South, and he accepted for the time being the popular idea in South Carolina that it was wise to secede, and that we had the constitutional right of secession."[4]

FULL DISCLOSURE: For eight Years James owned Ten Slaves that his Father Gave him.

The Darlington County census of 1860 records that James's father Caleb Coker, Jr., owned 114 slaves.[5] At no time did James ever buy any slaves himself, but in 1857, when he was 21, his father gave him, "ten or twelve slaves"[6] along with the

1000 acres of the Hartsville plantation. The Federal Census of 1860 shows that James had 13 slaves, including three under age three.[7] James was uncomfortable with slavery, but he reluctantly accepted these ten or so from his father with the land, probably because he did not want to appear ungrateful to his father. We know that James did not make his fortune on the backs of slaves, for he made no substantial fortune until after the Civil War.

Nevertheless, it must be plainly admitted that James Lide Coker did make use these ten slaves on his Hartsville farm for eight years, 1857-1865, and that this was wrong. Major Coker himself apologized, ending his book on his Civil War experience with these words: "There is one great result of the war between the States for which we are truly thankful: *Slavery is abolished.*"[8]

Abundant Evidence Showing that James Grew Beyond Prejudice

I want to thank my African American colleague, Rev. Henry Caldwell, pastor of First Church of God Ministries in Raleigh, NC for graciously helping me achieve what we believe is a balanced presentation of this subject. Rev. Caldwell, who grew up in Columbia, SC, is also a believer in the power forgiveness and in racial reconciliation under the cross. He wrote:

> Without trepidation, Major Coker transcended the racial barriers and societal norms of the time and created gainful employment opportunities for African Americans after the Civil War. In spite of hardships along the way, he lived so the light of Christ within him shone brightly in a time when light was so desperately needed. Surely, he was an example of what is good and

right in a world divided between good and evil
and right and wrong, even today.

As we examine his entire life, the evidence is abundant that
James never fit the stereotype of a slaveowner. That is just not
who James fundamentally was, as the testimony of abundant
accounts below of his goodness to African Americans indicates.

Social and Political Advocacy of African Americans

After the war, Major Coker's progressive stance and actions were
clearly Revealed. He had been a Democrat, but at that time of
Southern Reconstruction, he left the Democratic Party for a while,
because of their backward and repressive attitudes toward
freedmen. He joined and led the Union Reform Party, endorsing
a political platform calling for "full recognition of the legal and
political rights of the Negro." [9] His party also put at least one
African American on the ticket of each district in the state.[10]
Despite the Major's best efforts, his Union Reform Party did not
carry the day because he and his party went much further on
integration than most whites were willing to go at that time.

His Economic Advocacy of African Americans

Carolina Fiber Company paper machine, c. 1915, demonstrating the Major's desire for for cross-cultural emloyment. Picture courtesy of Sonoco Products, Inc.

As the leader of the
post-war Hartsville
Agricultural Committee,
Major Coker made
sure that freed slaves,
many of whom became
sharecroppers, received
"secure full compensation
and proper treatment of
the laborers employed."[11]

273

He further boosted the fortunes of African American sharecroppers by providing them with superior seeds and fertilizers, as described in Chapters 6 and 7. He also offered African Americans gainful employment in his industries, as described in Chapters 8 and 9. And he treated all his employees the same. Paul Rogers, secretary and treasury of the fiber company said: "Whenever any of these—superintendent or workers, black or white— came into the office, they usually went by the Major's office to have a friendly word or chat with him."[12]

African-Americans in Spartanburg, SC doing business with Coker Pedigreed Seed Co. and its Clemson affiliate, the SC Crop Improvement Association. These superior seeds helped SC's rural farmers see real profits and a better life. It all started in 1859 with Major Coker's fertilizer and crop experiments. Photo date is 1953. Permission of Linda Harris of Spartanburg.

His Spiritual Advocacy of African Americans

Major Coker was also concerned for African Americans spiritually. He and Sue expanded the Hartsville First Baptist Sunday School not only in Hartsville but by making two trips a month[13] to teach literacy and Bible lessons to barefoot country children, African American and white, in previously overlooked rural areas.

His Literary and Educational Advocacy of African Americans

In their rural Sunday Schools, James and Sue first taught the children to read out of Webster's Blue Back Speller, then taught them Bible. And as documented in Chapter 15, after Major Coker had gained his wealth, he donated some of his land near the end of Sixth Street to be used for a school for African Americans.

His Empathy for the Hardships of African Americans

Maum Delphi Chapman added: "Major Coker was a kind man – he sure was – and I'd be nursing the children (the grandchildren) and he'd come along and say, 'Had your breakfast?' 'No Sir.' 'Put that pan down before you do anything more and get your breakfast.' He was good to white and colored. …. The Major- he'd just walk around in the house- I'd see him coming or going and he'd see me coming and ask if I was tired. 'You set down and rest I know you're tired – you been running around here a long time.' 'You set down and rest,' he'd say to me."[14] For more on Major Coker's generosity, please see Generosity and Care for the Less Fortunate from Chapter 15 on his character qualities.

For discussion questions on the Major's influence on progress in race relations, see https://www.willjoslin.com/ major/questions/ racialprogess.

He Treated all People with the same Respect

Major Coker was never clannish, and in addition to African Americans, he showed concern for those from other backgrounds. In the course of the Major's sales of pulp and paper to the Atlanta Paper Company,

Carolina Fiber Co. employees chatting in Major Coker's Office. Illustration by professional artist Dan Nelson.

he developed a friendship with a Jewish paper executive, Mr. Lieberman. They became quite cordial, going to dinner together when the Major was in Atlanta, and they traded friendly jokes.[15]

Furman Professor Harvey T. Cook, contemporary of the Major, added: "On one occasion, a friend made unkind remarks about Roman Catholics in his presence. He immediately told of a kindness he received at the hands of Irish Roman Catholics [when he was severely injured] in Baltimore who knew him to be a Protestant and a paroled Rebel prisoner. His poise, common sense, and fair-mindedness were a cause of wonder." [16]

The Author 's Work in Racial Reconciliation

My parents, Bill and Mary Joslin, were enthusiastic supporters of Martin Luther King, Jr. When an African American attended our church in Raleigh, a rare occurrence in the late 1960's, my father was the first to shake his hand. Also, my mother, Major Coker's granddaughter, spent a good portion of her teaching career as a French Professor at St. Augustine's College in Raleigh, an African American school. Their social consciences rubbed off on their six children. My wife Becky is also from a family with civil rights sympathies, as her great-great grandfather, Elijah Tyson from Maryland, was an abolitionist.

All Believers of All Colors are One Under Christ

Since my conversion at age 20, I've found that sweet and lasting common ground is "the unity of the Spirit in the bond of peace" (Ephesians 4:3) through mutual faith in Jesus Christ. At the foot of the cross, no one, high or low born, from developed or underdeveloped nations, has any right to be prideful. And to me, therein lies the key to racial unity. Believers know that all humans have the same problem of selfishness rooted in sin, and we all have an equal need for forgiveness through the same Jesus: "You were called in one hope of your calling; one Lord, one faith...." (Eph. 4:4-6). And ultimately there's only one race – the human race: "And He has made from one blood every nation of men to dwell on all the face of the earth...." (Acts 17:26, NKJV).

Spiritual unity is no lame ethereal concept. It's the down to-earth power that reconciled two of the most dipolar men in history: President Nixon's hatchet man and "evil genius" Chuck Colson, one of the infamous "Watergate Seven," and former communist and bomb-throwing Black Panther, Eldridge Cleaver. After their conversions, they shook hands in fellowship and dined together as brothers in Washington, DC in 1975. Colson, just out of jail, brought along some inmates. "Hope you don't mind eating with eleven convicts, brother," Colson quipped. With a broad grin, Cleaver replied: "Hey man, you'll make me feel right at home." [17]

We Need Each Other

Just as whites direly need the contributions of gifted blacks, such as the piercing insights of escaped slave Frederick Douglass, the agricultural genius of George Washington Carver, and the courage of Rosa Parks, under the same banner of racial equality, blacks benefit from savvy white allies such as evangelist and emancipationist John Wesley, father of African American Episcopal churches, economic advocate for freedmen, James Lide Coker, and Harlem minister David Wilkerson, who liberated many urban youth from gang warfare and drug addiction.

The Table of Brotherhood

Martin Luther King said: "I have a dream that one day on the red hills of Georgia, the sons of former slaves and the sons of former slave owners will be able to sit down together at the table of brotherhood."[18] We all need to hear some of the really good news that is happening. Today The joyful union of African American and white believers together at "the table of brotherhood" is happening in the southern United States, even among traditionally hear some of the really good news that is already happening.

The joyful union of African American and white believers together at what Dr. King called "the table of brotherhood" is happening in the southern United States, even among traditionally white Southern Baptists. It's been a long time coming, but it's here! In November of 2019, for the first time, an African American pastor, Alex Sands, was elected head of South Carolina's Baptist Convention, a group of churches affiliated with the Southern Baptist Convention. Pastor Sands, who founded and leads Kingdom Life Church in Simpsonville, told South Carolina's *The Greenville News* "I didn't think we were at the point 10 years ago that an African American could be

Rev. Henry Caldwell and I are in the same city-wide men's fellowship. This is Rev. Caldwell's sanctuary at Raleigh's First Church of God. Henry played on UNC-Charlotte's 1977 Final Four Team with Cedrick "Cornbread" Maxwell.

president. I have seen a lot of changes, positive changes." [19] Along the way, it was racially progressive leaders like Major Coker who got the ball rolling toward reconciliation after the war who have hastened the arrival of this day.

I have seen the same God-ordained racial unity spring up in Raleigh, North Carolina at inter-racial churches like Crossroads Fellowship[20] and parachurch ministries like the Raleigh Dream

Center[21] and Clubs in the City.[22] I have had the privilege of being blessed in my participation with some of these cross-cultural ministries in Raleigh and elsewhere, as shown below.

I am a friend of Clubs In The City Inner City Ministry in downtown Raleigh, where I volunteered to lead an urban business club in 2016-2017. We taught the youth maketing, sales and profit / loss. Each youth took home his/her own earnings.

We train these urban youth in entrepreneurial principles such as Proverbs 31:16, 18: "She considers a field and buys it; from her earnings she plants a vineyard. She senses that her gain is good." We teach them about successful black entrepreneurs such as America's Earl Graves Jr., and Africa's Strive Masiyiwa. We encourage them to start their own businesses someday.

Youth in the author's business club at Clubs In The City in Raleigh, NC washing cars to earn their own money.

From 1984-1987, my wife and I led the Inner City Bible Church's children's ministry while we were at Dallas Theological Seminary.

ENDNOTES FOR APPENDIX 4: HOW MAJOR COKER GREW BEYOND THE MINDSET OF THE OLD SOUTH

1   Editor, Lumen, Educational Psychology, "Kohlberg's Stages of Moral Development," https://courses.lumenlearning.com/teachereducationx92x1/chapter/kohlbergs-stages-of-moral-development/, accessed 1/21.
2   Abraham Lincoln, History.com article edited by Sarah Pruitt, June 23, 2020, "5 Things You May Not Know About Abraham Lincoln, Slavery and Emancipation," https://www.history.com/news/5-things-you-may-not-know-about-lincoln-slavery-and-emancipation, accessed January 2021.
3   David John Marotta, and Megan Russell, June 23,2013 article "Protective tariffs: Primary cause of the Civil War," https://www.dailyprogress.com/opinion/guest_columnists/protective-tariffs-primary-cause-of-the-civil-war/article_63b77f5c-dc0c-11e2-8e99-001a4bcf6878.html, accessed December 29, 2019.
4   J. W. Norwood, op. cit., p. 425.
5   Darlington County census, 1860, on website https://sites.rootsweb.com/~ajac/scdarlington.htm (accessed December 29, 2019).
6   Will Coker, *Recollections*, p. 4.
7   Compiler, 1997-2020 article "All 1860 U.S. Federal Census – Slave Schedules results for James L. Coker, https://www.ancestry.com/search/collections/7668/?f-80000002=James+L.&f-80000003=Coker&gender=m&keyword=coker&keyword_x=1&residence=_hartsville-darlington-south+carolina-usa_22004&residence_x=_1-1-a. This census documents thirteen slaves, but three are three years old and younger, meaning James's father gave him ten slaves in 1857.
8   James Lide Coker, *History of Company G and E*, op. cit., p. 210.
9   Simpson, op. cit., pp. 90-91
10 Simpson, op. cit., pp. 90-91
11 George Lee Simpson Jr. op. cit., p. 88.
12 Paul Rogers, *Recollections*, p. 22.
13 Kate Chambers, op. cit., p. 78.
14 Ibid., pp. 88-89.
15 Paul Rogers, *Recollections*, pp. 24-25.
16 Harvey Toliver Cook, op. cit., p. 436.
17 Editor, Prison Fellowship web site, "A White Knight and a Black Panther," https://www.prisonfellowship.org/2016/03/white-knightblack-panther/, accessed 11/26/2020.
18 Dr. Martin Luther King, op. cit.

19   Mike Ellis, *The Greenville News*, November 22, 2019 article "SC Baptists elected their first black President," https://www.greenvilleonline.com/story/news/local/2019/11/22/sc-baptist-convention-elected-their-first-black-president/4248049002/ (accessed February 17,2020).

20   Editor, Crossroads Fellowship Church web site, 2018, 2020, https://www.crossroads.org/enespanol.

21   Editor, Raleigh Dream Center ministry web site, 2014, 2020, https://raleighdreamcenter.org/

22   Editor, Clubs In The City ministry web site, https://clubsinthecity.org/.

APPENDIX 5

THE MAJOR'S FAITH, SIMPSON'S CRITICISM, AND DARWIN

The Major's most complete statement of faith was his orthodox confession in his farm journal in January of 1859. Before this, and decades afterward, he affirmed this expression with corroborating statements. We will also examine a different opinion of Major Coker's faith by the late George Lee Simpson, Jr., author of *The Cokers of Carolina*, and in the process we touch on James's response to Darwin. Our outline will be:

A. The Major's Confessions of Faith in his Farm Journal and two other sources
B. George Lee Simpson's Criticisms of the Major's Faith, and Answers to them

A. The Major's Confessions of Faith in his Farm Journal and two other sources

James's confessions show that he believed God is personal and immanent. With the exception of the inserted headings, which do not change his meaning, his exact words are given below, unchanged from the way he penned them, and unchanged from how they presently stand in the archives of The South Caroliniana Room at the University of South Carolina in Columbia. His journal makes it plain that James had more than a passing acquaintance with the Bible.

Text of James's Farm Journal broken into Topics
The Holiness of God, and the Gravity of Discussing God

Showing both the faith of a child and the brain of a scholar, James wrote:

> Before a man engages in the consideration of a question whose merits involve the character and attributes of God, he may pause and consider. He is about to tread on sacred ground; he is about to touch that which is holy. In endeavoring to cope with the greatness of the subject, may he not assume too much, act with too much freedom, and even while making an effort to accomplish his purpose, commit the sin Uzzah did when he put forth his hand to touch the ark and called down upon him the displeasure of God for his presumptions. The character of the Supreme Being is a subject of such sanctity that we must, like the High Priest, when he would go within the veil of the temple, to purify ourselves, putting away all import and self-righteousness, and remember that our license thus to deal with

these sacred terms and penetrate into the most Holy place is derived from our communion with Christ our Lord and granted us through his most comprehensive merits. It is with such feelings that the writer has undertaken the present essay, and with the hope that he may be able to set forth in an appropriate and becoming manner, the views which he trusts are in accordance with the teaching of the divine word.

PHOTOGRAPHED SECTION FROM JAMES'S FARM JOURNAL

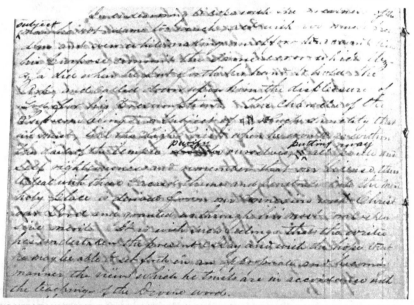

TWO LIBRARIANS FROMTHE ARCHIVES AT THE UNIVERSITY OF SOUTH CAROLINA'S CAROLINIANA ROOM HELPED ME TO READ AND RECORD THE WORDS OF THIS FARM JOURNAL AS ACCURATELY AS POSSIBLE:

"In endeavoring to cope with the greatness of the subject, may he [man] not assume too much, act with too much freedom, and even while making an effort to accomplish his purpose, commit the sin Uzzah did when he put forth his hand to touch the ark and called down upon him the displeasure of God for his presumptions. The character of the Supreme Beig is a subject of such sanctity that we must, like the High Priest, when he would go within the veil of the temple, purify ourselves, putting away all import and self righteousness, and remember that our license thus to deal with these sacred terms and penetrate into the most Holy place is derived from our communion with Christ our Lord and granted to us through His most comprehensive merits. It is with such feelings that the writer has undertaken the present essay, and with the hope that he may be able to set forth in an appropriate and becoming manner, the views which he trusts are in accordance with the teaching of the Divine word."

Courtesy of the South Caroliniana Library, University of South Carolina, Columbia, SC.

The Providence of God

James continued:

The doctrine of special providence teaches that God rules man not only in the general working of fixed laws but with special reference to the emotion and wants of each individual. That He marks our situation and dispenses directly such blessings and such punishments as will cause us to feel His presence and acknowledge His power. While in His existence previous to man's creation, He foreknew and had marked all the details incidental to the course of life our race was to pursue; He is none the less competent now to take the direction of these events and cause to occur by special interposition those things which had been decreed. It is a doctrine that is taught in the scriptures so plainly and so profusely that we are at a loss to select when we are called on to show the proof therein contained.

James actually did give his examples of Providence under "Examples of God's Providence" below.

God's Direct, Sudden, and Supernatural Creation of Man from Dust

We see in the scripture account of man's creation; we are clearly shown in language explicit and particular, that God was present there to direct and personally perform the work. We are not told that his laws, being established, operated, and produced that result. No! We are told that

God made Adam of the dust of the ground and breathed into his nostrils the breath of life; [next word illegible]. He placed him in Paradise and then appearing to him told him what were his duties – even what he should eat and should refrain from eating. Then God looked upon Adam's lonely condition and determined to relieve it and so caused a deep sleep to fall upon him, took a rib from his side, made a woman of the rib, and gave her to the man as a companion.

Examples of God's Providence – James continues his previous thoughts from "The Providence of God"

Do you suppose, my friend, that Adam, after that, doubted that God was always and would in person attend to his wants and crown him with blessings when it was proper that he should enjoy them? This truth is not less evidently taught in the account of Adam's fall and punishment, in the history of Noah and the flood, in the lives of Abram and Isaac and Jacob, of Moses, and all the prophets and kings mentioned in the Bible. Let us cite a few instances. Abraham, obeying the divine command and trusting in the faithful fulfillment of all God's promises, takes his son Isaac as an offering and prepares to sacrifice him upon the altar which he has erected. By the Special Providence of God, the intended victim is reprieved, and another prepared to take his place. Not only is it indicated to Abraham that a ram shall be slain instead of the youth, but God even provides the victim and secures him for the slaughter. When Joseph was cruelly torn from his devoted father and sold, poor Jacob mourned him as lost indeed, and even his brethren, who knew his fate, repented of[1] [the essay suddenly ended here, perhaps due to the necessities of the day].

The Major's on his belief in heaven, and hell, long after Darwin published

These last two quotes concerning James's confessions are not from his farm journal, but are added because they also express his orthodox beliefs. Major Coker strongly affirmed his belief in heaven when consoling his mother right after Charles' death when he wrote:

He is with the blessed Savior now, happier than when here, his fighting is over, his rest is come, eternal rest!"[1]

Later in life, Major Coker also said as much in his conversations. Professor Cook said the Major had told Dr. Osler that, in spite of Darwin causing some to question their faith in an afterlife, "he believed it anyway."[2]

As to his belief in hell, J. E. Norment of South Carolina's *News and Courier,* in his memorial tribute, "Major James L. Coker," quoted the Major as he described his own intentionally constructive life, James contrasted his life with an ominous destiny for the cowardly:

I have molded many bricks and have built them into serviceable beautiful walls. I envy no man who has sat unbruised amid the world's idler, dimmer, cooler corners, waiting for death to show him some justification for a record of empty days.[3]

---

[1] James Lide Coker's personal farming journal, op. cit., p. 28.

B. George Lee Simpson's Criticisms of the Major's Faith, and Answers to them

In *The Cokers of Carolina*, written in 1956, Simpson acknowledged some positive things about the Major's faith, but he misrepresented James regarding the farm journal. In fact, he criticized and minimized James's defense of Genesis.

Simpson went so far as to attack his motives for writing it, saying that "deep in himself" James knew what he wrote was wrong. Simpson also implied that the credibility of Christian faith ended with Darwin's "new science" (meaning the macroevolutionary part of Darwin's theory, which Simpson, but not James, took as fact). Ignoring James's well-documented statements of faith, Simpson tried to "rescue" Major Coker by reinventing James's faith according to Simpson's sentiments. Without substantiation, he proclaimed that James's journal entry amounted to his "one last, unsuccessful affirmation of the old faith."[4] We shall quote Simpson directly. The context in his book is Chapter 3, p. 50, right after James finished at Harvard:

> So in his farm journal that he began so confidently in the interests of a new world of science, he wrote one last and unsuccessful affirmation of the older faith. His subject was the doctrine of the special providence of God. He did not deny his science, and he had the simple loyalty to try and affirm the religion of his mother. But he had gone too far. Hannah believed. But James, in his tract, attempted to prove the special providence of God. That was the word that stood between two eras. Special providence can be believed in with the whole being, but it cannot be proved. Deep in himself, James must have known this, because the whole tract has the hollow sound of circular reasoning, totally out of tone with

anything he wrote before or after. He was a good many years in working this problem out, but in the end, it was to be science and the church, rather than Hannah's intuitional religion.[5] is His

This amounts to an attack on Major Coker's faith and spiritual legacy. For over sixty-four years Simpson's undocumented assessment has gone unchallenged. Honestly, it's time we compared and contrasted Simpson's assertions with what James actually said in his own writings.

1. Was James's farm journal entry of 1859 in fact his "one last and unsuccessful affirmation of the older faith?"

In 1862, three years after his journal entry, when his brother Charles died at Malvern Hill, the Major consoled his mother, saying, "Have we not, Mother, many causes for thanksgiving?... We know that Charles was a Christian, he professed to be one, and he lived as a follower of the Lamb."[6]

James wrote more confessions corroborating his farm journal in the year 1899, forty years afterward, and also forty years after Darwin's publication of *The Origin of Species*. In that year, at age sixty-two, the Major wrote a book on his company in the Civil War, entitled *History of Company G and E*. He described how much he admired the remarkable evangelic faith of Jefferson Davis, Stonewall Jackson, and Robert E. Lee. He also spoke in glowing terms of the "true conversion" of men in his company:

> President Davis was a devoted Christian; General Robert E. Lee possessed in extraordinary fullness the sweet characteristics of a true religion; Stonewall Jackson stands forth as a "burning and shining light," praying as he fought and

fighting as he prayed... Religious meetings were
always encouraged throughout the armies, and
thousands of men professed a true conversion
before the assembled congregations of their
comrades.[7]

In the same book, while grappling with the war's
devastation, Major Coker wrote in 1899 that he and other
Confederate Christians were "believing that they would not
be altogether forsaken of God, but would receive His guidance
in the dark night which enveloped their beloved Southland."[8]
He also founded his schools on the Christian faith and invited
William Jennings Bryan to speak at Coker College. So, my
reader, in 1859, did James gave "one last and unsuccessful
affirmation of the older faith"?

Simpson also claimed James's farm tract was "totally out of
tone with anything he wrote before or after." Let's consider this.
Before James wrote his farm journal confession in 1859, back at
The Citadel in 1856, James said of his conversion and baptism
that he was "indulging a hope." Then over a period of 62 years,
from 1856 to 1918, a scope of 62 years before, during, and after
his farm journal, Major Coker enthusiastically affirmed his
Christian faith.

Do you think James's own descriptions from 1856 of his
brother Charles as "a follower of the Lamb," and from 1899
of General Jackson as "'a burning and shining light, praying
as he fought and fighting as he prayed,'" and of the "true
conversions," of war comrades, and, that the post-war South
was, "not altogether forsaken of God, but would receive His
guidance in the dark night" actually represent someone who
had, as Simpson implied, rejected the hope and doctrines of
the Christian faith for "science?"

Victory of Faith over Doubt

As mentioned in the Introduction, James had a period of doubt about his faith that occurred in the wake of Darwin, between c. 1879 and 1994. Even for faithful Christians, a period of testing is not unusual. For different reasons, Mother Teresa, C. S. Lewis, Billy Graham, John Calvin, and John the Baptist each experienced doubts, and each emerged victorious.[9] For James, he confronted his doubts by carefully reconsidering *Origin of Species,* and, in the end, found no reason to doubt the faith. Like Christian in John Bunyan's classic, *Pilgrim's Progress,* James escaped the dungeon of "Doubting Castle," and the torments of "Giant Despair," and was glad to return to the pilgrim pathway.[10]

And his return to the pathway was sure. Soon after his death, his cousin Frank R. Chambers, who knew him for 57 years, twice addressed the victory of his faith over doubt in his speech at Coker College on Founder's Day on April 9, 1919:

> To a man of Major Coker's philosophical mind, it is not surprising that at one period his church activities were arrested by questions of theological dogma; but fundamentally his faith held fast, and in my late conversations with him, we were in perfect accord regarding the future life and its glorious expectations.

Chambers added:

> You are all aware how fully his faith was exemplified in placing Coker College, the special pride of his heart, under Christian control: that its character for all times should be distinctly religious.[11]

When we also consider that James faithfully taught Bible in Sunday school for thirty-eight of the years between 1857 and 1905, and was still teaching Bible at the Welsh Neck High School chapel in 1908, we may safely conclude that James's own writings and actions simply do not square with Simpson's statement that for him "in the end, it was to be science and the church, rather than Hannah's [so called] intuitional religion."[12] And honestly, does Major Coker, who invited William Jennings Bryan to speak at his college in 1911, sound, as Simpson alleged, like a man who had turned to science to replace his belief in the creator God?

2. Did James use "circular reasoning" when affirming the sovereignty of God?

Simpson wrote that "the whole [farm] tract has the hollow sound of circular reasoning." He said this because, in the first section of the essay, James says that the providence of God "is a doctrine that is taught in the scriptures so plainly and so profusely that we are at a loss to select when we are called on to show the proof therein contained." If this were all James had said on the matter, leaving off any examples, the charge of circular reasoning in that section might be justified. But that is not the case. For whatever reason, Simpson clearly missed the Major's examples of God's providence, which he clearly gave several lines further down in the same journal entry. The subsequent examples of providence James gave are:

a) God attended to Adam's loneliness by providing a wife.
b) God warned the world of the coming flood, told Noah to build the ark, and then saved Noah's family.
c) God provided a ram for Abraham, so that he need not sacrifice his son Isaac.

d) God worked in the patriarch Joseph's life, keeping him alive and well in Egypt while his father Jacob thought him dead.

3. In his apparent eagerness to discredit James's evangelic faith, Simpson wrote: "Special providence can be believed in with the whole being, but *it cannot be proved.*" Simpson was following a materialistic philosophy of education, which holds us that faith and reason are contradictory. Simpson would have been correct on unverifiability if James had tried to prove providence with mere personal examples from his life. But James did not mention personal examples. With his examples of Adam, Noah, Abraham, and Joseph above, James was tracing the history of God's providence in the lives of the patriarchs over thousands of years. James was saying that God is in ultimate control over all of history and that, as James wrote, He makes "interpositions" into history.

James's Belief in Providence, and Evidence for Providence

Major Coker's belief in providence was not, as Simpson strongly implied, naïve. I must admit that I take Simpson's condescending tone toward my great-grandfather's faith a bit personally, so I will demonstrate, by way of the Bible's prophetic fulfillments, that James's belief in providence was, and is, more than reasonable. The following prophecies were each fulfilled exactly, hundreds of years after being foretold. There's no circular reasoning here, for we include corroborating evidence of each prophecy's fulfillment from outside the Bible.

a) In 725 B.C., Micah predicted Messiah would be **born in Bethlehem**, an obscure, unlikely birthplace for a king (Micah 5:2), fulfilled with Jesus' birth in Bethlehem in Luke 2:4-7. Regarding extra-biblical evidence, in 2017, National Geographic writer Simon Worrall, after reviewing the tradition, wrote, "There is lots of evidence in its favor."[13]

b) In 700 B.C., Isaiah wrote: "A virgin shall be with child, and bear a son, and she will **call his name 'Immanuel**, meaning "God with us" (Isaiah 7:14). Not to discredit the virgin birth, but we'll focus on the second part of the prophecy, "Immanuel," which was fulfilled when Jesus was born of Mary in Matthew 1:23-25, and immediately called "Immanuel," This is still being fulfilled, since millions through the centuries, up to today, still refer to Him as "God with us."

c) In 1000 B.C., Nathan prophesied that Messiah would be a **direct descendant of Israel's King David** (2 Samuel 7a, 12-13), exactly fulfilled in Matthew 1:1-16 and Luke 3;23-38, where Jewish genealogies record both Mary and Joseph as direct descendants of David. This is why blind Bartimaeus called out: "Jesus, son of David, have mercy on me"(Mark 10:47). Outside the Bible, the Babylonian Talmud, a book of rabbinic traditions from before Christ onward, acknowledges His Davidic lineage, saying Jesus was "near to the kingship."[14]

d) In 700 B.C., Isaiah prophesied that the Christ would, unexpectedly, be, by and large, **rejected as King by his own people, the Israelites** (Isaiah 49:7; 53:3). In fulfillment, John 1:11 says that from the moment of His birth, "His own did not receive Him," because the chief Jewish priests and King Herod, a half-Jew, knew of His birth from the magi, but did not bother to accompany them on the short trip to Bethlehem. This rejection was complete in 30 AD, when the Jewish mob, incited by the priests, called for Christ's crucifixion with: "We have no king but Caesar" (John 19:14). Verification outside the Bible is evident. It is common knowledge most Jews have not yet accepted Christ as their Messiah and King.

e) In 700 BC, Isaiah prophesied Jesus would be **"a light to the *Gentiles*"** (Hebrew root word *"goy"* meaning non-Jews, or non-Jewish nations. This was not necessarily expected, since, in the Old Testament, Jews generally considered Gentiles unclean. Yet Gentile worship was fulfilled when the magi journeyed from Arabia to bow before Christ (Matt. 2:1-11), and more broadly at Christ's death, when the restrictive veil in the Jewish temple separating God's presence from all but the Jewish high priest, was torn in two from top to bottom. In that moment, God emphasized that His offer of salvation was universal and to all who all, Jew and non-Jew, who would receive it. Outside the Bible, the fulfillment is also historically evident; a much higher percentage of non-Jews than Jews have embraced Christ as Savior.

f) In 700 B.C., Isaiah prophesied that Messiah would **"proclaim liberty to the captives"** (Isaiah 61:1). Jesus initially fulfilled this role as liberator in his hometown synagogue in Luke 4:18-20, when He rose and quoted Isaiah: "The Spirit of the Lord is upon Me, because He has anointed me to... proclaim liberty to the captives...." Through the centuries, millions, including myself, give testimony that Christ liberated them from the worst of all captivities, the fear of death. Tens of thousands more add that Christ also freed them from alcoholism, drug abuse, and from other destructive addictions and fears.

g) In 700 B.C., Isaiah also prophesied **Christ would be crucified,** "pierced for our transgressions, and crushed for our iniquities." (Isaiah 53:5). This was fulfilled on Good Friday, the eve of the Passover, in His crucifixion (Luke 23:33). As corroborating evidence, the Babylonian Talmud says, "They hanged him on the eve of the Passover."[15]

h) In 1000 BC, King David predicted Christ's resurrection: "Thou wilt not allow Thy Holy one to undergo decay" (Psalm 16:9-11) and Isaiah prophesied the resurrection (Isaiah 25:8, 53:11-12). When Christ rose, He changed the life of his brother James. Previously, even after He had turned water to wine, James rejected his Messiahship (John 7:5). But when his risen brother appeared to him (1 Cor. 15:7), James believed, and so emboldened, went on to lead the Jerusalem church (Acts 15:13), a dangerous job in a hotbed of murderous persecution. This was not a job he'd have chosen unless strongly convinced Christ had conquered death for him. And modern scholars accept James's leadership of the Jerusalem church as historical.[16]

There is other evidence that, from the get-go, the infant church was strongly convinced Christ rose. First century Roman Senator, Cornelius Tacitus called Christians' belief in the resurrection "the pernicious superstition,"[17] and 2nd century Roman historian Suetonius referred to it as a "a new and mischievous superstition."[18]

Answering Objections to Providential Prophecy

Some deny the prophecies were written hundreds of years prior to fulfillments, alleging they were actually written after their fulfillments. This argument fails because the Septuagint, the translation of the entire Old Testament from Hebrew to Greek by Jewish scholars, containing all Old Testament prophecies, was completed under King Ptolemy II Philadelphus of Egypt by 246 BC, two and a half centuries before Christ,[19] and this Greek version of the Bible was widely used in the Graeco-Roman world before Jesus was born.

Others allege that Jesus faked His way into Messiahship, deliberately trying to fulfill the prophecies. Aside from making

Jesus into a malicious deceiver, which no one thinks, this acting scenario does not make sense. Christ had absolutely no control over his birthplace, over his genealogical lineage from David, over whether or his mother would call him Immanuel at his birth, and over whether scores of Gentiles would accept Him, a low-born Jew, as their Savior. So it was impossible for Him to fake these fulfillments.

Mathematical Odds in Favor of Major Coker's Belief in Providence

The proof of divine providence was elucidated by Peter Stoner, MS, and Robert C. Newman, Ph.D. in astrophysics, Cornell University, in their book *Science Speaks*. They performed a probability study of the likelihood of just eight of these prophecies being fulfilled hundreds of years later, apart from divine providence, in just one small part of the world, Judea, in just one person. Such a possibility is one in 10^{28}, or one in 10,00 0,000,000,000,000,000,000,000,000. That's one in ten octillions.[20] That is just for *eight* fulfilled prophecies, and the Bible records more than two hundred.[21] If we took half of those eight, four fulfilled prophecies, the odds are still one in 10 quintillion, or one in 1,000,000,000,000,000.

So despite George Lee Simpson's claim that providence "cannot be proved," strong evidence for providence is empirically proven well beyond any reasonable doubt, and Major Coker's faith in providence and in God's "interpositions" into history is vindicated. And as a noteworthy corollary, Bible prophesies proving providence simultaneously prove the divine inspiration of the Bible, in which Major Coker also believed.

4. Was James, as Simpson alleged, suppressing his knowledge of so-called "new science" and trying to defend his mother's

faith out of some kind of misguided loyalty that amounted to dishonesty?

Simpson: "He had been raised under the pervasive religion of his mother and in what must be called a devout community... All this background contributed to a compelling personal sense of God and tied him quite closely to literal Christianity. He had gone to Harvard to study science... These were the times when evolution... was in the scientific air... Deep within himself, James must have known [notice that Simpson gives no evidence supporting this contention] this, because the whole tract has a hollow sound of circular reasoning.... In the end, it was to be science and the church, rather than Hannah's intuitional religion."[22]

Apart from his mother's faith, James clearly took personal ownership of Jesus Christ and the faith from his conversion in 1856 to the end of his life. He did not just casually adopt his mother's faith, as Simpson alleged. If his personal ownership of the faith is not yet clear, please review the above, "Was James's farm journal entry in fact his one last and unsuccessful affirmation of the older faith?"

Simpson's comment that his mother Hannah's faith was "intuitional" was likely his polite way of saying she was naïve. Furthermore, in that statement, Simpson was disregarding the kind of historical evidence for providence and biblical inspiration given above, which was available in his day as well.

5. Simpson stated that James's only subject in the journal entry was the special providence of God, saying: "His subject was the doctrine of special providence."[23] Is this true?

Oddly, in his apparent eagerness to convince us that James used circular reasoning on providence, Simpson never acknowledged the three other important points that James made in the journal regarding Genesis and the Bible:

a) **James wrote reverently of the holiness of God**: "In endeavoring to cope with the greatness of the subject, may he [an inquiring person] not assume too much, act with too much freedom, and even while making an effort to accomplish his purpose, commit the sin Uzzah did when he touched the ark and called down upon him the displeasure of God for his presumptions."

b) **James wrote of the absolute necessity of coming to God only through the merits of His Son for pardon of sins**: "Remember that our license thus to deal with these sacred terms and penetrate into the most Holy place is derived from our communion with Christ our Lord and his most comprehensive merits."

c) **James spoke of God's direct supernatural creation of Adam and Eve.** James took special care to say that God created the first couple apart from naturalistic processes: "We are not told that His laws being established, operated and produce that result. No! We are told that God made Adam of the dust of the ground and breathed into his nostrils the breath of life."

So it is clear that Simpson's critique does not represent, present, or even address James's own words in his farm journal, and neither does it represent James's faith. **In fact, when we look carefully at what Simpson said, *he failed to quote even one phrase from James's words in the journal itself,* nor did he quote from even one of the numerous other written confessions of faith which James made throughout his life, before and after the farm journal.**

6. Finally, Simpson said that James wrote his farm journal "in the interest of the world of the new science."[24]

 I found no record that James ever even used Simpson's term, "new science," in the journal or anywhere else. Other than James's theological thoughts, the journal was mainly a practical record of plantings, fertilizers, harvests, animals, etc., written in the interest of increasing profitability in his farming ventures.

But let there be no doubt about it - James was in favor of true empirical, operational science! He could recite exact chemical formulas and used them in his lab experiments to produce superior seeds and fertilizers. As boosters of farming in the South, he and D. R. used the scientific method of repetition and controlled breeding. They noted well the variations within a seed species, and used this data to create advanced seed breeds boosting farming across the South. The Major also noticed that no matter how he bred them, his seeds did not graduate to another species. There were no macroevolutionay changes - they were still seeds! So as microevolutionary adaptions go, James agreed with Darwin, who correctly observed intra-special variations in the beaks of the finches of the Galapagos Islands. But by "new science," Simpson meant more than that. He meant the naturalistic religion of macroevolution, a yet unproven hypothesis of "molecules to man" across species. Apparently, Simpson could not bear the thought that James disbelieved in "new science," and tried to "rescue" him from the evangelic faith by obscuring what James actually wrote and believed. But there is simply no evidence that Major Coker believed macroevolution; on the contrary, in his farm journal above, he stated he believed in the literal, sudden, personal, and direct creation of man and woman by God.

James read *Origin of Species*, including Darwin's free admission that the transitional fossils between species needed to justify macroevolution had not been found. In his Chapter 6, "Difficulties of the Theory," the English biologist wrote: "Why, if species have descended from other species by fine gradations, do we not everywhere see innumerable transitional forms?"[25] James's own scientific lab and field work optimizing seeds also showed him the apparent limits of evolution. No matter how well he bred cotton for optimization, it was still the same species, that is, cotton. And not matter how superior his pedigreed corn was, it was still corn.

Darwin staked his theory on a leap of faith that transitional forms between species would be found. But 160 years of ensuing paleontology have not been kind to Darwin. Evolutionary anthropologist Dr. Jeffrey H. Schwartz of the University of Pittsburgh admitted as much in 1999, writing: "Instead of filling in the gaps in the fossil record with so-called missing links, most paleontologists found themselves facing a situation in which there were only gaps in the fossil record, with no evidence of transformational intermediates between documented fossil species."[26]

With the absence of transitional forms, Dr. Schwartz and other macroevolutionists of recent decades, refusing to abandon their assumption of only naturalistic processes, changed the "new science." They resorted to a neo-Darwinian idea called "punctuated equilibrium," hypothesizing that one species must have suddenly "jumped" up to another. Perhaps if Simpson had lived a few decades later, he too would have discarded Darwin's "new science" in favor of the "new 'new science,'" and had Major Coker still been around, tried to "rescue" him from disbelieving in that as well. (;

Once again, I recognize there have been further developments in evolutionary and creationist thinking in the 21st century, and that there are also intermediate positions, falling under theistic evolution, held by many Christians, then and now.

I will go into no further detail on James's faith in this Appendix, but others from The Major's time, including his son Will Coker, J.W. Norwood, E. V. Baldy, and James's granddaughter Hannah Lide Coker, commented on his faith, and how orthodox they thought it was or wasn't. I have posted their comments on the book's web site at https://www. willjoslin.com/major/questions/moreonfaith.

In summary, James confessed Christ as his Savior and also affirmed his belief in the orthodox doctrines: the sudden creation of a literal Adam and Eve, the holiness of God, the reality of sin, the existence of hell and heaven, the need for repentance and the gracious forgiveness offered by Christ. Excepting one period of doubt, the Major affirmed these beliefs not only at the time of his conversion, but throughout his life, in the founding papers of his schools, and at the end of his life.

ENDNOTES FOR APPENDIX 5: THE MAJOR'S FAITH, SIMPSON'S CRITICISM, AND DARWIN

1   From Darlington County Historical Commission, Darlington, SC, Personal Letters of James L. Coker.

2   Cook, op. cit., p. 436.

3   J. E. Norment. op. cit.

4   Simpson, op. cit., p. 51.

5   Ibid., p. 51.

6   Simpson, op. cit., p. 65.

7   James Lide Coker, op. cit., pp. 204-205.

8   James Lide Coker, *History of Company G and E*, op. cit., p. 206.

9   Jesse Carey, *Relevant* magazine, 2019 article "Seven Prominent Christian thinkers who wrestled with doubts,"https://relevantmagazine. com/god/7-prominent-christian-thinkers-who-wrestled-doubt (accessed December 29, 2019). Also see the Billy Graham Evangelistic Association's 2014 web article by Will Graham called "The Tree Stump Prayer: When Billy Graham Overcame Doubt." As to John the Baptist's doubts, they are found in Matthew 11:2-3.

10 John Bunyan, The Pilgrim's Progress (Public Domain, 1678), Chapter 29.

11 Frank R. Chambers, *Founder's Day Speeches, April 9, 1919*, op. cit., p. 60.

12 Ibid., p. 52.

13 Simon Worrall, National Geographic, December 23, 2017 article "The Little Town of Bethlehem Has a Surprising History" (accessed August 22, 2020).

14 Editor described as one of the Sanhedrin, *The Babylonian Talmud*, 43a, as quoted by Josh McDowell and Bill Wilson, *He Walked Among Us, Evidence for the Historical Jesus* (Thomas Nelson Publishers, Nashville, TN), 1993, p. 64

15 Ibid, p. 65

16 Finney Philip, *The Origins of Pauline Pneumatology: the Eschatological Bestowal of the Spirit*, Wissenschaftliche Untersuchungen zum Neuen Testament 2, Reihe, p. 205 (2005). Mohr Siebeck, https://www.google.com/ books/edition/_/HFuc-lzhmCgC?hl=en&gbpv=1&bsq=increasing%20 trend, last accessed 9/4/2020.

17 Cornelius Tacitus, *Annals*, originally penned c. 116 AD, Loeb Edition. 15.44, as quoted by Josh McDowell and Bill Wilson, op. cit., p. 49.

18 Editor, Early Christian Writings, 2020 article "Suetonius," http://www. earlychristianwritings.com/suetonius.html.

19 Paul Lawrence, Ph.D., website of The Shiloh Excavations, 2016 article "A Brief History of the Septuagint," https://biblearchaeology.org/

research/new-testament-era/4022-a-brief-history-of-the-septuagint (accessed December 29, 2019).

20 Peter Stoner, M.S., and Robert C. Newman, Ph.D., *Science Speaks: Scientific Proof of the Accuracy of the Bible*, (Moody Press: Chicago IL), 1968, 1976, p. 106.

21 Josh McDowell, *Evidence that Demands a Verdict*, Here's Life Publishers, San Bernardino, CA, 1972, 1979, pp. 141-176, and pp. 267-320.

22 Simpson, op. cit., pp. 51-52.

23 Ibid., p. 50.

24 Simpson, op. cit., p. 51.

25 Mortimer Adler, editor, *Great Books of the Western World* (Encyclopedia Britannica, Inc: Chicago, 1952), vol. 49, "Darwin," Charles Darwin, *Origin of Species*, 1859, Chapter 6, "Difficulties of the Theory," p. 80.

26 Jeffrey H. Schwartz, *Sudden Origins* (New York, John Wiley, 1999), p. 300., as quoted by Henry D. Morris, Ph.D., 2020 article "The Scientific Case Against Evolution," https://www.icr.org/home/resources/resources_tracts_scientificcaseagainstevolution/, last accessed Sept. 20, 2020.

Bibliography

Archivist. (n.d.). Coker College Archives, Charles W. and Joan S. Coker Library-Information Technology Center. Hartsville, SC.

Ashby, C. (2013, April 19). *A Depressingly 'Ecclesiastical Perspective' by Mark Twain*. Retrieved November 15, 2019, from After+Math: https://chadashby.com/2013/04/19/a-depressingly-ecclesiastical-perspective-by-mark-twain/

Aubert, B. (2016, October). *J. Gresham Machen's The Virgin Birth of Christ: Then and Now*. Retrieved February 20, 2020, from Uniocc. com: https://uniocc.com/archive/j-gresham-machen-the-virgin-birth-of-christ-then-and-now

Baldoni, J. (2012, February 2012). *Leadership Lessons from The Iron Lady*. Retrieved from Inc.com: https://www.inc.com/john-baldoni/the-pride-and-peril-of-the-iron-lady-margaret-thatcher-leadership-lesson.html

Baldy, R. E. (1918, June 26). James Lide Coker. *Funeral Service of James Lide Coker*. Hartsville, SC: Hartsville First Baptist Church.

Baumgarten, A. (2019, November 20). *Grand Forks Herald*. Retrieved December 29, 2019, from https://www.grandforksherald.com/lifestyle/health/4779091-With-nations-highest-suicide-rate-middle-aged-white-men-often-dont-seek-mental-health-care

Beecher, H. W. (2001-2010). *Henry Ward Beecher Quotes*. Retrieved December 29, 2019, from https://www.brainyquote.com/quotes/henry_ward_beecher_124703

Behre, R. (2017, September 9). *Saving Society Hill: The birthplace of the Pee Dee looks to its past for new life*. Retrieved December 29,

2019, from Preservation South Carolina: https://preservesc.org/saving-society-hill-the-birthplace-of-the-pee-dee-looks-to-its-past-for-new-life/

Blake, T. (2001, October). *Darlinton County Census, 1860, slaveholding.* (T. Blak, Editor) Retrieved December 2019, 2019, from Rootsweb. com: https://sites.rootsweb.com/~ajac/scdarlington.htm

Bos, C. (2019). *Francis Marion, "Swamp Fox".* Retrieved February 29, 2019, from Awesome Stories: https://www.awesomestories.com/asset/view/Francis-Marion-Swamp-Fox-//1

Brakas, G. (2010, June 25). *Foundations Study Guide for Ancient Greek Philosophy.* Retrieved October 12, 2019, from The Atlas Society: https://atlassociety.org/commentary/commentary-blog/3766-foundations-study-guide-ancient-greek-philosophy

Brown, T. (2018, December 11). *Coker College Has a New Name.* Retrieved from ABC15News: https://wpde.com/news/local/Coker-college-has-a-new-name

Brown, W. E. (2011,2019). *David Hume.* Retrieved December 16 2019, from Stanford Encyclopedia of Philosophy: https://plato. stanford.edu/entries/hume/

Campell, R. (2011, April 29). *Thought Provoking John Wesley Quotes.* (R. Campbell, Editor) Retrieved March 5, 2020, from Logos Talk: https://blog.logos.com/2011/04/ten_thought-provoking_john_wesley_quotes/

Carey, J. (2019). *Seven Prominent Christian thinkers who wrestled with doubts.* Retrieved December 29, 2019, from Relevant Magazine: https://relevantmagazine.com/god/7-prominent-christian-thinkers-who-wrestled-doubt

Chambers, K. (1919, 2004). *Chronicles of A Worthwhile Family.* Hartsville, SC: Coker College with help from Edgar J. Lawton, Jr., Frank Bush.

Chisolm, J. J. (1864). A manual of military surgery, for the use of surgeons in the Confederate States army; with explanatory plates of all useful operations. 119.

Cinema, N. L. (Producer), Tolkien, J. R. (Writer), & Jackson, P. (Director). (2003). *The Return of the King* [Motion Picture].

Coclanis, P. A. (1999, Fall). David R. Coker, Pedigreed Seeds, and the Limits of Arigbusiness in Early-Twentieth-Century South Carolina. *Business and Economic History, 28*(2).

Coker, H. L. (1887). *A Story of the Late War, Written at the request of Her Children, Grandchildren, and Many Friends.* Charleston, SC: Walker, Evans, and Cogswell Company Printers.

Coker, H. L. (1915). Chapel Messages at Coker College. Hartsville, SC: Coker College.

Coker, J. L. (1858, January 28). *Farm Journal,* handwritten by James Lide Coker, Coker family boxes, The South Caroliniana Library, University of South Carolina, Columbia, SC.

Coker, J. L. (1899). *History of Company G, Ninth Regiment, Infantry, SC Army and of Company E, Sixth SC Regiment, Infantry, SC Army.* Greenwood, SC: Attic Press.

Coker, J. L. (1899,1990). *Hartsville: Its Early Settlers.* Winmark, Inc. / Jiffy Print.

Coker, J. L. (1913, October 10). Letter of James Lide Coker to J. W. Perrin. *James Lide Coker Collection.* (U. o.-B. South Caroliniana Library, Compiler) Hartsville, SC.

Coker, J. L. (1916, May 16). Last Will and Testament. Hartsville, SC.

Coker, J. L. (c. 1857-c.1817). Personal Papers. (U. o. Courtesy of South Caroliniana Library, Compiler) Hartsville, SC: James Lide Coker.

Compiler. (1997-2020). *All 1860 U.S. Federal Census – Slave Schedules results for James L. Coker.* Retrieved from ancestry. com: https://www.ancestry.com/search/collections/7668/?f-80000002=James+L.&f-80000003=Coker&gender=m&keywo rd=coker&keyword_x=1&residence=_hartsville-darlington-south+carolina-usa_22004&

Cook, H. T. (1926). *Rambles in the Peed Dee Basin, South Carolina* (Vol. 1). Columbia: The State Company.

Cralle, R. D. (1888). *Speeches of John C. Calhoun.* (R. K. Cralle, Ed.) New York, NY: D. Appleton and Co. Retrieved March 5, 2019, from

Google Books: https://books.googleusercontent.com/books/ content?req=AKW5QadyTn8FkXrjQjBgXWwyA_lIeBqHl_4JFh-FpGsQPKMeLtMyeQGr7ATHFjfgL0XuQF--Er_T_UY6BgkHFQm--v6yQuhzWZ7Q4_DRPXGlZHxBsZXj2EHs-RMalu7f9RDLFU9sB ZOIAwpOI6WPkEl0ON2MfaUMQt515ghTZ0FsJwJkov5szoxSkB BQdBek2SCNAD1oU

Cunningham, J. M. (n.d.). *Saint Justin Martyr, Christian Apologist.* Retrieved November 22, 2019, from Brittanica.com: britannica.com

Darwin, C. (1859, 1952, Charles Darwin, The Origin of Species By Means of Natural Selection (Encyclopedia Britannica, Inc. [Great Books Series, #49]: Chicago, London, Toronto,), 1952, pp. 80-87.). *The Origin of Species By Means of Natural Selection* (Vol. 49). (p. William Benton, Ed.) Chicago, IL: Encyclopedia Brittanica Great Books.

David Mention, P. (2017, August 25). *Natural Selection and Macroevolution.* Retrieved September 2, 2019, from Answers in Genesis: https://answersingenesis.org/natural-selection/ natural-selection-and-macroevolution/

Doubles, M. C. (2005). *A Century Plus: A History of Sonoco Products Company.* Hartsville, SC: Coker College Press.

Doubles, M. C. (2008). *In Quest of Excellence.* Hartsville, SC: Coker College Press.

Economy, P. (2015, June 5). *44 Inspiring John C. Maxwell Quotes for Leadership Success.* Retrieved December 29, 2019, from Inc.: https://www.inc.com/peter-economy/44-inspiring-john-c-maxwell-quotes-that-will-take-you-to-leadership-success.html

Edgar, W. (1988). *South Carolina: A History.* Columbia, SC: South Carolina Press.

Editor. (n.d.). Retrieved March 5, 2020, from Wikiquote: https:// en.wikiquote.org

Editor. (n.d.). *"The Prince of Peace," text of speech by William Jennings Bryan.* Retrieved December 29, 2019, from Trisagionseraph. tripod.com: http://trisagionseraph.tripod.com/Texts/Prince. html

Editor. (1911, June 19). Bryan at Hartsville. *Newspaper- Leader and Vindicator*. Bishopville, SC: Leader and Vindicator.

Editor. (1915). *Who's Who in America, 1914-1915*. Berkeley Heights, NJ: Marquis Press.

Editor. (1920). *James Lide Coker*. (James T. White and Company) Retrieved September 17, 2019, from The National Cyclopedia of Amerian Biography.

Editor. (1922). *International Banking Directory*. (Editor, Editor, & N. Y. Bankers Publishing Co., Producer) Retrieved December 29, 2019, from Google Books - pdf: https://books.googleusercontent.com/books/content?req=AKW5QafT6jFiXq7zPSCI7yv338U3qIt-kMA ExUCgNeJAJpppXm9FizNfx4zcp67PmMBrHMPRdGpQyNJxC JgT6ghM6-EnpkgaJMDeJfYYZiBlinrcn_sjd_pJfWpG47q91AxqQ VuOMDhbqnGnOASmEs5iqn5dppdD8Lo1EkpAI-ZihvSPAd_ KO7uSlWbGArZHdnzzqxJCO

Editor. (1928, May 28). *Founder's Day Exercises, as quoted by Malcom Doubles in A Century of Excellence*. Hartsville, SC: Coker College.

Editor. (1934). Coker College Catalogue, "Spirit and Control".

Editor. (1935). Coker College Catalogue, "Spirit and Control".

Editor. (1936). Coker College Catalogue, "Spirit and Control".

Editor. (1956, April 27). Founder's Day Exercises. (Editor, Ed.)

Editor. (1960, April 27). Founder's Day Exercises. Hartsville, SC: Coker College.

Editor. (1997). *Recollections of The Major*. Hartsville, NC: Hartsville Museum.

Editor. (2007f). *Spontaneous Generation*. Retrieved February 15, 2019, from Lumen Microbiology: https://courses.lumenlearning.com/microbiology/chapter/spontaneous-generation/

Editor. (2008). *Fulfilled Prophecy as Evidence for the Bible's Divine Origin*. Retrieved May 14, 2019, from Faith Facts: http://www.faithfacts.org/search-for-truth/maps/fulfilled-prophecy-as-evidence

Editor. (2008, August). *List of Unconvinced Scientists*. Retrieved November 1, 2019, from Evolution is Not Science: https://evolutionisntscience. wordpress.com/list-of-unconvinced-scientists/

Editor. (2009, February 2). *Last Gladiator Fight*. Retrieved from bible. org: https://bible.org/illustration/last-gladiator-fight

Editor. (2010,2017). *Hartsville Oil Mill*. Retrieved December 4, 2019, from Next Exit History: http://www.nextexithistory.com/ explore/historical-sites/hartsville-oil-mill/

Editor. (2011, 2016, May 3). Retrieved 2020, from History: https:// www.history.com

Editor. (2013, November 12). *List of Presidents of Clemson*. Retrieved November 20, 2019, from ClemsonWiki: https://clemsonwiki. com/wiki/List_of_Presidents_of_Clemson

Editor. (2013). *The WPA Guide to South Carolina: The Palmetto State*. San Antonio, TX: Trinity University Press. Retrieved from https:// books.google.com/books?id=YbLpCAAAQBAJ&dq=saint +david%2 7s+society+society+hill+named+for+patron+saint& source=gbs_navlinks_s.

Editor. (2014). *Hartsville, City of.* Retrieved July 30, 2019, from South Carolina Department of Archives and History: http://rediscov. sc.gov/scar/default.asp?IDCFile=DETAILSG.IDC,SPECI FIC=5624,DATABASE=GROUP,

Editor. (2017, June 19). *American Slavery: Separating Fact from Myth*. Retrieved February 28, 2019, from The Conversation: http:// theconversation.com/american-slavery-separating-fact-from- myth-79620

Editor. (2018). *Best Colleges, US News Rankings, Coker College, Coker College Academics*. Retrieved December 29, 2019, from US News: https://www.usnews.com/best-colleges/coker-college-3427/ academics

Editor. (2018, May 21). *Eastern Carolina Silver Company*. Retrieved November 11, 2019, from The Hartsville Museum: https:// hartsvillemuseum.org/posts/2018/1/19/eastern-carolina- silver-company

Editor. (2018). *Sonoco Inroduces Enviro-Sense Sustainable Packaging Development Initiative.* Retrieved February 2020, 2020, from Sonoco Products: https://investor.sonoco.com/news-releases/news-release-details/sonoco-introduces-envirosensetm-sustainable-packaging

Editor. (2018, August 4). *The Physical Resurrection a Historical Fact Part One.* Retrieved April 5, 2019, from Associates for Bible Research: http://www.biblearchaeology.org/post/2011/08/04/The-Physical-Resurrection-a-Historical-Fact-Part-One.aspx

Editor. (2018). *TODAY IN SOUTH CAROLINA HISTORY: THE PATRIOT WITH MEL GIBSON.* Retrieved December 29, 2019, from The Historical Commission: https://dchcblog.net/2017/06/30/today-in-south-carolina-history-the-patriot-with-mel-gibson

Editor. (2018, 2 20). *UNIVERSITY OF LOUISVILLE STRIPPED ON NAT'L CHAMPTIONSHIP...Over Sex Party Scandal.* Retrieved December 29, 2019, from TMZ Sports: https://www.tmz.com/2018/02/20/university-of-louisville-stripped-of-national-championship-sex-party-scandal/

Editor. (2019). Retrieved December 29, 2019, from Goodreads.com: https://www.goodreads.com/

Editor. (2019). *2019 College Admissions Scandal.* Retrieved from Wikipdedia.

Editor. (2019, May 18). *Benjamin Franklin Whittemore, the SCGOP's first Chairman.* Retrieved Febrary 19, 2020, from Grand Old: https://grandoldpartisan.typepad.com/blog/2019/05/benjamin-franklin-whittemore.html

Editor. (2019). *Coker Family History.* Retrieved December 29, 2019, from Ancestry.com: https://www.ancestry.com/name-origin?surname=Coker

Editor. (2019). How Sonoco Reduces its Environmental Impact. *Sonoco Publication.* Hartsville, SC: Sonoco.

Editor. (2019). *Indulge, defintion of.* Retrieved December 29, 2019, from Merriam Webster: https://www.merriam-webster.com/dictionary/indulge

Editor. (2019). *John Lide Hart*. Retrieved December 29, 2019, from WikiTree: https://www.wikitree.com/wiki/Hart-10757

Editor. (2019, November 12). *Nullification Procalamation*. (Editor, Editor) Retrieved December 29, 2019, from Library of Congress Web Guides: https://history.house.gov/Historical-Highlights/1800-1850/The-Tariff-of-Abominations/

Editor. (2019). *Plotinus*. Retrieved from New World Encyclopdia: https://www.newworldencyclopedia.org

Editor. (2019, December 18). *Robert E. Lee*. Retrieved December 29, 2019, from Wikiquote: https://en.wikiquote.org/w/index.php?title=Robert_E._Lee&action=history

Editor. (2019). *Sonoco Named One of America's Best Large Employers 2019*. Retrieved March 7, 2020, from Sonoco: https://investor.sonoco.com/news-releases/news-release-details/sonoco-named-one-americas-best-large-employers-2019

Editor. (2019). *Sonoco Products*. Retrieved Febrary 17, 2020, from Fortune: https://fortune.com/fortune500/2019/sonoco-products/

Editor. (2019, Winter). *South Carolina Historical Markers*. Retrieved 2020, from South Carolina Department of Archives and History: https://scdah.sc.gov/sites/default/files/Documents/Historic%20Preservation%20(SHPO)/Programs/Programs/Historical%20Markers/SC%20Historical%20Marker%20Program%20Guidebook%20-%20Winter%202019%20(12-9-19).pdf

Editor. (2019). *South Carolina Plantations*. Retrieved December 29, 2019, from SCIWAY.NET: https://south-carolina-plantations.com/darlington/hartsville.html

Editor. (2019, April 17). *The Emancipation Proclamation*. Retrieved December 29, 2019, from National Archives: https://www.archives.gov/exhibits/featured-documents/emancipation-proclamation

Editor. (2019). *Thomas E. Hart House - Hartsville, South Carolina*. Retrieved June 29, 2019, from SC Picture Project, Documenting our History: https://www.scpictureproject.org/darlington-county/thomas-e-hart-house.html

Editor. (2020). *Answers to Your Civil War Questions*. Retrieved December 29, 2020, from American Battlefield Trust: https://www.battlefields.org/learn/articles/civil-war-facts

Editor. (2020). *Christianity and the Civil War: Did You Know?* Retrieved March 5, 2019, from Christianity Today: https://www.christianitytoday.com/history/issues/issue-33/christianity-and-civil-war-did-you-know.html

Editor. (2020). *Eveyln Mayo Snider*. Retrieved December 29, 2019, from Coastal Carolina University: https://www.coastal.edu/aboutccu/historytraditions/founders/honorees/evelynsnider/

Editor. (2020). *Matthew Arnold on Learning 'The Best Which Has Been Thought and Said"*. Retrieved January 14, 2020, from New Learning: New Learning

Editor. (2020, January 8). *Sonoco Named One of America's Most Responsible Companies*. Retrieved January 12, 2019, from Barron's: https://www.barrons.com/articles/PR-CO-20200108-908361?tesla=y&tesla=y

Editor. (2020). *THE 10 WORST CORPORATE ACCOUNTING SCANDALS OF ALL TIME*. Retrieved December 29, 2019, from Accouting Degree: https://www.accounting-degree.org/scandals/

Editor. (2020). *The Southern 'Black Codes' of 1865-66*. Retrieved December 29, 2019, from Constitutional Rights Foundation: http://www.crf-usa.org/brown-v-board-50th-anniversary/southern-black-codes.html

Editor. (n.d.). *AZ Quotes*. Retrieved December 29, 2019, from Dwight L. Moody Quotes: https://www.azquotes.com/quote/694525

Editor. (n.d.). *Christianity Today*. Retrieved from christianitytoday.com

Editor. (n.d.). *Civil War Facts*. Retrieved December 29, 2019, from American Battlefield Trust: https://www.battlefields.org/learn/articles/civil-war-facts

Editor. (n.d.). *Coker House and Familty History*. Retrieved February 17, 2019, from United Brokerage Real Estate Services: Coker House and Familty History

Editor. (n.d.). *Coker University Web Site*. Retrieved from https://www.coker.edu

Editor. (n.d.). *James H. Carlisle History of SC Slide Collection*. Retrieved December 29, 2019, from Knowitall.org: https://www.knowitall. org/photo/james-h-carlisle-history-sc-slide-collection (

Editor. (n.d.). *Lide Family History*. Retrieved December 29, 2019, from Ancestry.com: https://www.ancestry.com/name-origin? surname=lide

Editor. (n.d.). *Lincoln's Gettysburg and Second Inaugural Address*. Retrieved December 2019, 2019, from Biblescripture.net: http:// biblescripture.net/Address.html

Editor. (n.d.). William Jennings Bryan's book contaning his speech, *Prince of Peace*. Retrieved December 29, 2020, from archive.org: https://archive.org/details/princeofpeace00brya/page/n8

Editor. (n.d.). *Scientific Dissent from Darwinism*. Retrieved December 29, 2019, from dissentfromdarwin.org: https://dissentfromdarwin.org/

Editor. (n.d.). *Significant Civil War Battles*. Retrieved March 5, 2020, from PBS, American Experience: https://www.pbs.org/wgbh/ americanexperience/features/timeline-death/

Editor. (n.d.). *Singleton Family*. Retrieved March 5, 2020, from Major Robert Lide: http://www.singletonfamily.org/getperson. php?personID=I4021&tree=1

Editor. (n.d.). *The Intuition Mission*. Retrieved from Avlis Publishing: https://www.intuitionmission.com/fight_apathy.htm

Editor. (n.d.). *The North's Last POW Camp*. Retrieved December 2019, 2019, from History.net: http://www.historynet.com/norths-last- pow-camp.htm

Editor. (n.d.). *The Tariff of Abominsatons: The Effects*. Retrieved March 5, 2020, from History, Art, and Archives: https://history.house.gov/ Historical-Highlights/1800-1850/The-Tariff-of-Abominations/

Ellis, M. (2019, November 22). *The Greenville News*. Retrieved from SC Baptists elected their first black President: https://www. greenvilleonline.com/story/news/local/2019/11/22/sc-baptist- convention-elected-their-first-black-president/4248049002/

Ellison, M. E. (1936, June 1). Major Coker Eulogized. Hartsville, SC: Coker College, now in Coker College Archives.

Fogel, R. W. (n.d.). *Phases of the Four Great Awakenings*. Retrieved December 29, 2019, from University of Chicago: https://www.press.uchicago.edu/Misc/Chicago/256626.html

Gainey, A. (n.d.). Recollections of the Sunday School. Darlington, SC: Angus Gainey as and adult.

Garrett, S. W. (n.d.). South Caroliniana Library, University of South Carolina, Columbia, SC, Letter 2, p. 4. *Letters by Samuel W. Garrett* XE "Samuel W. Garrett" *(early Dean of Coker College)*. Hartsville, SC.

George MacLeod, R. (2013). *Where He died, What He Died For*. (R. Ortland, Editor) Retrieved November 30, 2019, from Gospel Coaltion: https://www.thegospelcoalition.org/blogs/ray-ortlund/where-he-died-what-he-died-for/

Gerson, L. P. (1990). *God and Greek Philosophy, Studies in the Early History of Natural Theology*. London and New York: Routledge.

Graham, W. (2014). *The Tree Stump Prayer: When Billy Graham Overcame Doubt*. Retrieved December 29, 2019, from billygraham.org: https://billygraham.org/story/the-tree-stump-prayer-where-billy-graham-overcame-doubt/

Green, S. (Ed.). (1937, February). *Centennial Celebration, subsection entitled Addresses on Other Occasions*. Hartsville, SC: Coker College.

Guelzo, A. C. (2018). *Reconstruction, A Concise History*. New York, New York: Oxford Press.

Horgan, J. (2011). *Pssst! Don't tell the creationists, but scientists don't have a clue how life began*. Retrieved October 3, 2019, from Scientific American: https://blogs.scientificamerican.com/cross-check/pssst-dont-tell-the-creationists-but-scientists-dont-have-a-clue-how-life-began/

Irwin, N. L. (2016, April 15). *Coker, Charles Westfield*. Retrieved December 29, 2019, from South Carolina Encyclopedia: South Caroliniana Library, University of South Carolina, Columbia, SC, File 3778-B.

Irwin, N. L. (2016, August 10). *Coker, James Lide, Sr.* Retrieved March 4, 2020, from South Carolina Encyclopedia: http://www.scencyclopedia.org/sce/entries/coker-james-lide-sr/

Joslin, M. C. (2003). *Essays on William Chambers Coker, Passionate Botanist.* Chapel Hill, NC: Botanical Garden Foundation.

Kay, B. C. (2010). *The Civil War from A to Z: Two Points of View.* (A. House, Producer, & Bloomington, IN) Retrieved December 2019, 2019, from Google Books: https://books.google.com/books?id=0MsrwRga3hQC&pg=PT18&lpg=PT18&dq=stonewall+Jackson+standing+as+a+stone+wall+Yankee+skedaddle+to+Washington&source=bl&ots=Pq-m8_Vsm-&sig=ACfU3U1SjrEvdJEHDovYzqmOoqPcFeGjUQ&hl=en&sa=X&ved=2ahUKEwin3IaUiv3hAhUOh-AKHaF_AY8Q6A

Kennon, J. (2011, July 23). *How Extended Adolescence Is Changing the United States (and Takes a Much Higher Toll on Women.* Retrieved December 16, 2019, from joshuakennon.com: https://www.joshuakennon.com/how-extended-adolescence-is-changing-the-united-states-and-takes-a-much-higher-toll-on-women/

Knighton, A. (2017, July 21). *How the Confederacy Almost Won the American Civil War.* Retrieved December 29, 2019, from War History Online: https://www.warhistoryonline.com/american-civil-war/confederacy-almost-won-american-civil-war.html

Komisar, E. (2019). *Masculinity Isn't a Sickness.* Retrieved December 29, 2019, from wsj.com Wall Street Journal: https://www.wsj.com/articles/masculinity-isnt-a-sickness-11547682809

Law, T. H. (1859,1941). *the Journal of Cadel Tom Law.* (A. Law, Ed.) Clinton, SC: Presbyterian College Press.

Lawton, N. (2020). *History - A Little bit of this and that about our Town (Hartsville) and its Begininngs.* Thursday Study Club. Hartsville: From boxes of papers from Hartsville Oil Mill.

Les Benedict, M. (1980). Southern Democrats in the Crisis of 1876-1977: A Reconsideration of Reunion and Reaction. *The Journal of Southern History, 46*(4), 489-524. Retrieved from www.jstor.org/stable/2207200. Accessed 14 June 2020.

Lewin, R. (1980, November). *Evolutionary Theory Under Fire*. Retrieved December 29, 2019, from science.sciencemag.org: https://science.sciencemag.org/content/210/4472/883

Lewis, J. D. (2019). *Darlington County, SC*. Retrieved from Carolana.com: https://www.carolana.com/SC/Counties/darlington_county_sc.html

Lide, Miss Jane, "An Attempted Character Sketch," Founder's Day Speech, Coker College, Friday April 27, 1956, college archives.

Linville, S. G. (1983). *Jennie: A Biography of Jenny Coker Gay*. SC: Not Given.

Lohn, A. (n.d.). *What to Do*. Retrieved from Wealth Management: Andrew Lohn, Wealth Management, Sep 12, 2017 article "What to Do When There's No Clear Successor," https://www.wealthmanagement.com/high-net-worth/what-do-when-there-s-no-clear-successor.

Lyles, S. (2017, October 24). *Historical Society Celebrates 80th Anniversary*. Retrieved June 14, 2019, from Darlington's News and Press: http://www.newsandpress.net/historical-society-celebrates-80th-anniversary/:

Magness, P. W. (2020). *Tariffs and the American Civil War*. Retrieved December 29, 2019, from Essential Civil War Curriculum: http://www.marottaonmoney.com/protective-tariffs-the-primary-cause-of-the-civil-war/

Martin Luther King, J. (n.d.). *Martin Luther King, Jr. > Quotes*. Retrieved March 9, 2020, from goodreads.com: https://www.goodreads.com/quotes/134001-i-have-a-dream-that-one-day-this-nation-will

Martin, P. (2019, November 19). *CRITICAL MASS: The Rolling Stones' 'Let It Bleed' marks end of the '60s*. Retrieved December 29, 2019, from Arkansas Democrat Gazette: https://www.arkansasonline.com/news/2019/nov/10/let-it-bleed-marks-end-of-the-60s-20191/?entertainment

McDowell, J. (1972,1979). *Evidence That Demands a Verdict*. San Bernadino, CA: Here's Life Publishers.

McDowell, J., & Wilson, B. (1993). *He Walked Among Us, Evidence for the Historical Jesus*. Nashville, TN: Thomas Nelson Publishers.

Miller, E. C. (2010, March 1). *Review of DR. HARRY EMERSON FOSDICK, "SHALL THE FUNDAMENTALISTS WIN?"*. Retrieved February 2, 2020, from Voices of Democracy: https://voicesofdemocracy.umd. edu/wp-content/uploads/2019/06/VOD-Miller-6.3.19.pdf

Mitcham, S. (2019, July 15). *A History Lesson for Ted Cruz*. Retrieved December 1, 2019, from The Abbeville Blog: https://www. abbevilleinstitute.org/blog/a-history-lesson-for-ted-cruz/

Montgomery, M. (1949, December 18). Major James Lide Coker. *The State*, 1-8.

Morris, L. a. (2020, June 15). *How whiite Americans used lynchings to terrorize and control black people*. Retrieved from The Guardian: https://www.theguardian.com/us-news/2018/apr/26/ lynchings-memorial-us-south-montgomery-alabama

Nelson, L. E. (2016). *Coker's Pedigreed Seed Co.* Retrieved August 5, 2019, from South Carolina Encyclopedia: http://www.scencyclopedia. org/sce/entries/Cokers-pedigreed-seed-company/

Nestel, M. (2018, June 20). *Charleston formally apologizes for its role in slavery*. Retrieved from ABC News: https://abcnews.go.com/US/ charleston-formally-apologizes-role-slavery/story?id=56026589

Newman, P. S. (1968, 1976). *Science Speaks: Scientific Proof for the Accuracy of the Bible*. Chicago, IL: Moody Press.

Norwood, J. W. (1919, April 19). Major James Lide Coker as a Citizen and Businessman. *Memorial Day*. (Editor, Ed.) Hartsville: Coker College.

O'Keefe, T. (n.d.). *Epicurus (341-271 BC)*. Retrieved from Internet Encyclopedia of Philosophy: https://www.iep.utm.edu/epicur/

Papas, S. (n.d.). *APA issues first-ever guidelines for practice with men and boys*. Retrieved from American Pyschological Association: https://www.apa.org/monitor/2019/01/ce-corner

Paul Lawrence, P. (2016). *a Brief History of the Septuagint*. Retrieved from https://biblearchaeology.org/research/ new-testament-era/4022-a-brief-history-of-the-septuagint

Penney, J. C. (1956). *Lines of a Layman*. Grand Rapids, MI: Eerdman's.

Ramsey, D. (2019). *Millionaire Spending Habits That Will Surprise You.* Retrieved November 16, 2019, from Daveramsey.com: https://www.daveramsey.com/blog/millionaire-spending-habits

Rank, S. M. (200, November). *Industrial Revolution Working Conditons.* (P. Scott Michael Rank, Editor) Retrieved December 2, 2019, from History on the Net: https://www.historyonthenet.com/industrial-revolution-working-conditions

Reynolds, D. S. (2008). *First Baptist Church Scrapbook.* Hartsville, SC: History Committee Books.

Ricky Ciapha Dennis, J. (2018, October 22). *Black and white SC churches combine in weekly worship, open to all.* Retrieved February 5, 2020, from Post and Courier: https://www.postandcourier.com/news/black-and-white-sc-churches-combine-in-weekly-worship-open/article_a3a2e71a-d606-11e8-9184-e78926acef71.html

Rizm, J. C. (n.d.). *What Has Athens to do with Jerusalem?* Retrieved December 2019, 2019, from Rizm.org: https://www.rzim.org/read/a-slice-of-infinity/what-has-athens-to-do-with-jerusalem

Rogers, J., & Nelson, L. (1994). *Mr. D. R.: A Biography of David R. Coker.* Hartsville: Coker College Press.

Ropp, M. (1997, Winter). *Charles Hodge and His Objection to Darwinism: The Exclusion of Intelligent Design.* Retrieved December 29, 2019, from theropps.com: http://www.theropps.com/papers/Winter1997/CharlesHodge.htm#Hodge's%20Case%20Against%20Darwinism

Russell, D. J. (2013, June 23). Retrieved December 29, 2019, from https://www.dailyprogress.com/opinion/guest_columnists/protective-tariffs-primary-cause-of-the-civil-war/article_63b77f5c-dc0c-11e2-8e99-001a4bcf6878.html

Sandburg, C. (1939). *Abraham Lincoln: The War Years* (Vol. III). New York, NY: Harcourt Brace & Company.

Schultz, B. (2004). *Boyhood and Beyond.* Eugene, OR: Great Expectations Books.

Schwartz, J. H. (1999). *Sudden Origins*. Hoboken, New Jersey: John Wiley Press. As quoted by Henry Morris, https://www.icr.org/article/scientific-case-against-evolution-summary-part-1/.

Sherman, M. (2019). *Everything you need to know about the college basketball scandal*. Retrieved December 29, 2019, from http://www.espn.com/mens-college-basketball/story/_/id/22555512/explaining-ncaa-college-basketball-scandal-players-coaches-agents

Sikes, E. W. (1919, April 19). Major J. L. Coker, Leader in Education. *Memorial Exercises*. Hartsville, SC: Coker College.

Sikes, E. W. (September, 15 1918). Tribute to Major Coker's Contribution to Hartsville First Baptist Church in Church Minutes. (E. Sikes, Ed., & G. S. Furman University, Compiler) Hartsville, SC: Harstville First Baptist Church.

Simpson, G. L. (1956). *Cokers of Carolina*. Chapel Hill, NC: University of North Carolina Press.

Simpson, R. R. (1994). *A Century of Education: Welsh Neck High School and Coker College*. Hartsville, SC: Coker College and R. L. Bryan Presses.

Snider, E. (1939). From Coker Backstage. 1-2. (c. o. Box 2 of the James Lide Coker Collection, Compiler) Hartsville, SC: Evelyn Snider.

Snyzer, A. C. (1980). *Ugaritic Religion*. Leiden, Netherlands: E. J. Brill. Retrieved from https://books.google.com/books?id=S4geAAAA IAAJ&pg=PA3&lpg=PA3&dq=baal+Ugaritic+tablets+that+date+back+to+the+middle+of+the+second+century+B.C.&source=bl&ots=RgeR0M0QOj&sig=ACfU3U2NKdl

Stith, E. (1912, June). Editor. *Euterpean, Series Two*(Number Two).

Stout, H. C. (2008, March). *Religion in the Civil War*. Retrieved December 29, 2019, from TeacherServe® Home Page, National Humanities Center: TeacherServe® Home Page, National Humanities Center,

Tacitus, C. (1993). Annals, Loeb Edition. In J. M. Wilson, *He Walked Among Us, Evidence for the Historical Jesus*. Nashville: Thomas Nelson.

The Washington Post. (11/18/2011 and 8/11/2012).

Tom Blake, T. (Ed.). (2001, October 28). *Darlington County Census, 1860, slaveholding.* Retrieved December 29, 2019, from sites.rootsweb. com: https://sites.rootsweb.com/~ajac/scdarlington.htm

Traywick, H. V. (2019, June 19). *The Apostate.* Retrieved December 29, 2019, from Reckonin': https://www.reckonin.com/hv-traywick-jr/ the-apostate

Trumbull, H. C. (1896). *Prayer, Its Nature and Scope.* New York, NY: Fleming H. Revell Co.

Twain, M., & Webmaster. (1924. posted on Hubevents web siteAugust 11, 2018). *Autobiography of Mark Twain.* Retrieved August 20, 2020, from Hubevents: http://hubeventsnotes.blogspot.com/2018/07/ autobiography-of-mark-twain-volume-i.html

United States Congress of 1828. (1828, May 29). *A Century of Lawmaking for a New Nation: US Congressional Documents and Debates, 1774-1875.* Retrieved from American Memory: https:// memory.loc.gov/cgi-bin/ampage?collId=llsl&fileName=004/ llsl004.db&recNum=317

Wallace, J. W. (2019). *How Ancient Eyewitness Testimony Became the New Testament Gospel Record.* Retrieved November 30, 2019, from Cold Case Christianity: https://coldcasechristianity.com/ writings/how-ancient-eyewitness-testimony-became-the-new-testament-gospel-record/

Waters, Emory L. *The City We Knew But Everybody Forgot, Hartsville, the African American Experience* (Lyndon Williams, Saving Ourselves Publications, 2020).

Webb, R. (2010, August 10). *Story of the Song: Beautiful Day, U2, 2000.* (U2) Retrieved from Independent: https://www.independent. co.uk/arts-entertainment/music/features/story-of-the-song-beautiful-day-u2-2000-2050946.html

Wilson, J. L. (1910). *Memories of Society Hill, SC.* SC: Pee Dee Historical Society.

Zauzmer, J. (2017, February 27). *What happened when a black and white church merged in Florida.* Retrieved February 9, 2020, from

Post and Courier: https://www.washingtonpost.com/local/social-issues/two-fla-churches--one-black-one-white--merge-in-racial-reconciliation-effort/2017/02/07/a95dde72-e287-11e6-a547-5fb9411d332c_story.html

$\mathcal{I}ndex$

A

Abraham Lincoln xi, xiii
agnostic 5, 185
Agnostic 185
Alabama 10, 27, 28, 29, 35, 38
A. L. M. Wiggins 123, 129, 244
American Sulphite Paper
        Company 131
Angus Gainey 152, 159, 161, 163,
        167, 168, 169
Atlantic Coast Line Railroad 94
authority 119

B

B. A. McIlhany, 230, 239, 248
Bank of Hartsville 101, 103
barefoot 7, 77, 156, 274
Ben Hur- A Tale of the Christ 56
Bertrand Russell 185
Bible xxi, 53, 77, 150, 154, 165, 180,
        182, 197, 203, 259, 260, 274,
        287, 293, 294, 298
Black Codes 105
Black Creek 134, 136, 156, 171, 240
Blue Back Speller 274
bluebird 222
bootleggers 233
born again 19
breeding 24, 32, 33, 97, 98

B

Bright Williamson 93, 108
business leadership 112

C

Caleb Coker, Jr. 5, 271
calling xi, xx, 32, 84, 126, 188, 196,
        271, 273, 277
Carpetbaggers 79, 81, 84
carriage 93, 165, 191, 192, 193
Carrie Lee Erwin Kalber 125, 191,
        192, 204, 205
catalog 182, 198, 199
Catholic 200
Central Baptist Church 162
chapel 188, 197, 204, 293
chapel messages 188, 204
Charles H. Campbell 143
Charleston 6, 10, 12, 16, 42, 44, 57,
        60, 90, 91, 92, 125, 144, 188,
        198, 200, 261
Charles W. Coker 101, 142
Charles Westfield
        Charles Westfield Coker, the
                Major's Brother 13, 148
Charles Westfield Coker 33, 140
Charlie Coker 137, 143, 147, 148
chemistry 24
Chickamauga 43, 48, 261
Christian service 184, 195, 196,
        197, 198

CPSIA information can be obtained
at www.ICGtesting.com
Printed in the USA
BVHW031943200221
600662BV00006B/20